JACKSON
LANZING

COLLIN
KELLY

MARCUS
TO

IRMA
KNIIVILA

JOYRIDE™

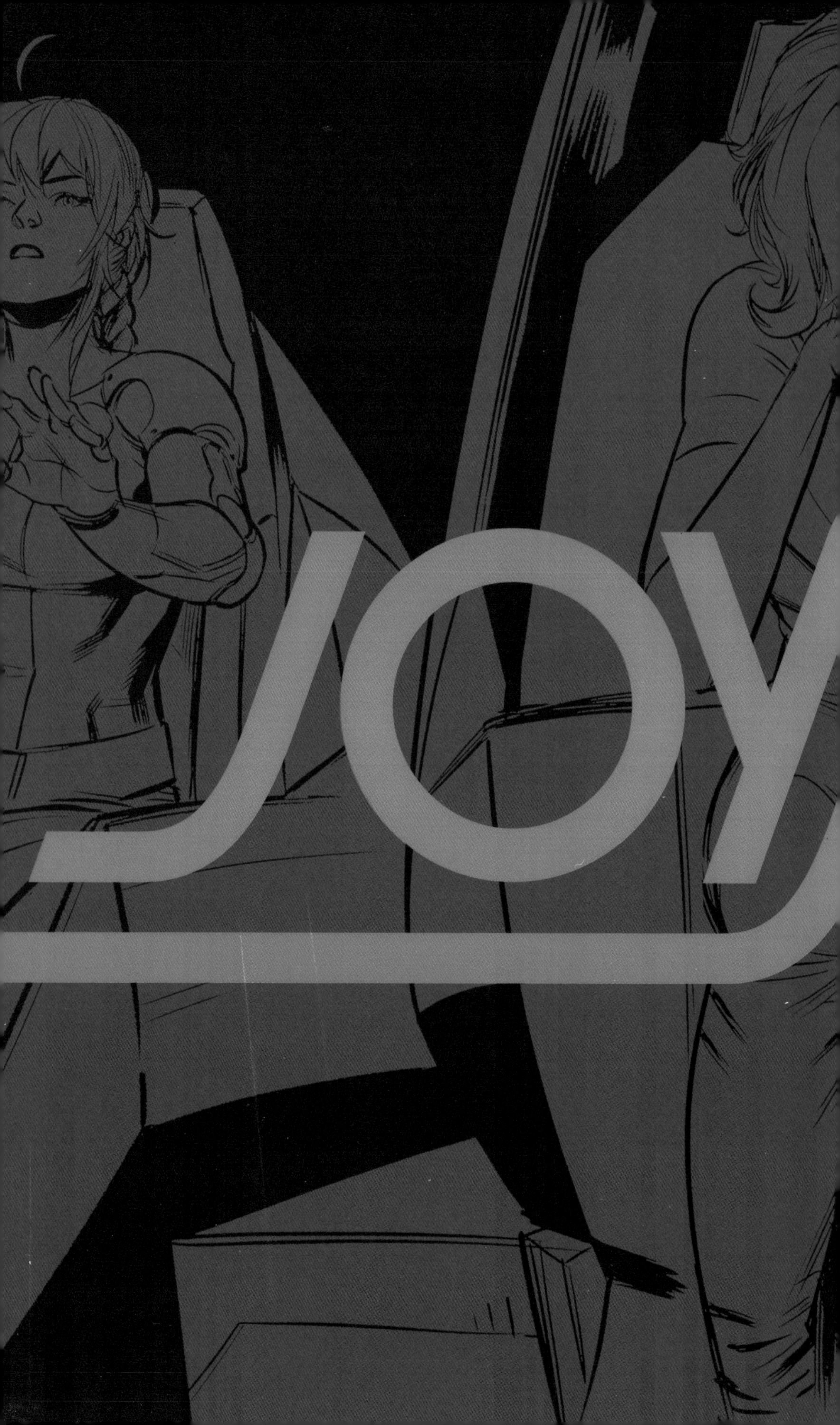
JOY

RIDE™

VOL. 2: TEENAGE SPACELAND

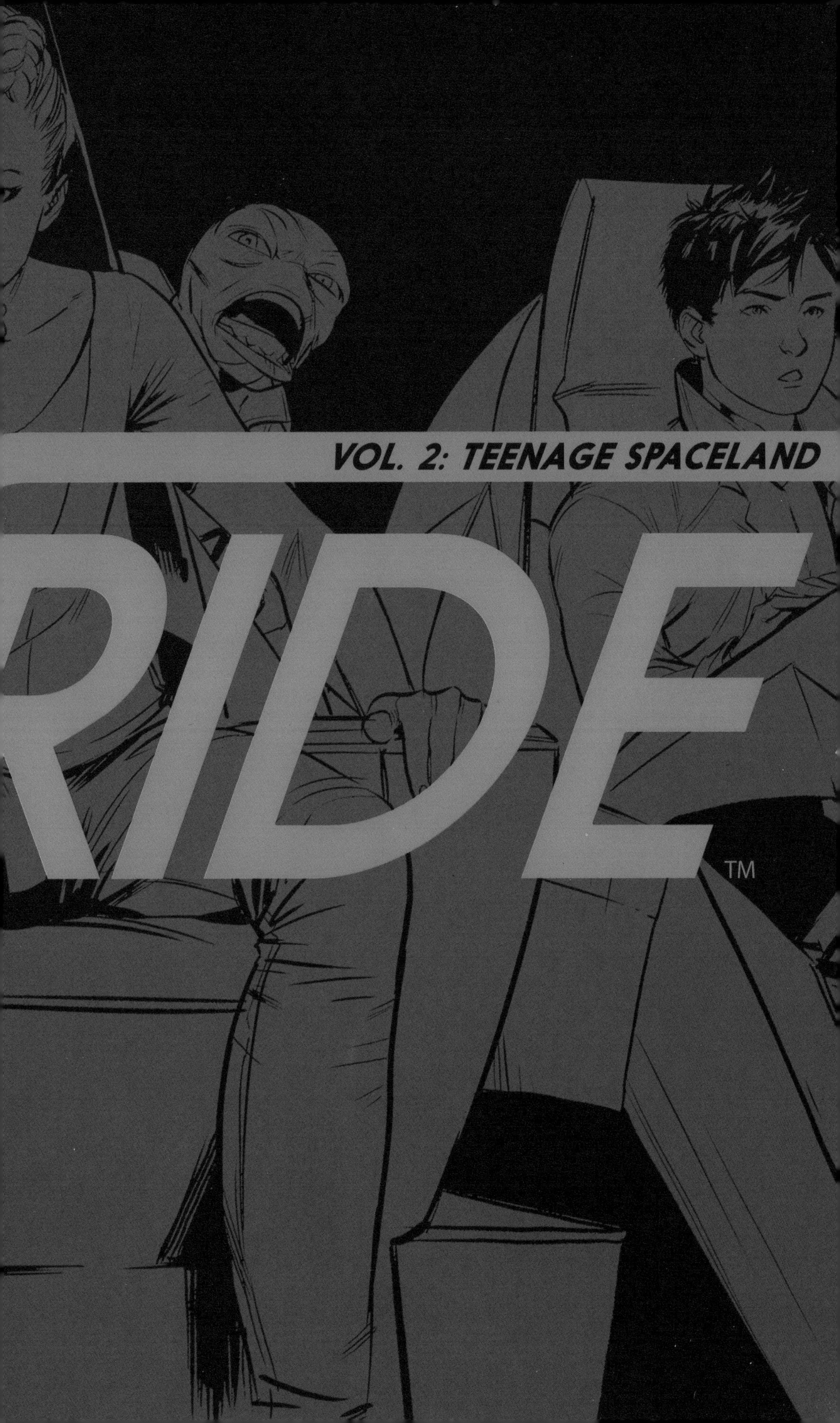

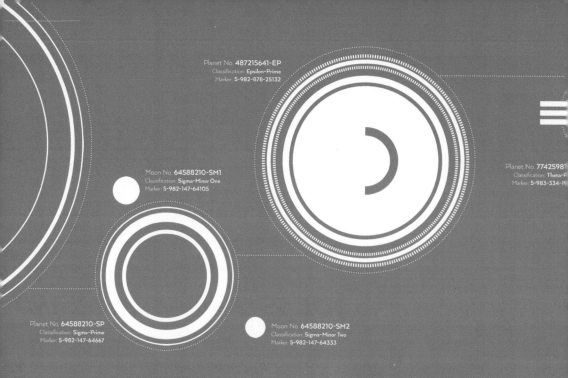

Planet No. **487215641-EP**
Classification: **Epsilon-Prime**
Marker: **5-982-878-25132**

Moon No. **64588210-SM1**
Classification: **Sigma-Minor One**
Marker: **5-982-147-64105**

Planet No. **7742598**
Classification: **Theta-P**
Marker: **5-983-334-1**

Planet No. **64588210-SP**
Classification: **Sigma-Prime**
Marker: **5-982-147-64667**

Moon No. **64588210-SM2**
Classification: **Sigma-Minor Two**
Marker: **5-982-147-64333**

ROSS RICHIE CEO & Founder
MATT GAGNON Editor-in-Chief
FILIP SABLIK President of Publishing & Marketing
STEPHEN CHRISTY President of Development
LANCE KREITER VP of Licensing & Merchandising
PHIL BARBARO VP of Finance
BRYCE CARLSON Managing Editor
MEL CAYLO Marketing Manager
SCOTT NEWMAN Production Design Manager
KATE HENNING Operations Manager
SIERRA HAHN Senior Editor
DAFNA PLEBAN Editor, Talent Development
SHANNON WATTERS Editor
ERIC HARBURN Editor
WHITNEY LEOPARD Associate Editor
JASMINE AMIRI Associate Editor
CHRIS ROSA Associate Editor
ALEX GALER Associate Editor
CAMERON CHITTOCK Associate Editor
MATTHEW LEVINE Assistant Editor
SOPHIE PHILIPS-ROBERTS Assistant Editor
KELSEY DIETERICH Production Designer
JILLIAN CRAB Production Designer
MICHELLE ANKLEY Production Designer
GRACE PARK Production Design Assistant
ELIZABETH LOUGHRIDGE Accounting Coordinator
STEPHANIE HOCUTT Social Media Coordinator
JOSÉ MEZA Sales Assistant
JAMES ARRIOLA Mailroom Assistant
HOLLY AITCHISON Operations Assistant
SAM KUSEK Direct Market Representative
AMBER PARKER Administrative Assistant

VISUAL RESEARCH ASSISTANT
DANI V

DESIGNER
SCOTT NEWMAN

ASSOCIATE EDITOR
CAMERON CHITTOCK

EDITOR
DAFNA PLEBAN

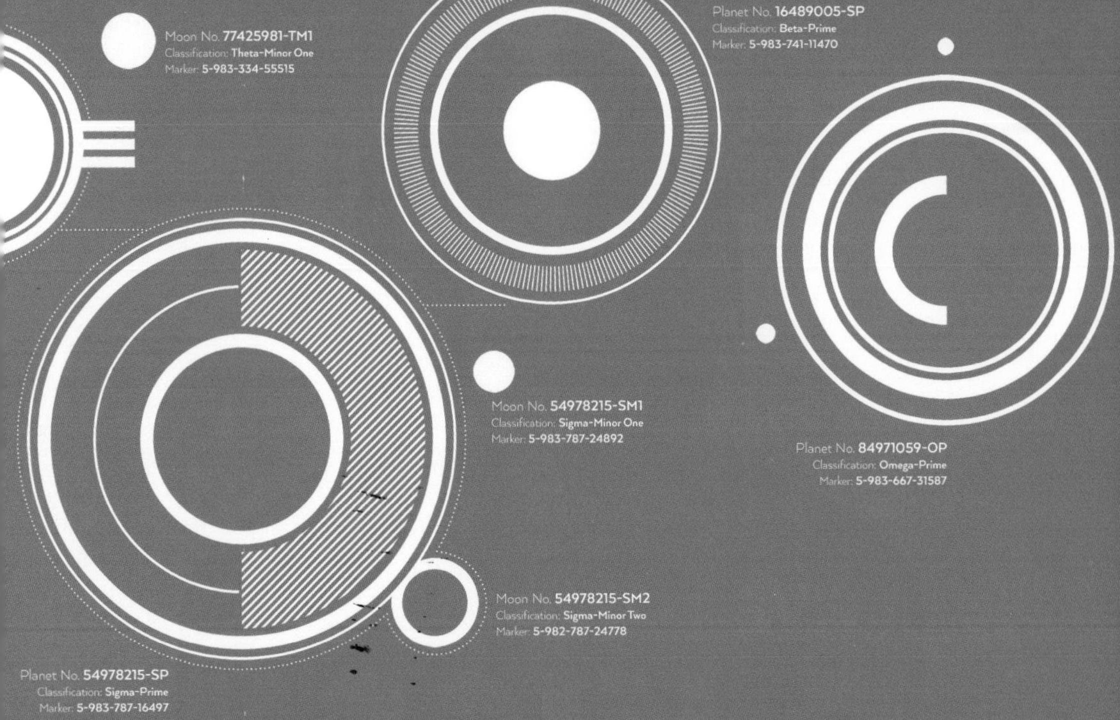
Moon No. 77425981-TM1
Classification: Theta-Minor One
Marker: 5-983-334-55515
Planet No. 16489005-SP
Classification: Beta-Prime
Marker: 5-983-741-11470
Moon No. 54978215-SM1
Classification: Sigma-Minor One
Marker: 5-983-787-24892
Planet No. 84971059-OP
Classification: Omega-Prime
Marker: 5-983-667-31587
Moon No. 54978215-SM2
Classification: Sigma-Minor Two
Marker: 5-982-787-24778
Planet No. 54978215-SP
Classification: Sigma-Prime
Marker: 5-983-787-16497

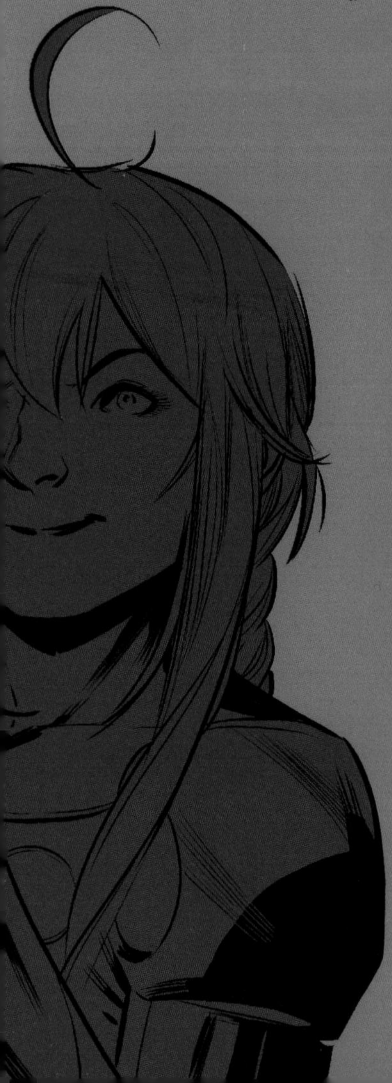

SCRIPT BY
JACKSON LANZING
& COLLIN KELLY

ART BY
MARCUS TO

COLORS BY
IRMA KNIIVILA

LETTERS BY
JIM CAMPBELL

COVER BY
MARCUS TO
WITH COLORS BY **IRMA KNIIVILA**

CREATED BY
MARCUS TO, JACKSON LANZING & COLLIN KELLY

CHAPTER **FIVE**

THE KISSING PLANET

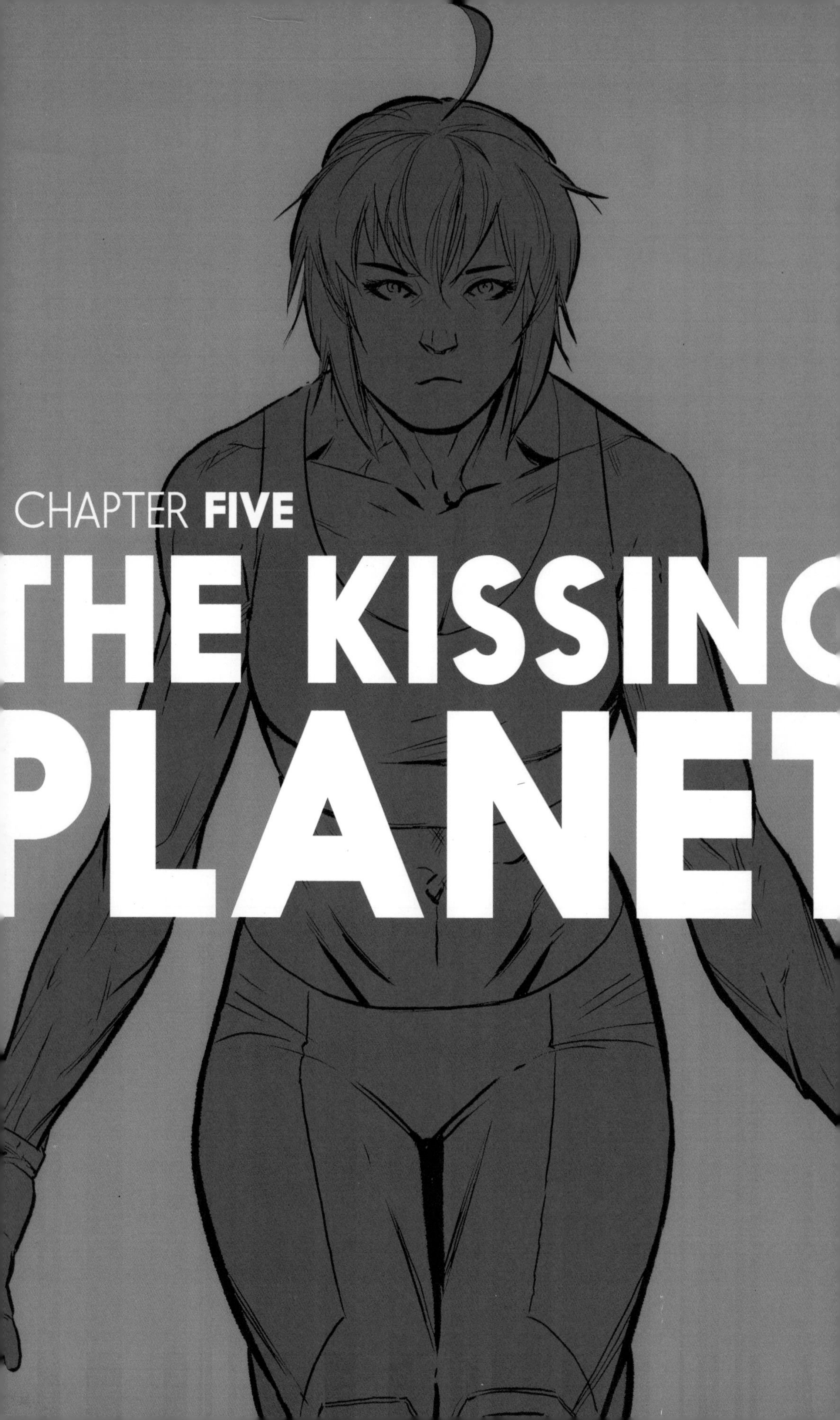

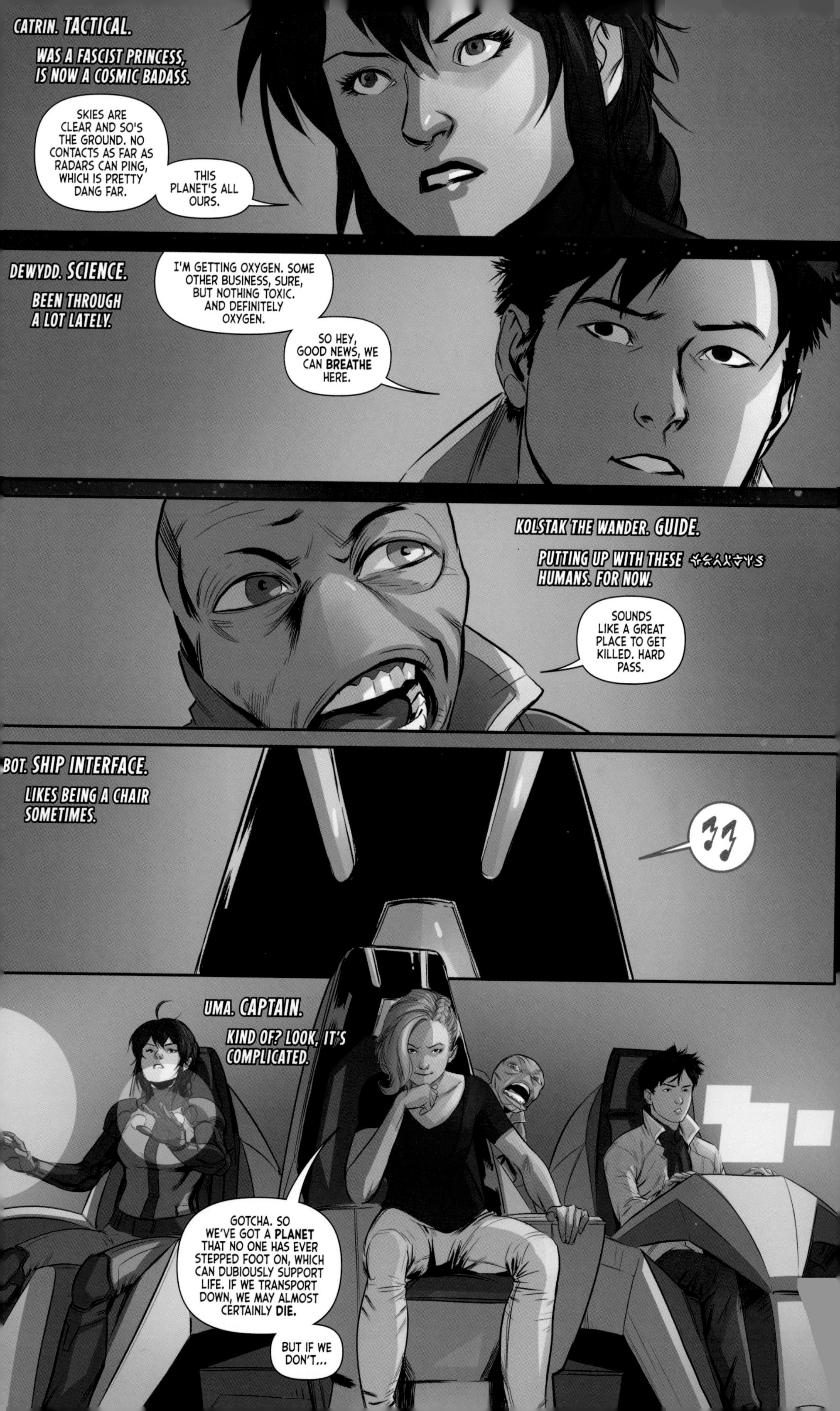
CATRIN. TACTICAL.
WAS A FASCIST PRINCESS, IS NOW A COSMIC BADASS.
SKIES ARE CLEAR AND SO'S THE GROUND. NO CONTACTS AS FAR AS RADARS CAN PING, WHICH IS PRETTY DANG FAR.
THIS PLANET'S ALL OURS.
DEWYDD. SCIENCE.
BEEN THROUGH A LOT LATELY.
I'M GETTING OXYGEN. SOME OTHER BUSINESS, SURE, BUT NOTHING TOXIC. AND DEFINITELY OXYGEN.
SO HEY, GOOD NEWS, WE CAN BREATHE HERE.
KOLSTAK THE WANDER. GUIDE.
PUTTING UP WITH THESE HUMANS. FOR NOW.
SOUNDS LIKE A GREAT PLACE TO GET KILLED. HARD PASS.
BOT. SHIP INTERFACE.
LIKES BEING A CHAIR SOMETIMES.
UMA. CAPTAIN.
KIND OF? LOOK, IT'S COMPLICATED.
GOTCHA. SO WE'VE GOT A PLANET THAT NO ONE HAS EVER STEPPED FOOT ON, WHICH CAN DUBIOUSLY SUPPORT LIFE. IF WE TRANSPORT DOWN, WE MAY ALMOST CERTAINLY DIE.
BUT IF WE DON'T...

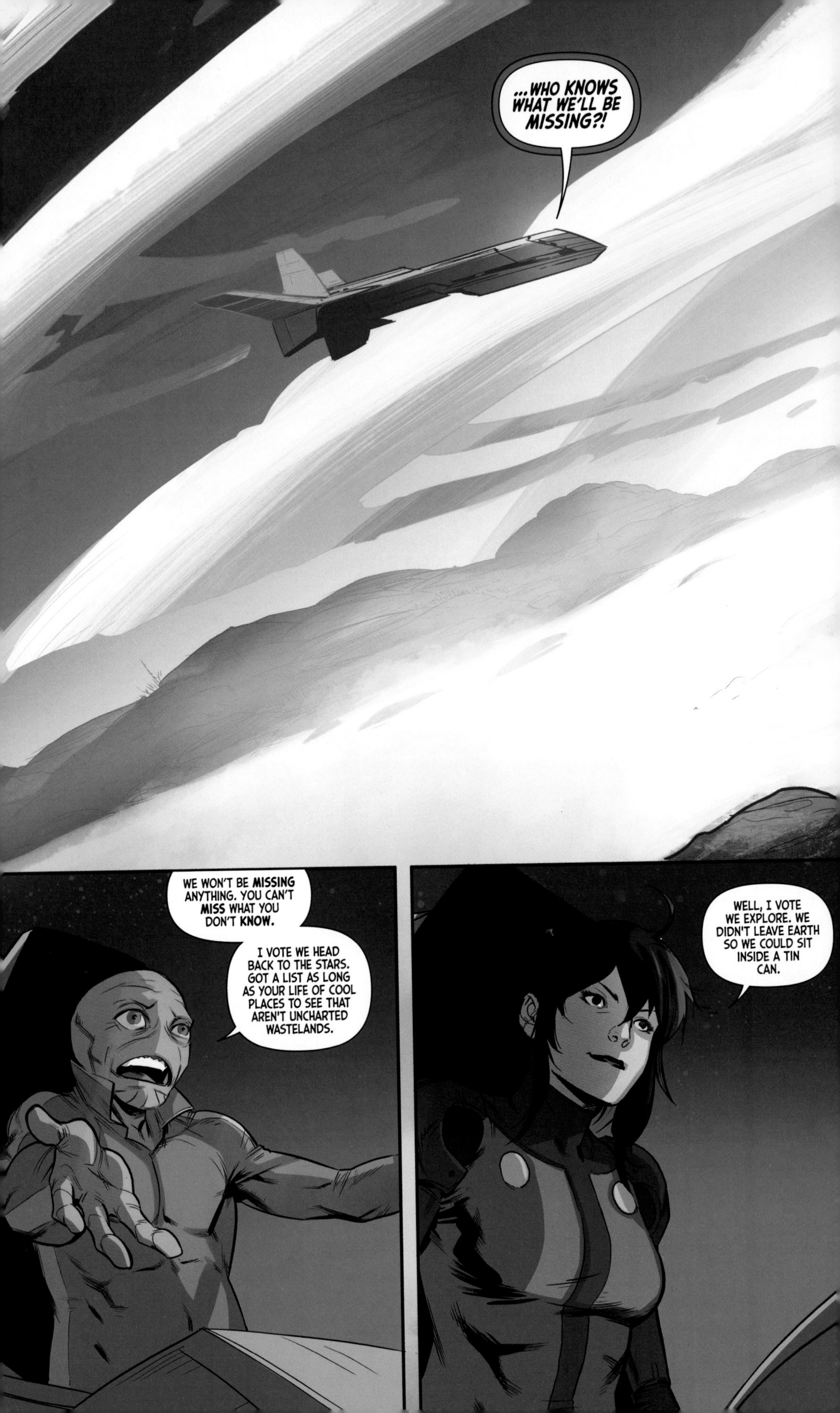
...WHO KNOWS WHAT WE'LL BE MISSING?!
WE WON'T BE MISSING ANYTHING. YOU CAN'T MISS WHAT YOU DON'T KNOW.
I VOTE WE HEAD BACK TO THE STARS. GOT A LIST AS LONG AS YOUR LIFE OF COOL PLACES TO SEE THAT AREN'T UNCHARTED WASTELANDS.
WELL, I VOTE WE EXPLORE. WE DIDN'T LEAVE EARTH SO WE COULD SIT INSIDE A TIN CAN.

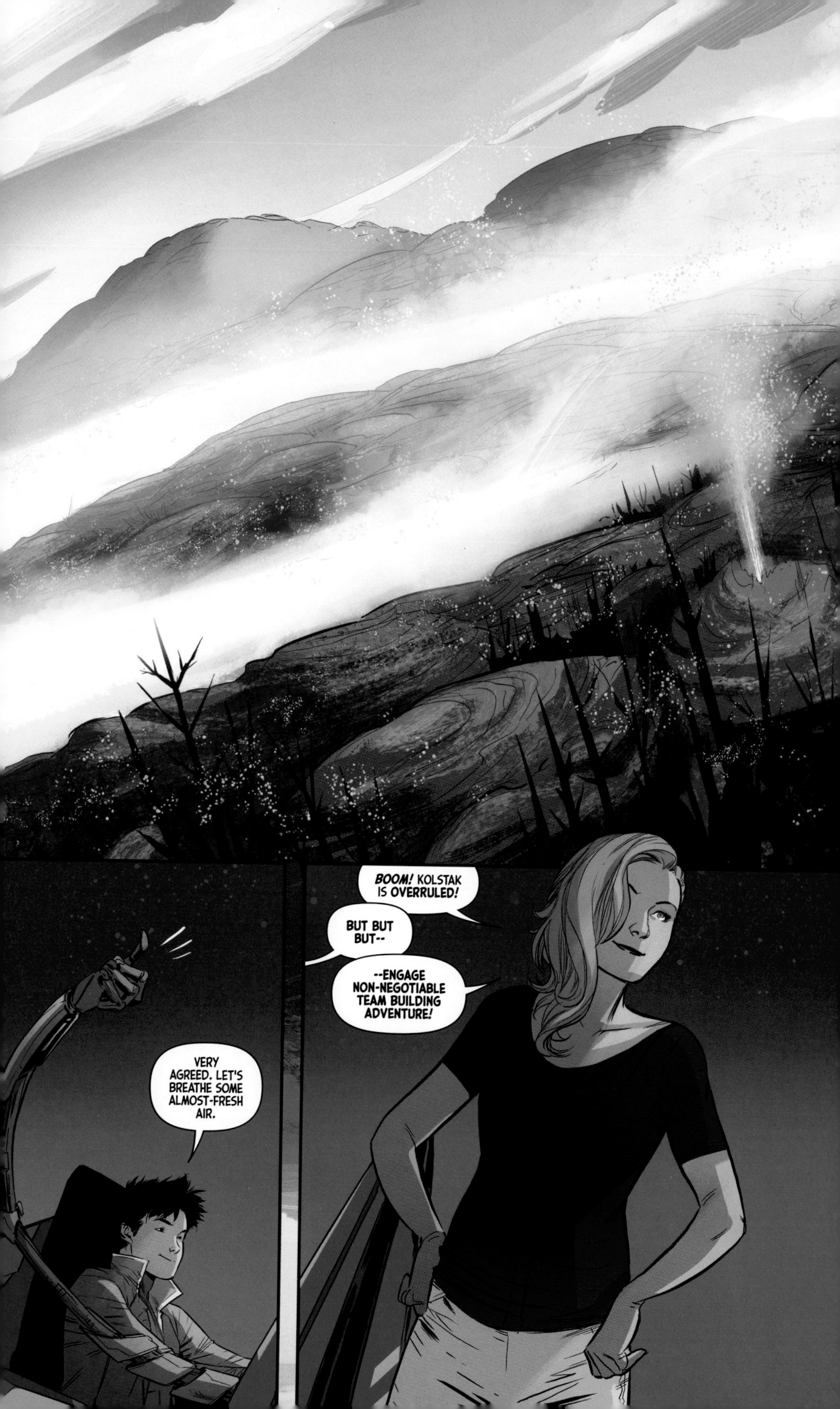
VERY AGREED. LET'S BREATHE SOME ALMOST-FRESH AIR.
BOOM! KOLSTAK IS OVERRULED!
BUT BUT BUT--
--ENGAGE NON-NEGOTIABLE TEAM BUILDING ADVENTURE!

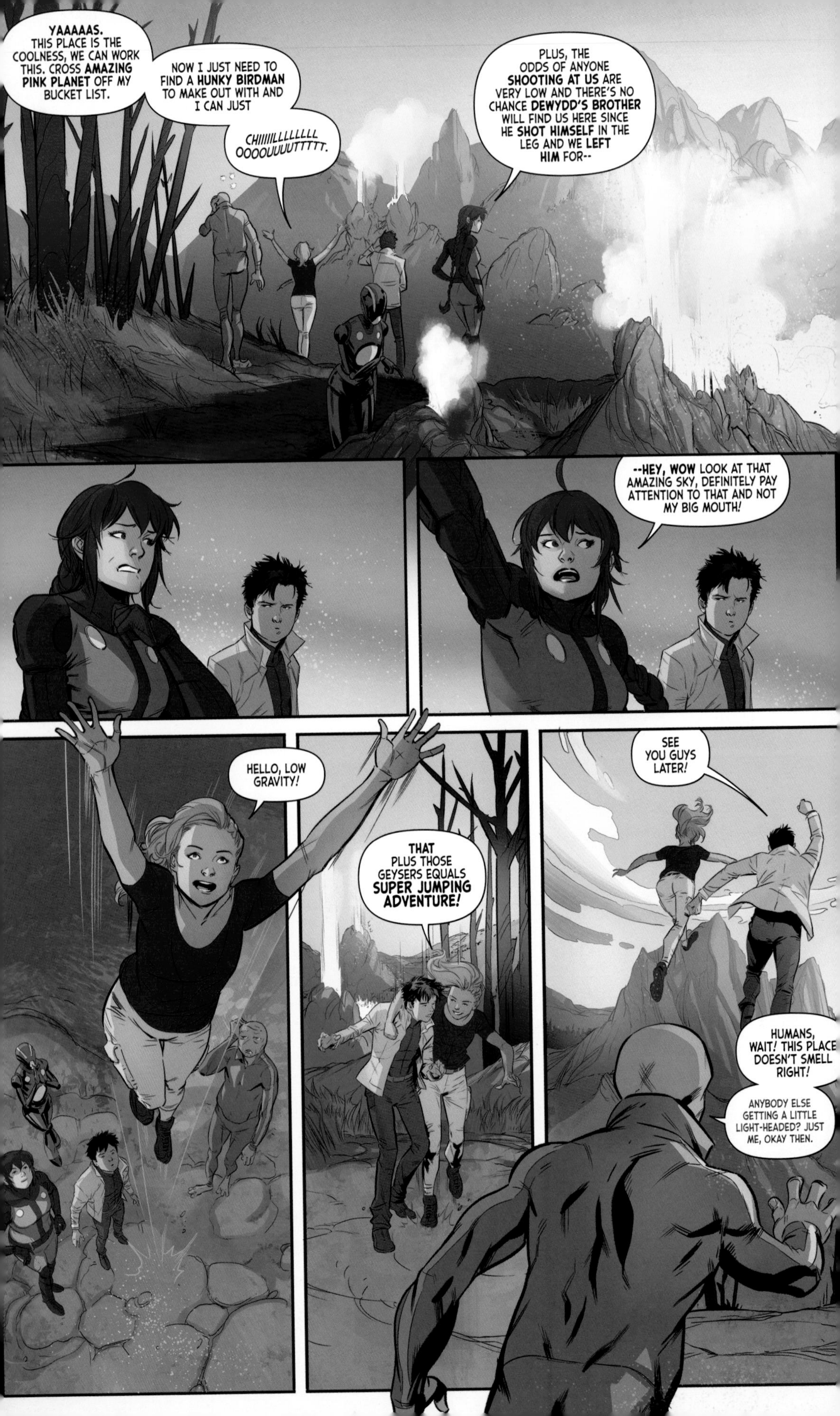
YAAAAAS. THIS PLACE IS THE COOLNESS, WE CAN WORK THIS. CROSS AMAZING PINK PLANET OFF MY BUCKET LIST.
NOW I JUST NEED TO FIND A HUNKY BIRDMAN TO MAKE OUT WITH AND I CAN JUST
CHIIIIILLLLLLLL OOOOUUUUTTTTTT.
PLUS, THE ODDS OF ANYONE SHOOTING AT US ARE VERY LOW AND THERE'S NO CHANCE DEWYDD'S BROTHER WILL FIND US HERE SINCE HE SHOT HIMSELF IN THE LEG AND WE LEFT HIM FOR--
--HEY, WOW LOOK AT THAT AMAZING SKY, DEFINITELY PAY ATTENTION TO THAT AND NOT MY BIG MOUTH!
HELLO, LOW GRAVITY!
THAT PLUS THOSE GEYSERS EQUALS SUPER JUMPING ADVENTURE!
SEE YOU GUYS LATER!
HUMANS, WAIT! THIS PLACE DOESN'T SMELL RIGHT!
ANYBODY ELSE GETTING A LITTLE LIGHT-HEADED? JUST ME, OKAY THEN.

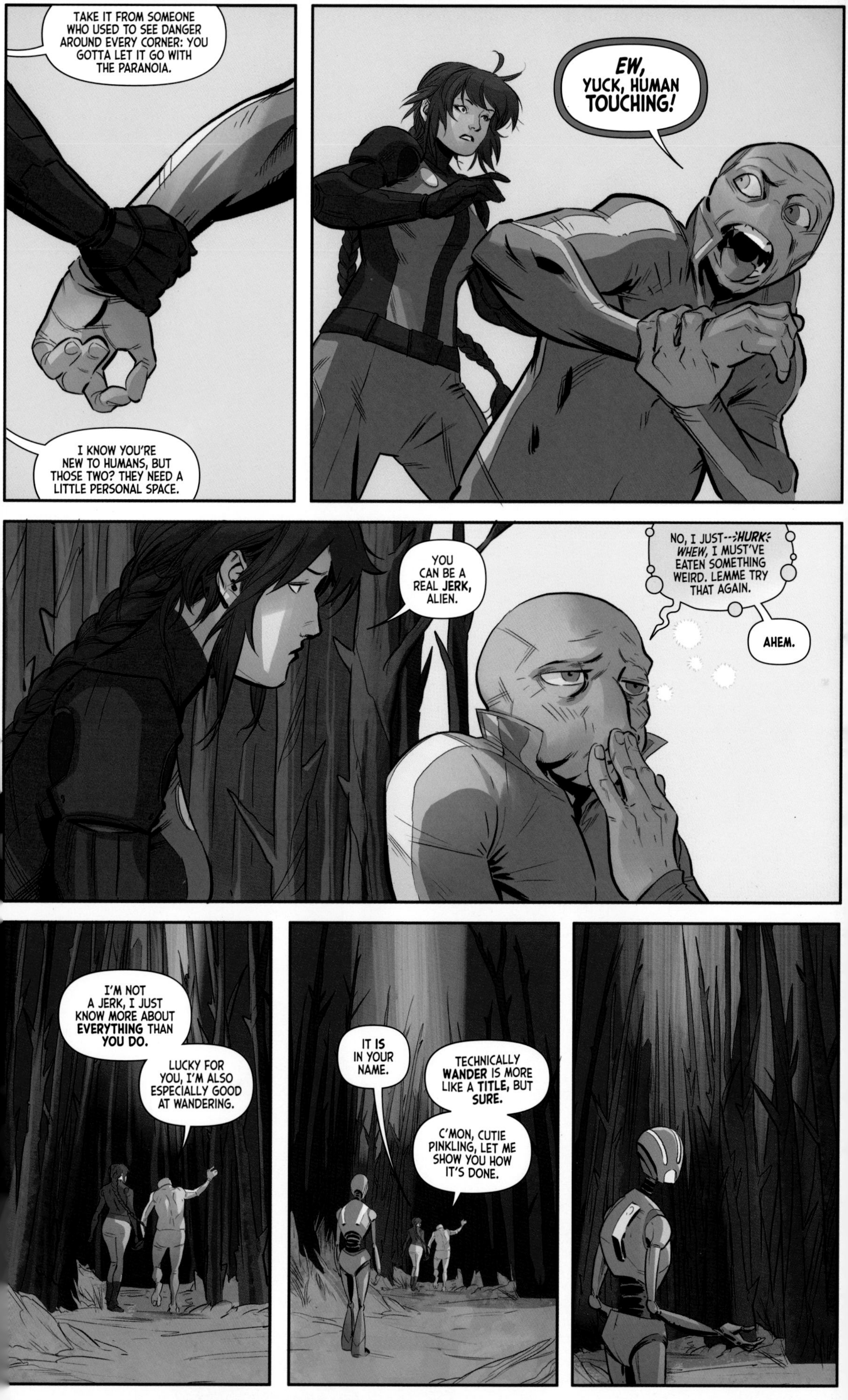
TAKE IT FROM SOMEONE WHO USED TO SEE DANGER AROUND EVERY CORNER: YOU GOTTA LET IT GO WITH THE PARANOIA.
I KNOW YOU'RE NEW TO HUMANS, BUT THOSE TWO? THEY NEED A LITTLE PERSONAL SPACE.
EW, YUCK, HUMAN TOUCHING!
YOU CAN BE A REAL JERK, ALIEN.
NO, I JUST--HURK WHEW, I MUST'VE EATEN SOMETHING WEIRD. LEMME TRY THAT AGAIN.
AHEM.
I'M NOT A JERK, I JUST KNOW MORE ABOUT EVERYTHING THAN YOU DO.
LUCKY FOR YOU, I'M ALSO ESPECIALLY GOOD AT WANDERING.
IT IS IN YOUR NAME.
TECHNICALLY WANDER IS MORE LIKE A TITLE, BUT SURE.
C'MON, CUTIE PINKLING, LET ME SHOW YOU HOW IT'S DONE.

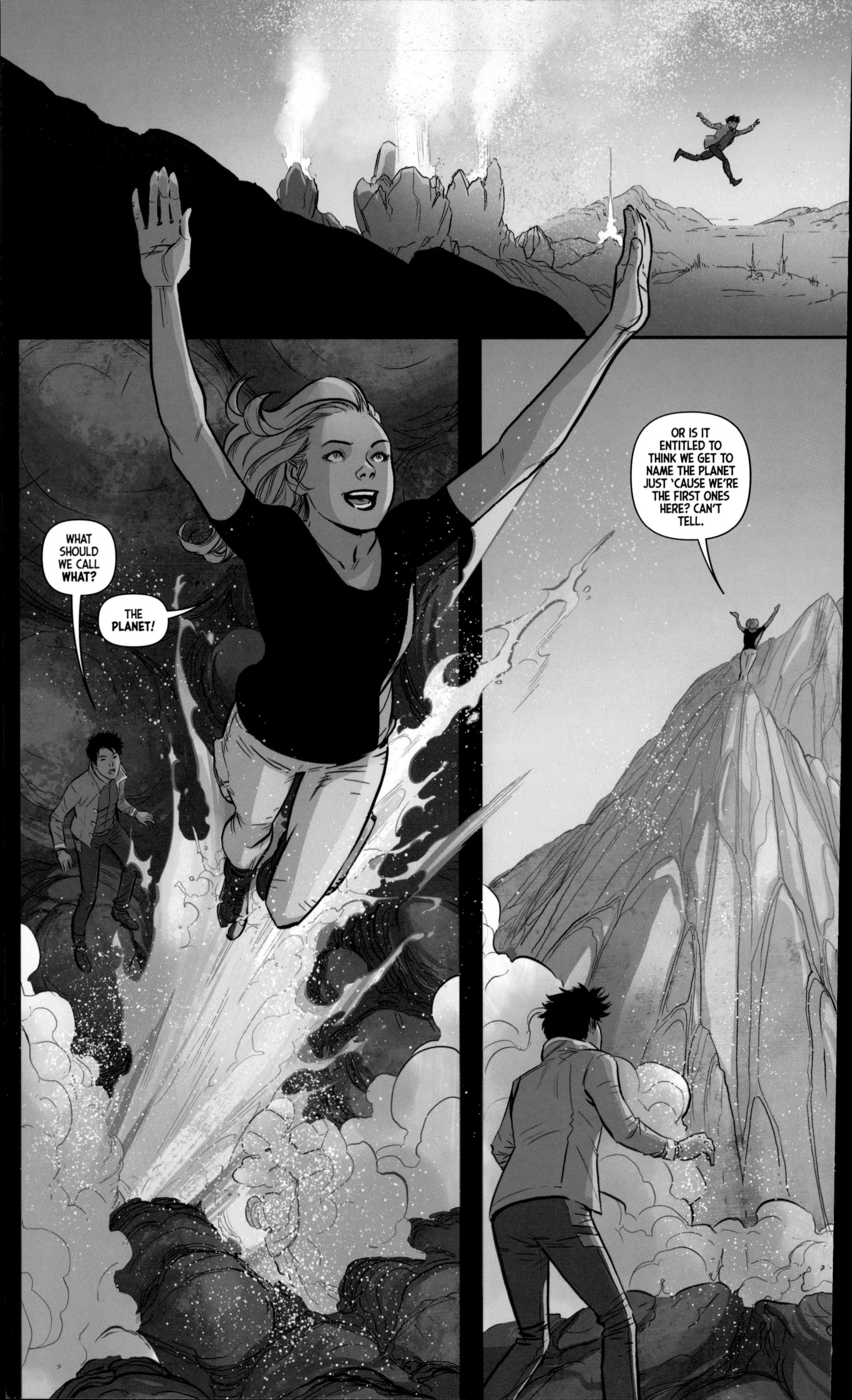
WHAT SHOULD WE CALL WHAT?
THE PLANET!
OR IS IT ENTITLED TO THINK WE GET TO NAME THE PLANET JUST 'CAUSE WE'RE THE FIRST ONES HERE? CAN'T TELL.

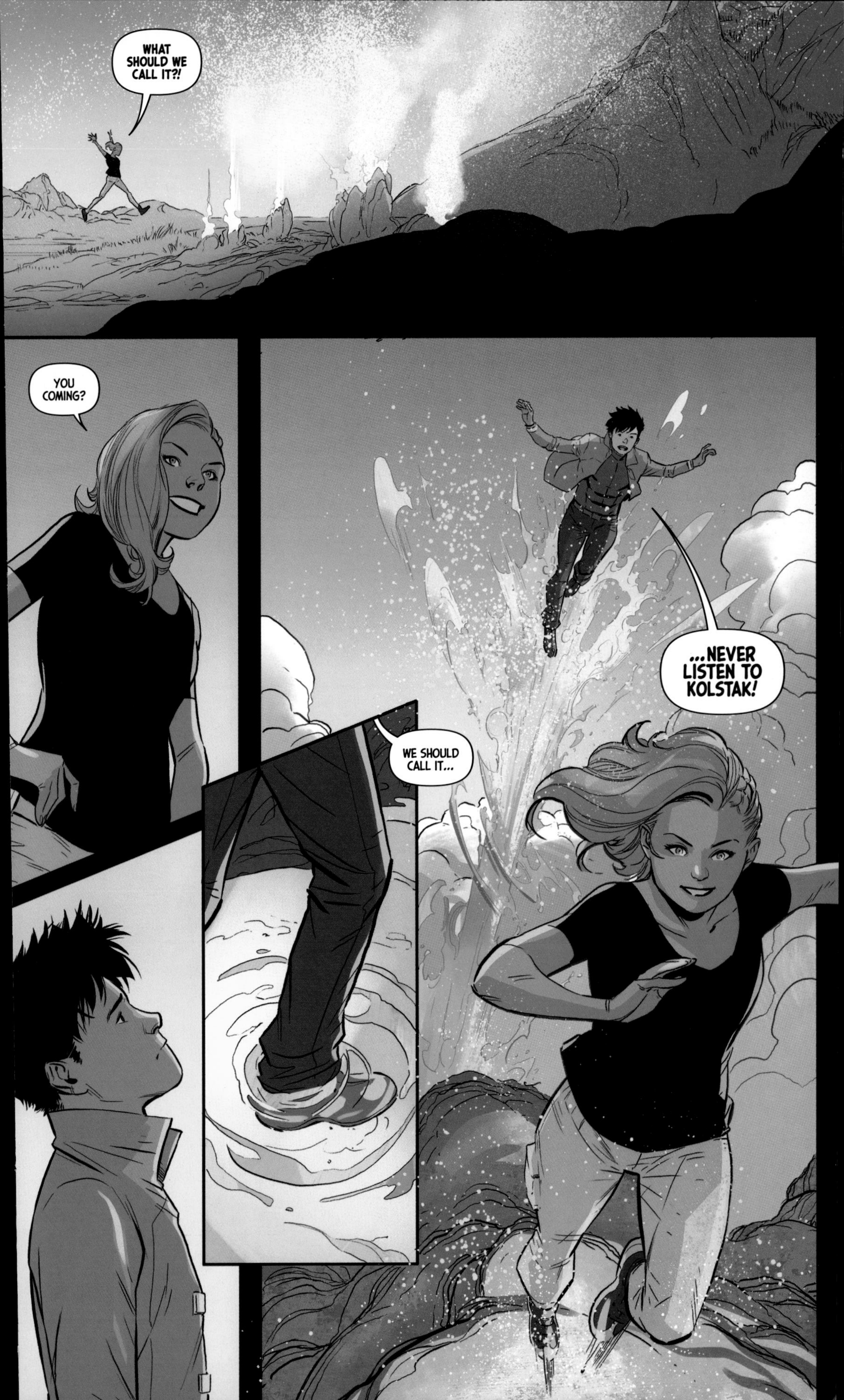
WHAT SHOULD WE CALL IT?!
YOU COMING?
WE SHOULD CALL IT...
...NEVER LISTEN TO KOLSTAK!

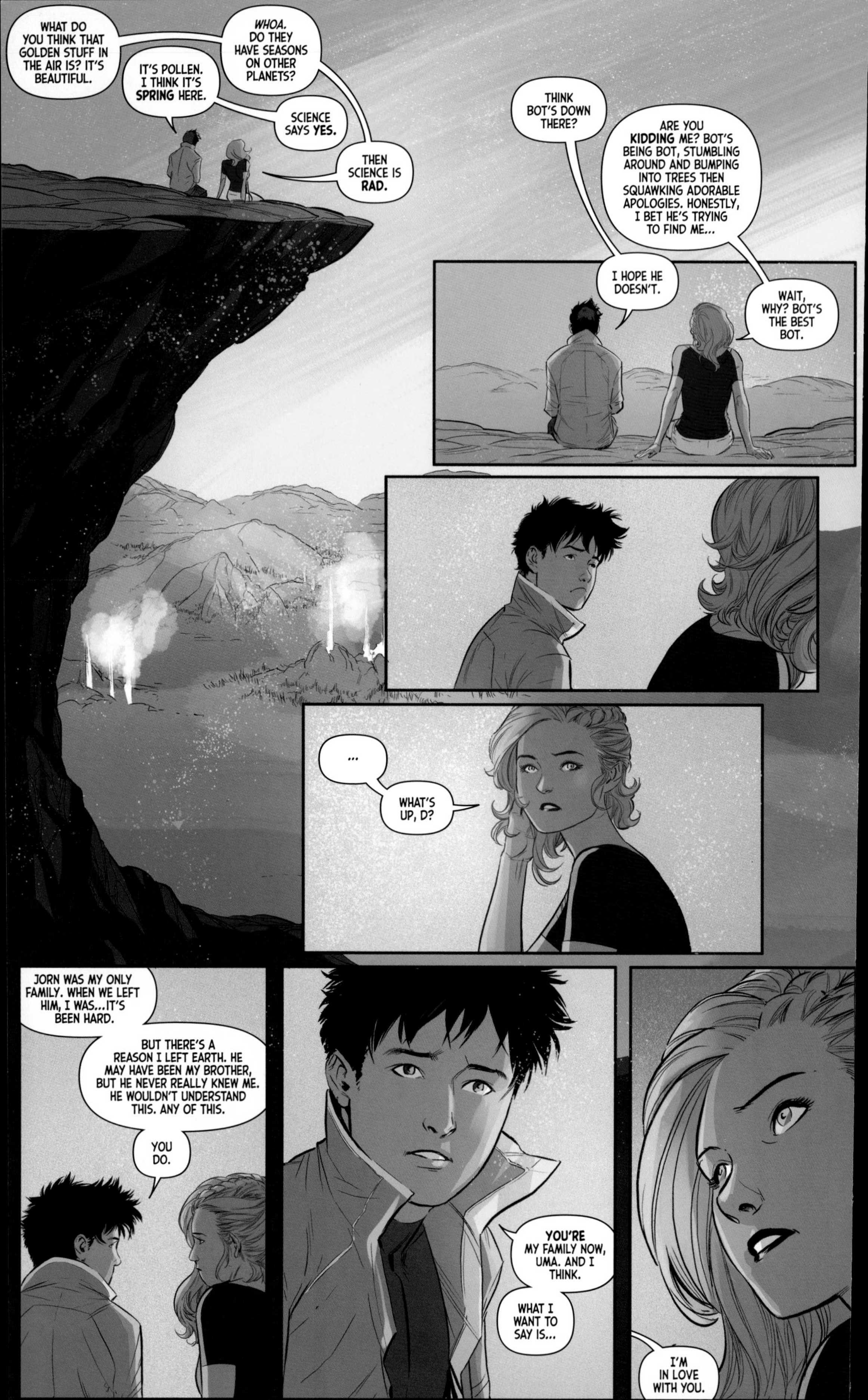
WHAT DO YOU THINK THAT GOLDEN STUFF IN THE AIR IS? IT'S BEAUTIFUL.
IT'S POLLEN. I THINK IT'S **SPRING** HERE.
WHOA. DO THEY HAVE SEASONS ON OTHER PLANETS?
SCIENCE SAYS **YES.**
THEN SCIENCE IS **RAD.**
THINK BOT'S DOWN THERE?
ARE YOU **KIDDING** ME? BOT'S BEING BOT, STUMBLING AROUND AND BUMPING INTO TREES THEN SQUAWKING ADORABLE APOLOGIES. HONESTLY, I BET HE'S TRYING TO FIND ME...
I HOPE HE DOESN'T.
WAIT, WHY? BOT'S THE BEST BOT.
...
WHAT'S UP, D?
JORN WAS MY ONLY FAMILY. WHEN WE LEFT HIM, I WAS...IT'S BEEN HARD.
BUT THERE'S A REASON I LEFT EARTH. HE MAY HAVE BEEN MY BROTHER, BUT HE NEVER REALLY KNEW ME. HE WOULDN'T UNDERSTAND THIS. ANY OF THIS.
YOU DO.
YOU'RE MY FAMILY NOW, UMA. AND I THINK.
WHAT I WANT TO SAY IS...
I'M IN LOVE WITH YOU.

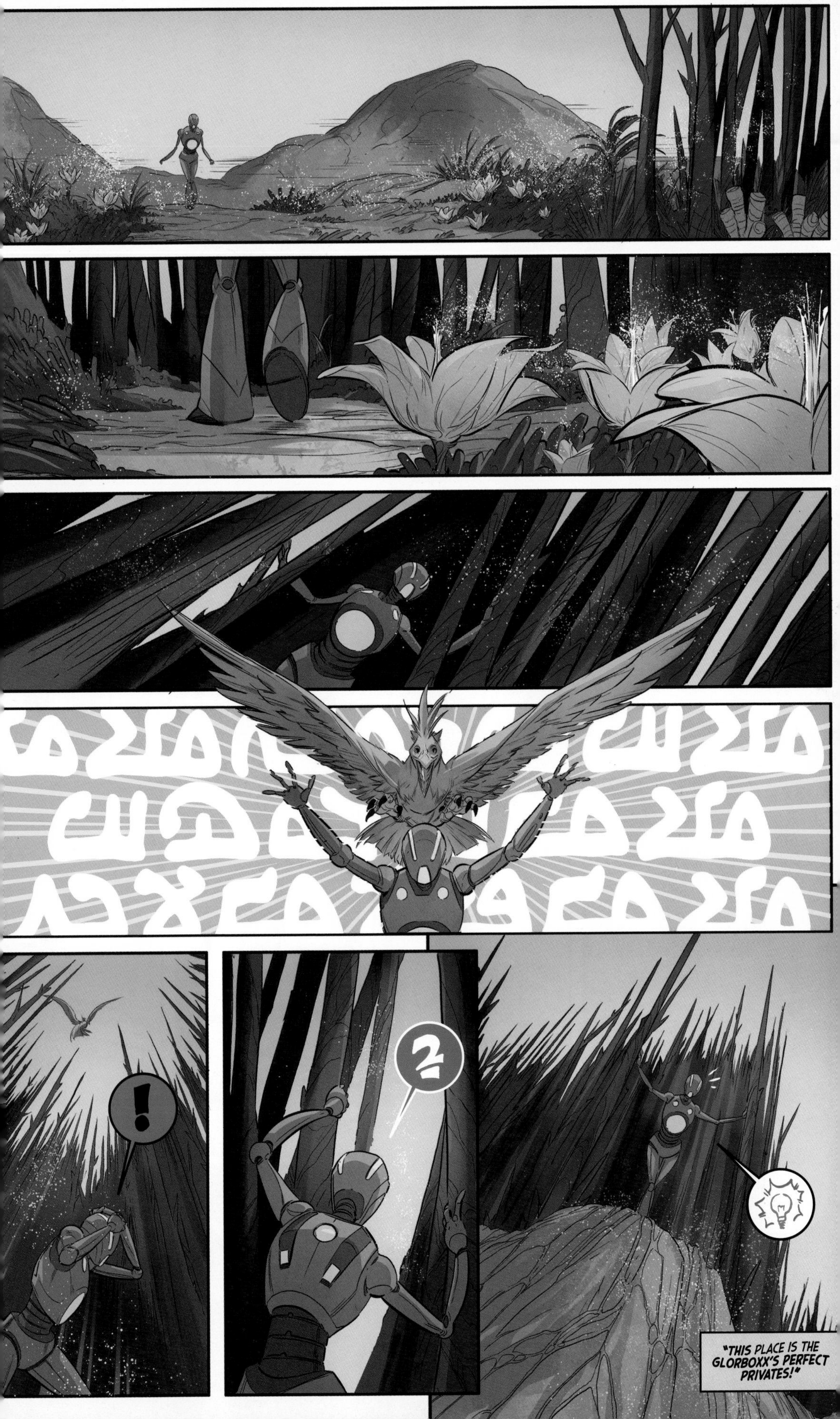
!
"THIS PLACE IS THE GLORBOXX'S PERFECT PRIVATES!"

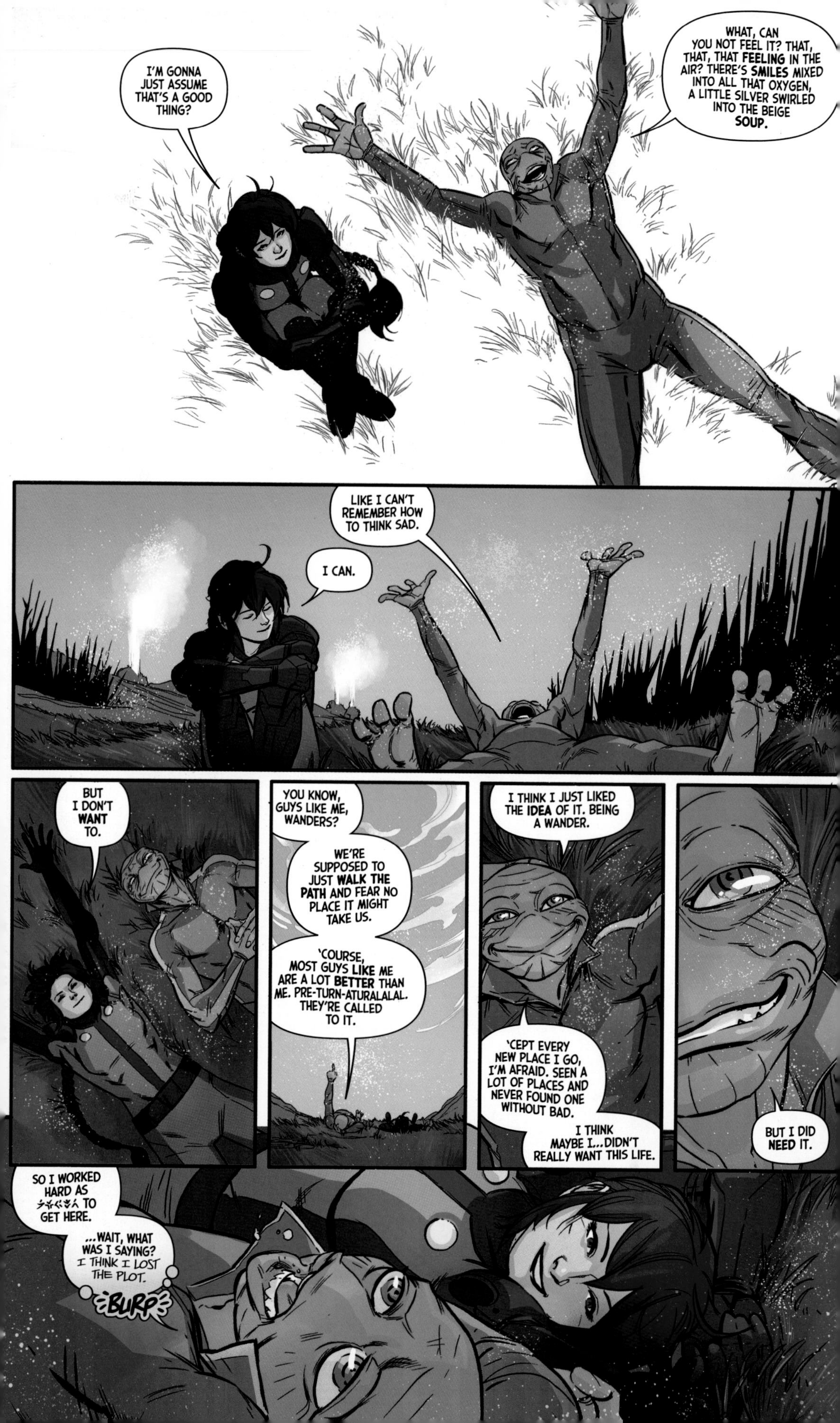

I'M GONNA JUST ASSUME THAT'S A GOOD THING?
WHAT, CAN YOU NOT FEEL IT? THAT, THAT, THAT FEELING IN THE AIR? THERE'S SMILES MIXED INTO ALL THAT OXYGEN, A LITTLE SILVER SWIRLED INTO THE BEIGE SOUP.
LIKE I CAN'T REMEMBER HOW TO THINK SAD.
I CAN.
BUT I DON'T WANT TO.
YOU KNOW, GUYS LIKE ME, WANDERS?
WE'RE SUPPOSED TO JUST WALK THE PATH AND FEAR NO PLACE IT MIGHT TAKE US.
'COURSE, MOST GUYS LIKE ME ARE A LOT BETTER THAN ME. PRE-TURN-ATURALALAL. THEY'RE CALLED TO IT.
I THINK I JUST LIKED THE IDEA OF IT. BEING A WANDER.
'CEPT EVERY NEW PLACE I GO, I'M AFRAID. SEEN A LOT OF PLACES AND NEVER FOUND ONE WITHOUT BAD.
I THINK MAYBE I...DIDN'T REALLY WANT THIS LIFE.
BUT I DID NEED IT.
SO I WORKED HARD AS TO GET HERE.
...WAIT, WHAT WAS I SAYING?
I THINK I LOST THE PLOT.
BURP

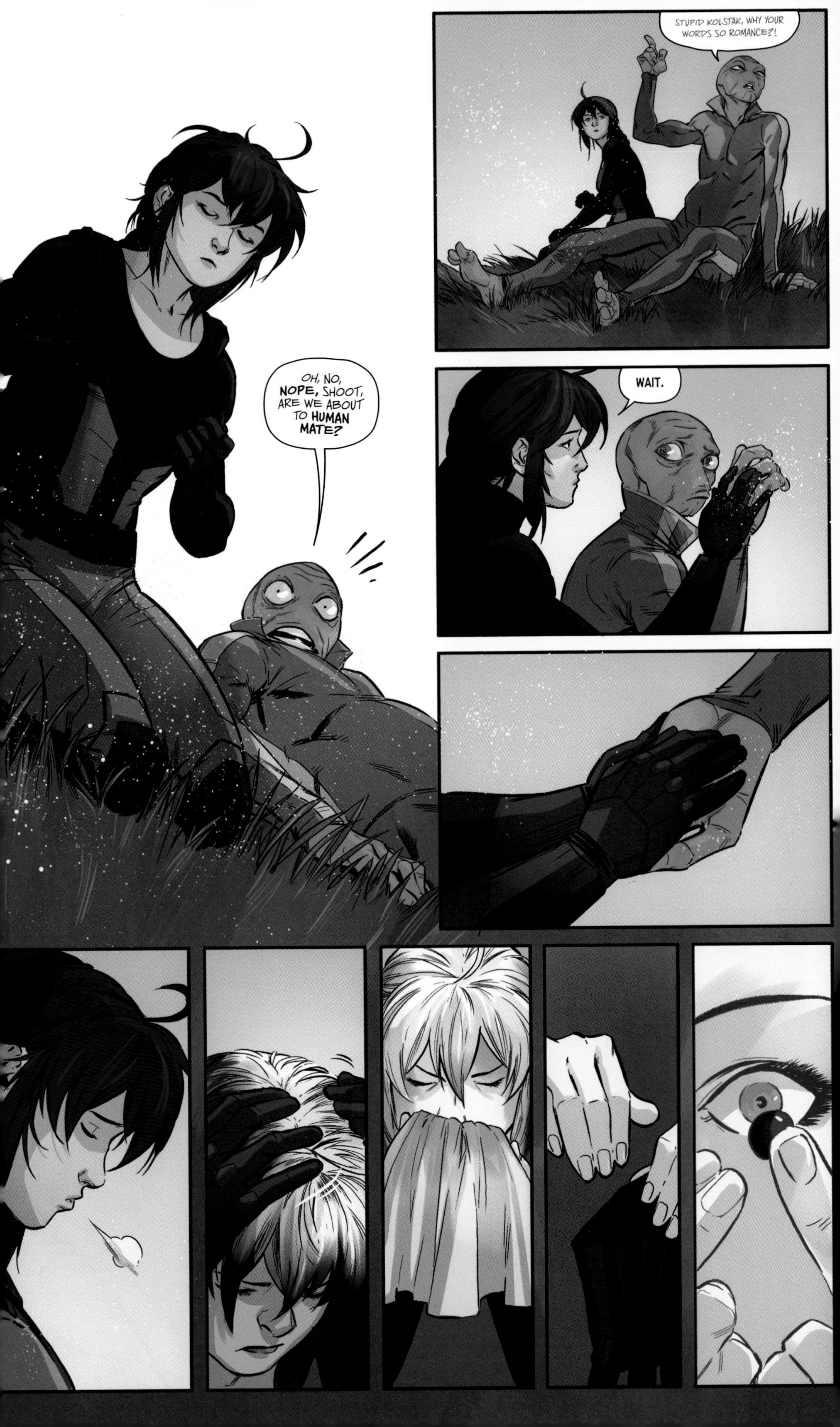

STUPID KOLSTAK, WHY YOUR WORDS SO ROMANCE?!
OH, NO, NOPE, SHOOT, ARE WE ABOUT TO HUMAN MATE?
WAIT.

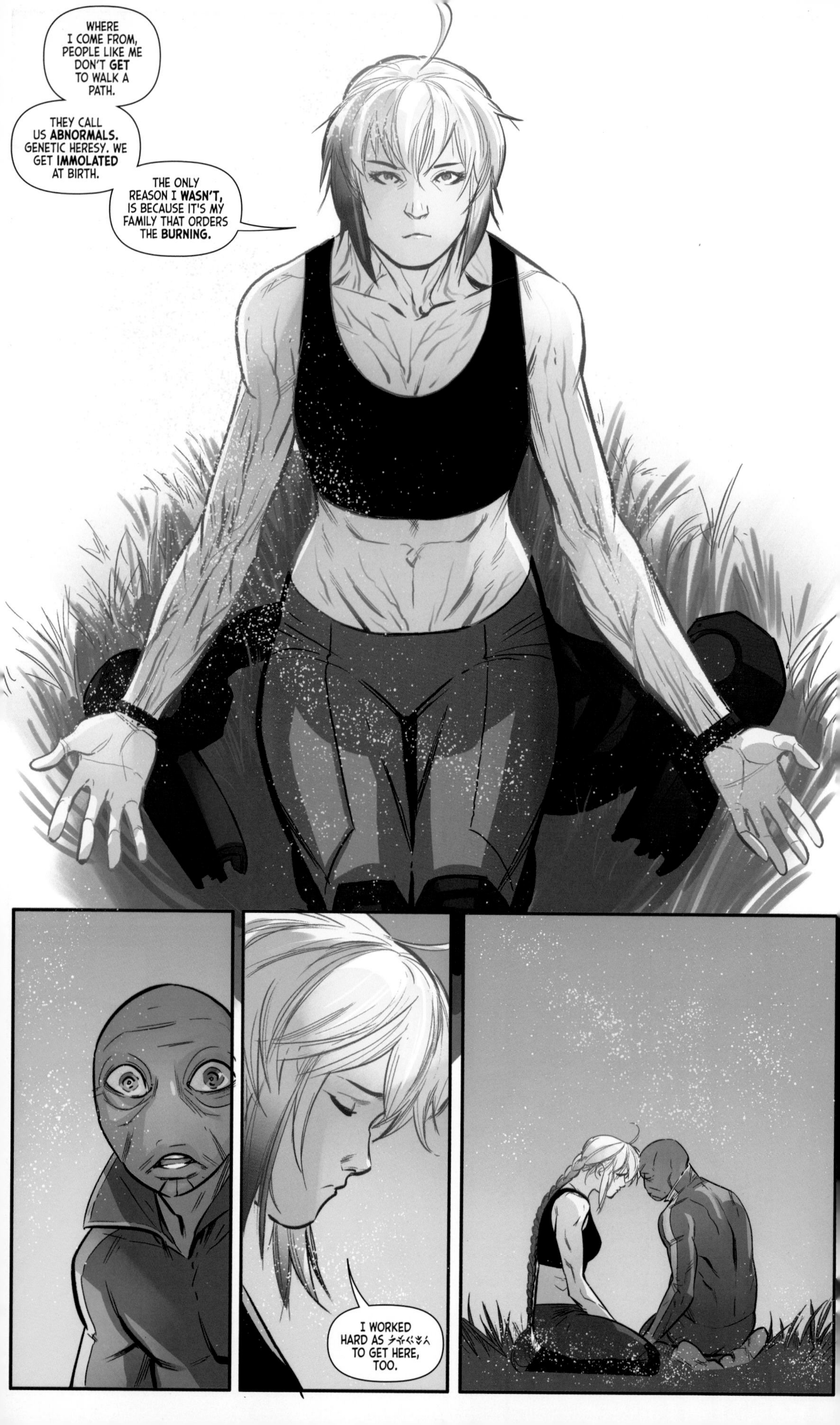
WHERE I COME FROM, PEOPLE LIKE ME DON'T GET TO WALK A PATH.
THEY CALL US ABNORMALS. GENETIC HERESY. WE GET IMMOLATED AT BIRTH.
THE ONLY REASON I WASN'T, IS BECAUSE IT'S MY FAMILY THAT ORDERS THE BURNING.
I WORKED HARD AS TO GET HERE, TOO.

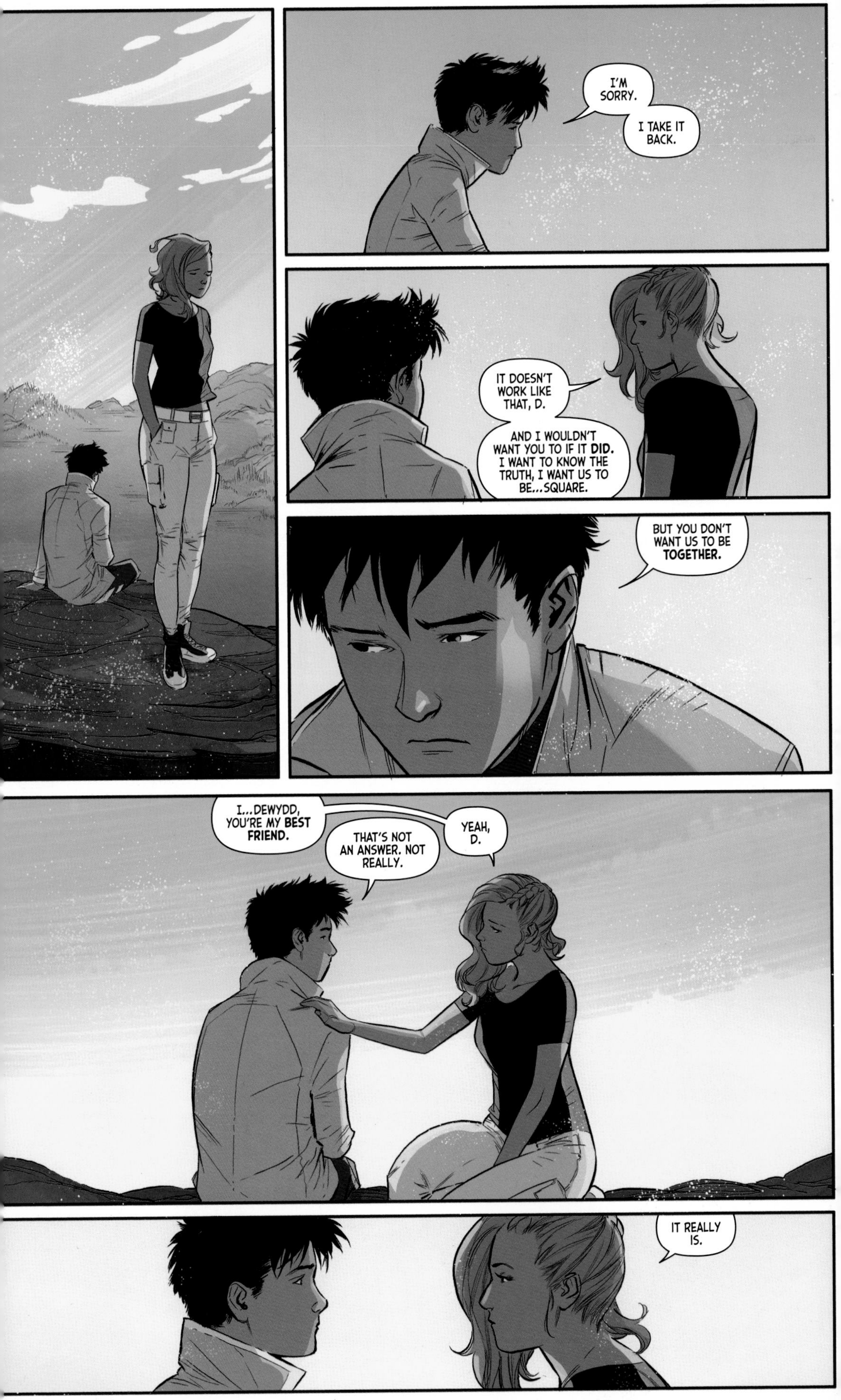
I'M SORRY.
I TAKE IT BACK.
IT DOESN'T WORK LIKE THAT, D.
AND I WOULDN'T WANT YOU TO IF IT **DID.** I WANT TO KNOW THE TRUTH, I WANT US TO BE...SQUARE.
BUT YOU DON'T WANT US TO BE **TOGETHER.**
I...DEWYDD, YOU'RE MY **BEST FRIEND.**
THAT'S NOT AN ANSWER. NOT REALLY.
YEAH, D.
IT REALLY IS.

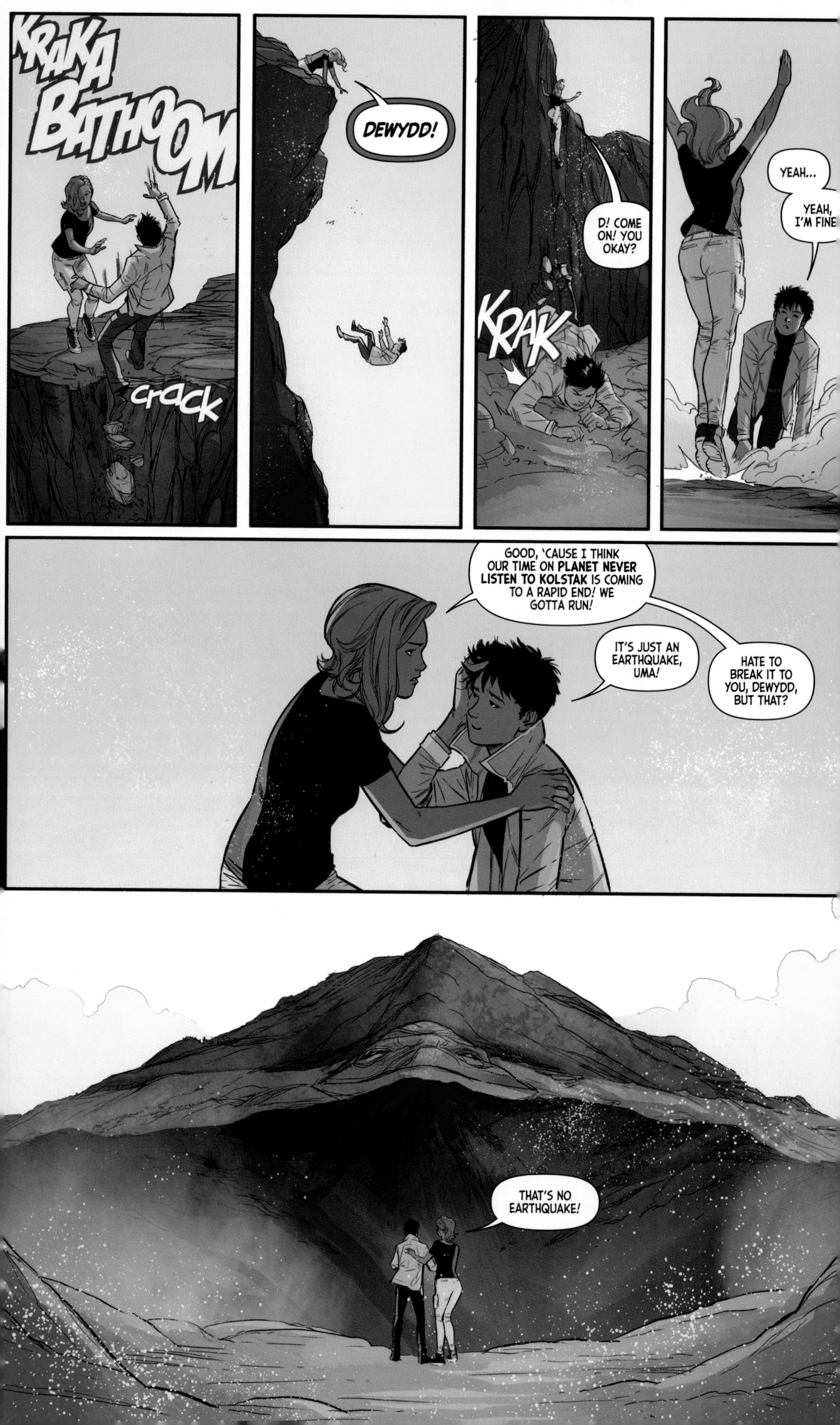
KRAKA BATHOOM
CRACK
DEWYDD!
D! COME ON! YOU OKAY?
KRAK
YEAH...
YEAH, I'M FINE
GOOD, 'CAUSE I THINK OUR TIME ON PLANET NEVER LISTEN TO KOLSTAK IS COMING TO A RAPID END! WE GOTTA RUN!
IT'S JUST AN EARTHQUAKE, UMA!
HATE TO BREAK IT TO YOU, DEWYDD, BUT THAT?
THAT'S NO EARTHQUAKE!

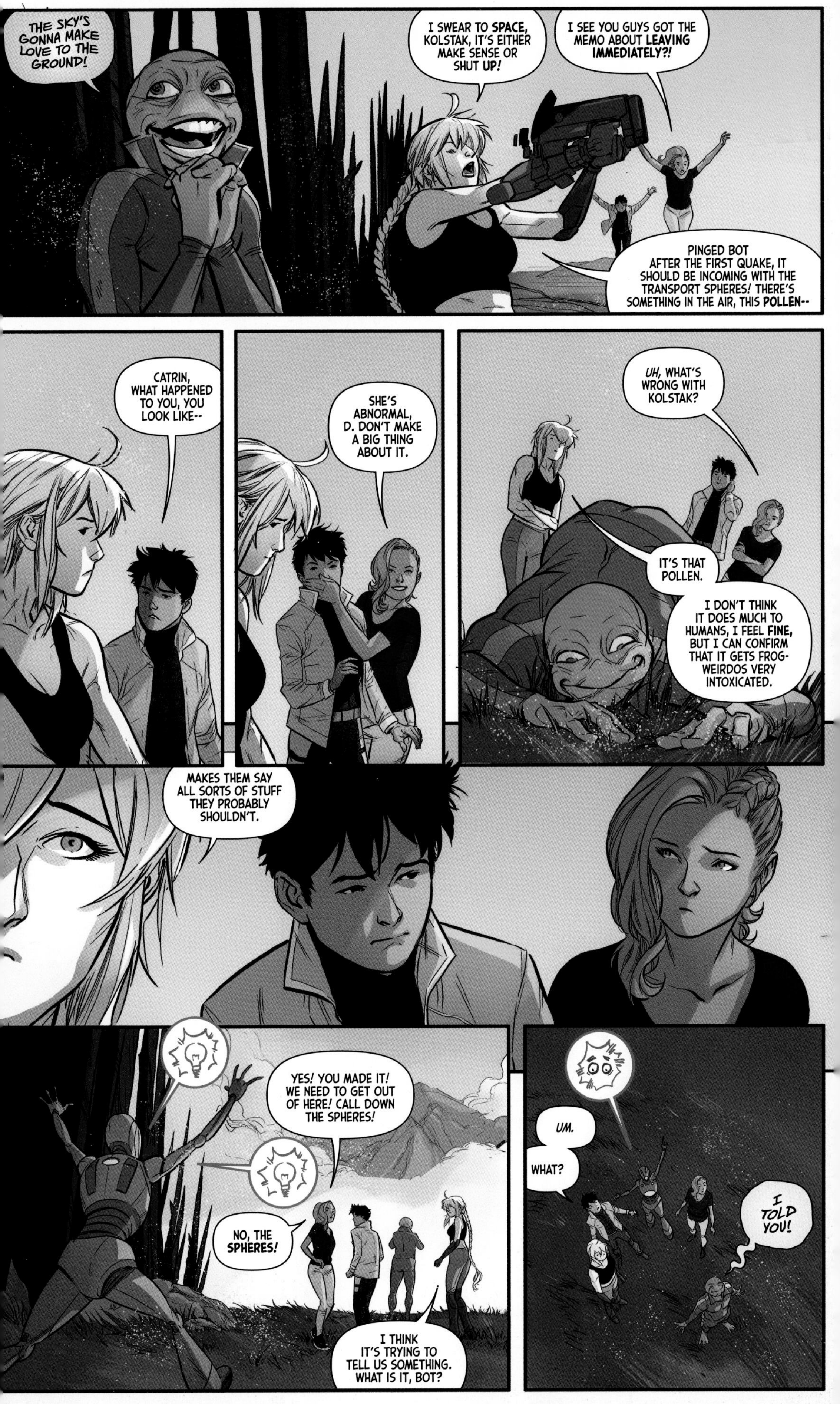
THE SKY'S GONNA MAKE LOVE TO THE GROUND!
I SWEAR TO SPACE, KOLSTAK, IT'S EITHER MAKE SENSE OR SHUT UP!
I SEE YOU GUYS GOT THE MEMO ABOUT LEAVING IMMEDIATELY?!
PINGED BOT AFTER THE FIRST QUAKE, IT SHOULD BE INCOMING WITH THE TRANSPORT SPHERES! THERE'S SOMETHING IN THE AIR, THIS POLLEN--
CATRIN, WHAT HAPPENED TO YOU, YOU LOOK LIKE--
SHE'S ABNORMAL, D. DON'T MAKE A BIG THING ABOUT IT.
UH, WHAT'S WRONG WITH KOLSTAK?
IT'S THAT POLLEN.
I DON'T THINK IT DOES MUCH TO HUMANS, I FEEL FINE, BUT I CAN CONFIRM THAT IT GETS FROG-WEIRDOS VERY INTOXICATED.
MAKES THEM SAY ALL SORTS OF STUFF THEY PROBABLY SHOULDN'T.
YES! YOU MADE IT! WE NEED TO GET OUT OF HERE! CALL DOWN THE SPHERES!
NO, THE SPHERES!
I THINK IT'S TRYING TO TELL US SOMETHING. WHAT IS IT, BOT?
UM.
WHAT?
I TOLD YOU!

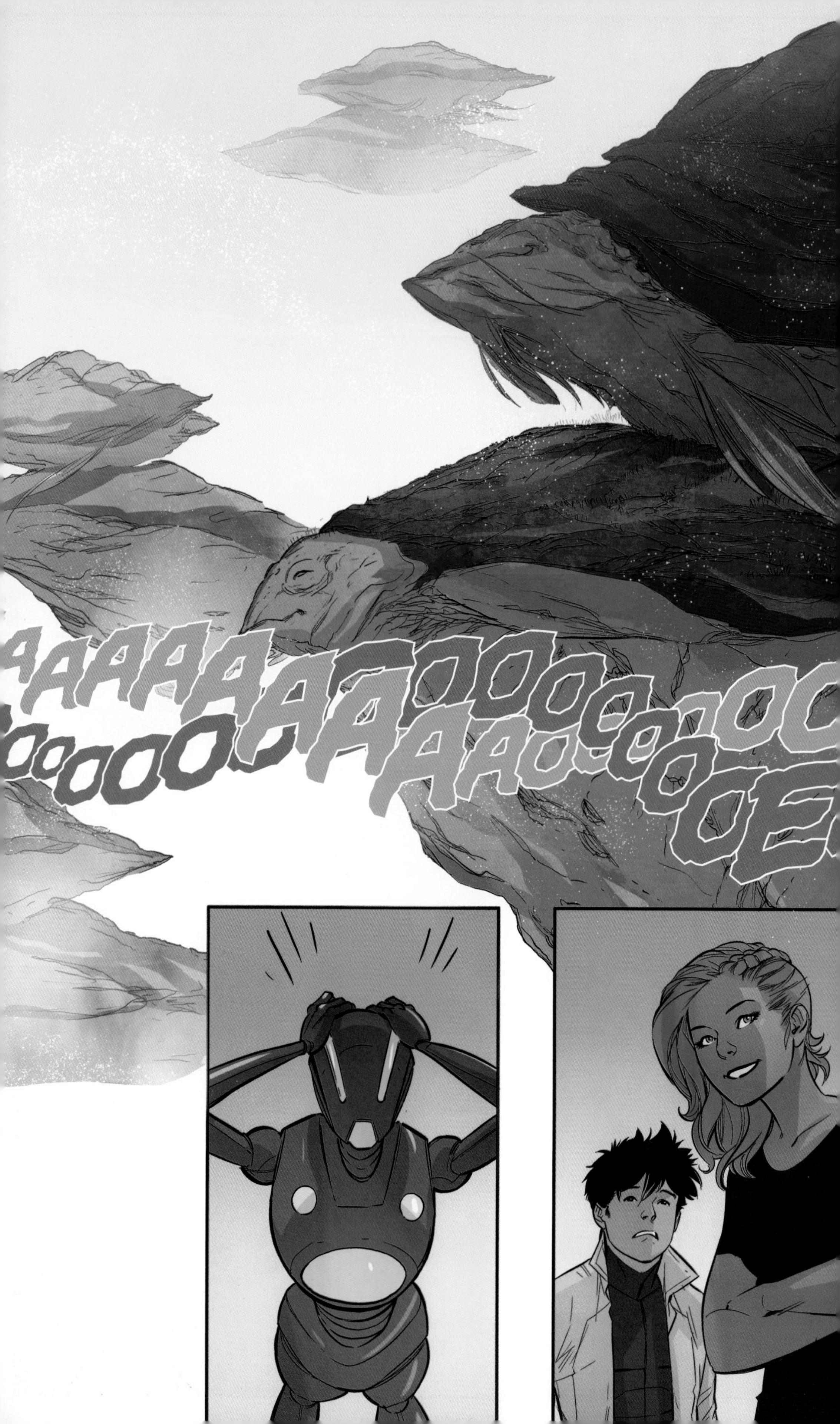
AAAAAAAOOOOOOO
OOOOOOAAAAOOOOOE

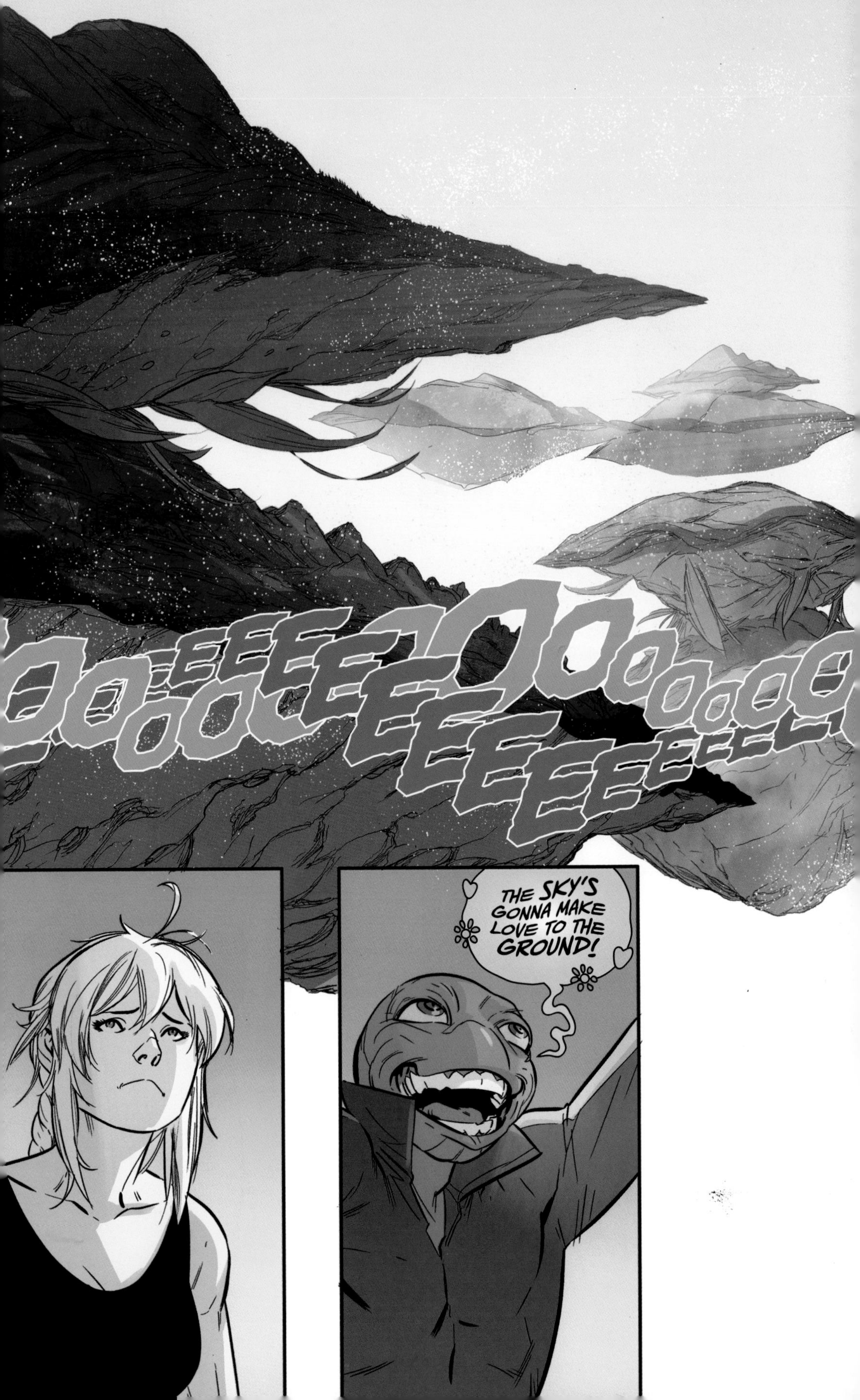
OOOEEEEEEOOOOOOOOOOOEEEEEEEEEEE
THE SKY'S GONNA MAKE LOVE TO THE GROUND!

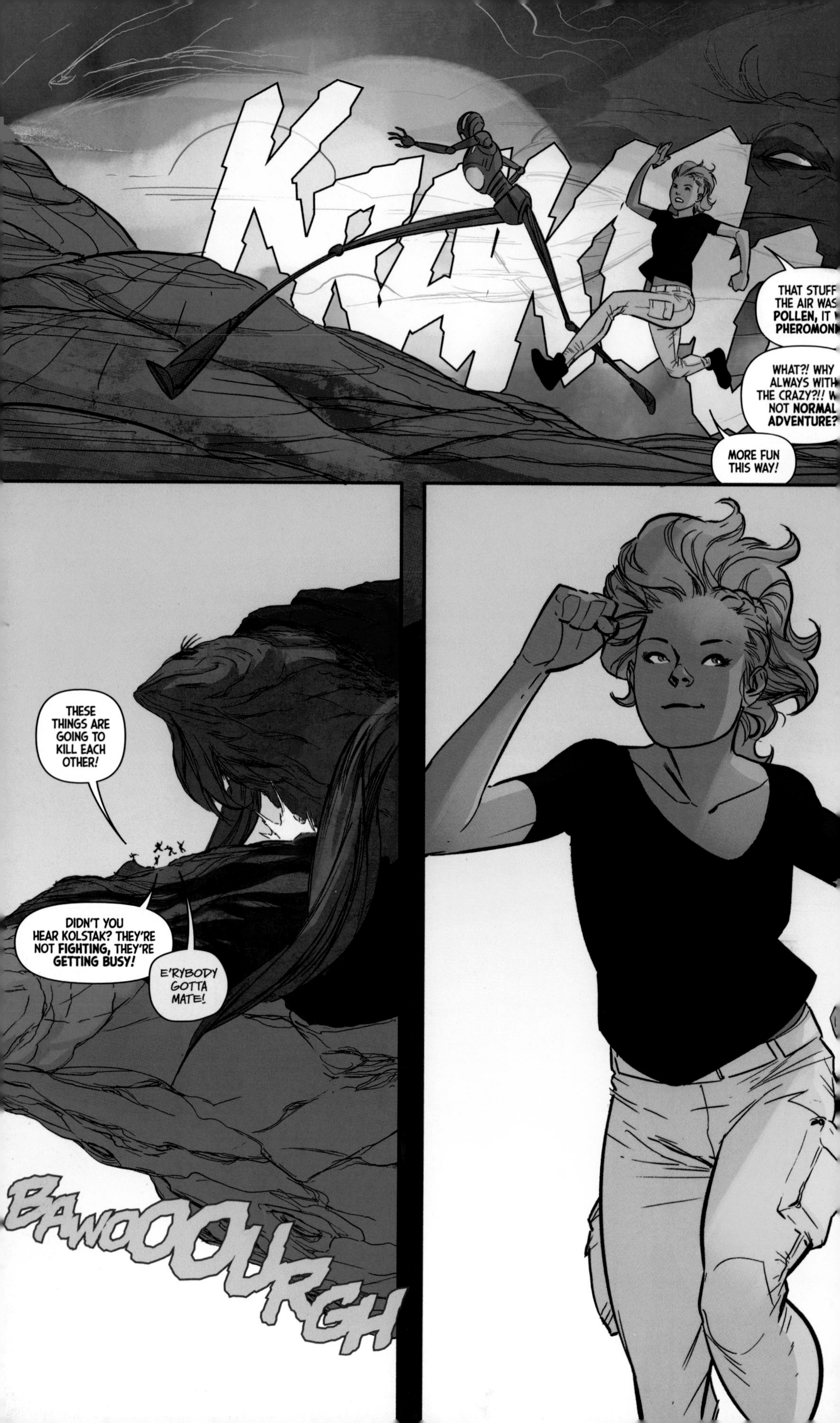

THAT STUFF THE AIR WAS POLLEN, IT PHEROMON
WHAT?! WHY ALWAYS WITH THE CRAZY?!! W NOT NORMAL ADVENTURE?
MORE FUN THIS WAY!
THESE THINGS ARE GOING TO KILL EACH OTHER!
DIDN'T YOU HEAR KOLSTAK? THEY'RE NOT FIGHTING, THEY'RE GETTING BUSY!
E'RYBODY GOTTA MATE!
BAWOOOURGH

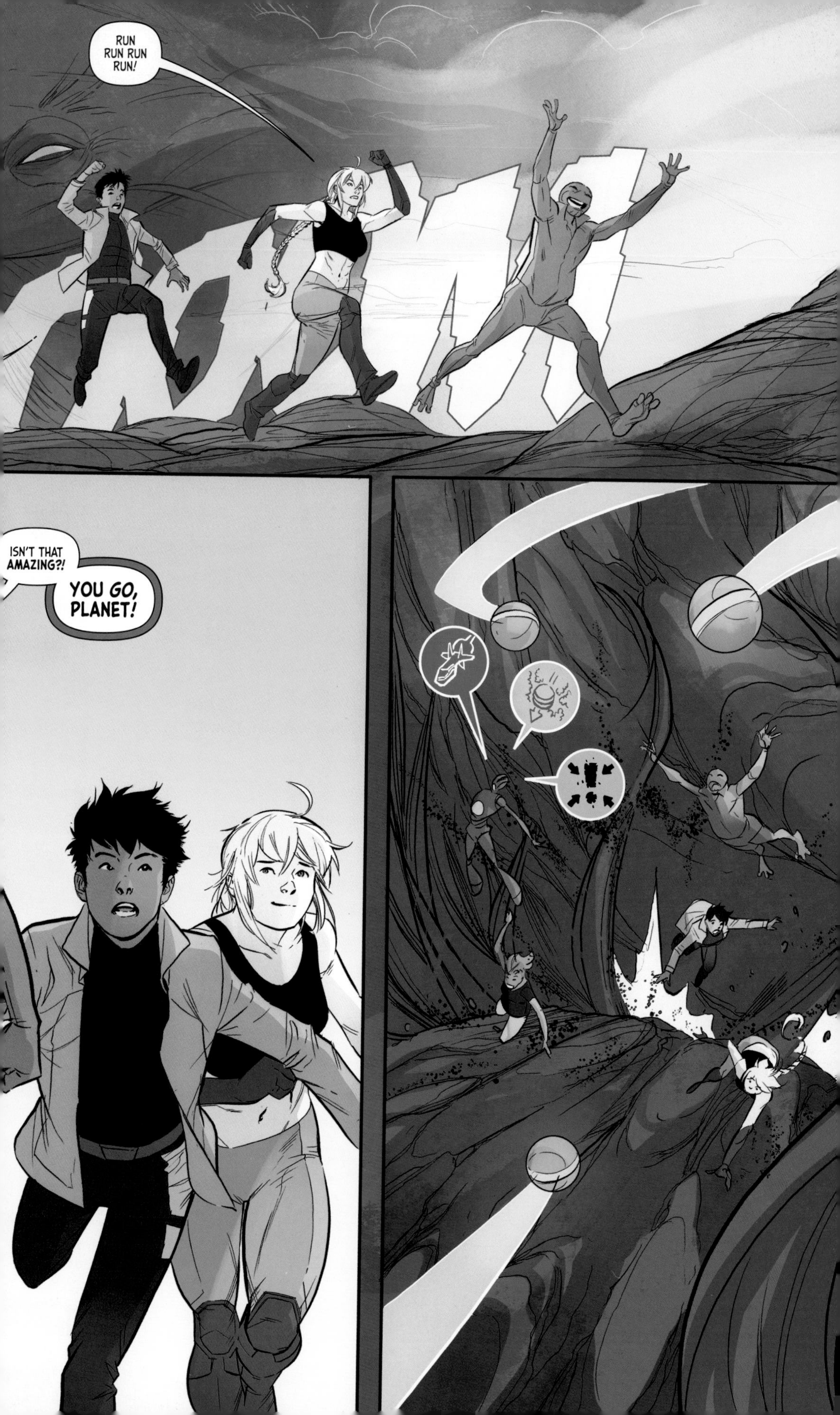
RUN RUN RUN RUN!
ISN'T THAT AMAZING?!
YOU GO, PLANET!

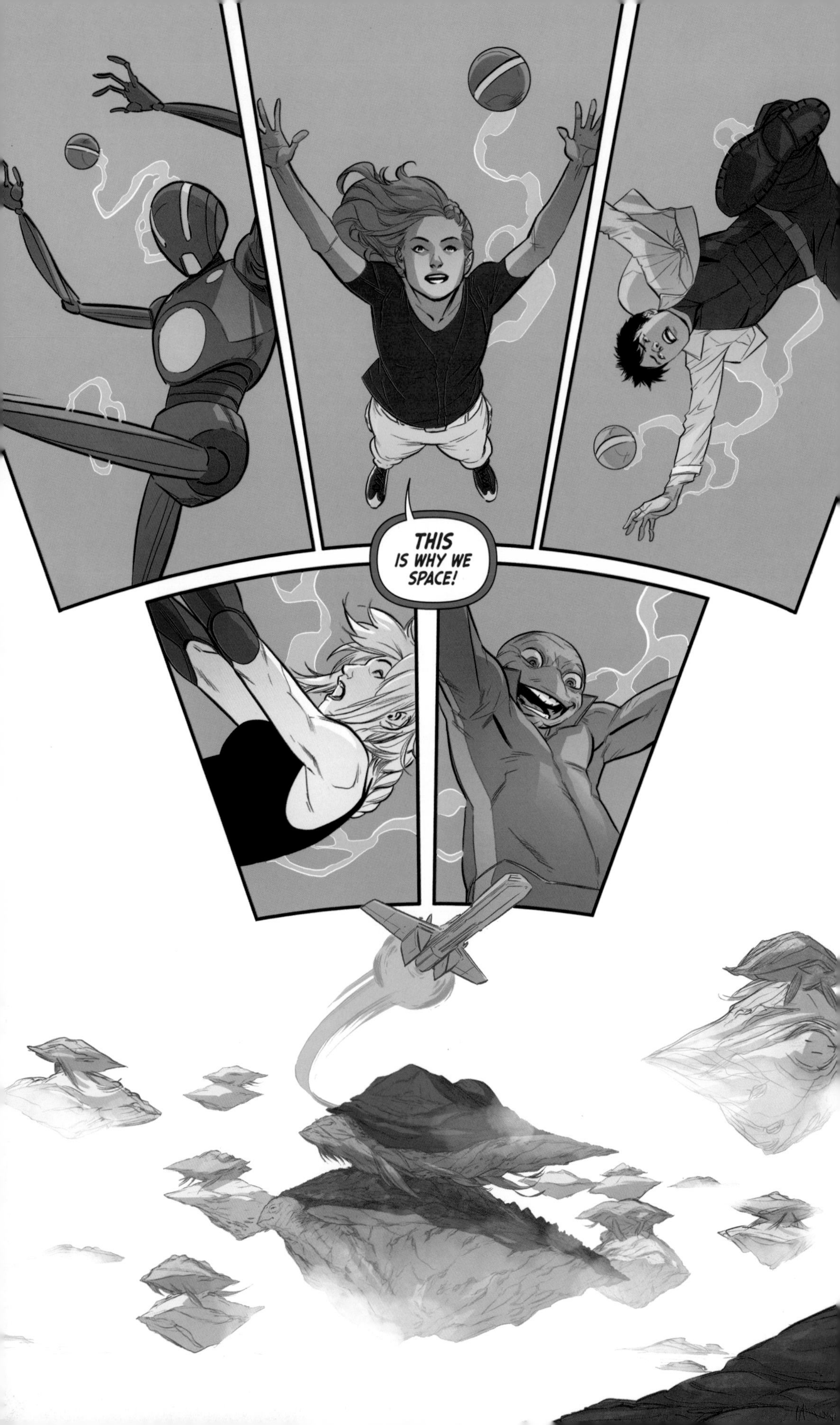
THIS IS WHY WE SPACE!

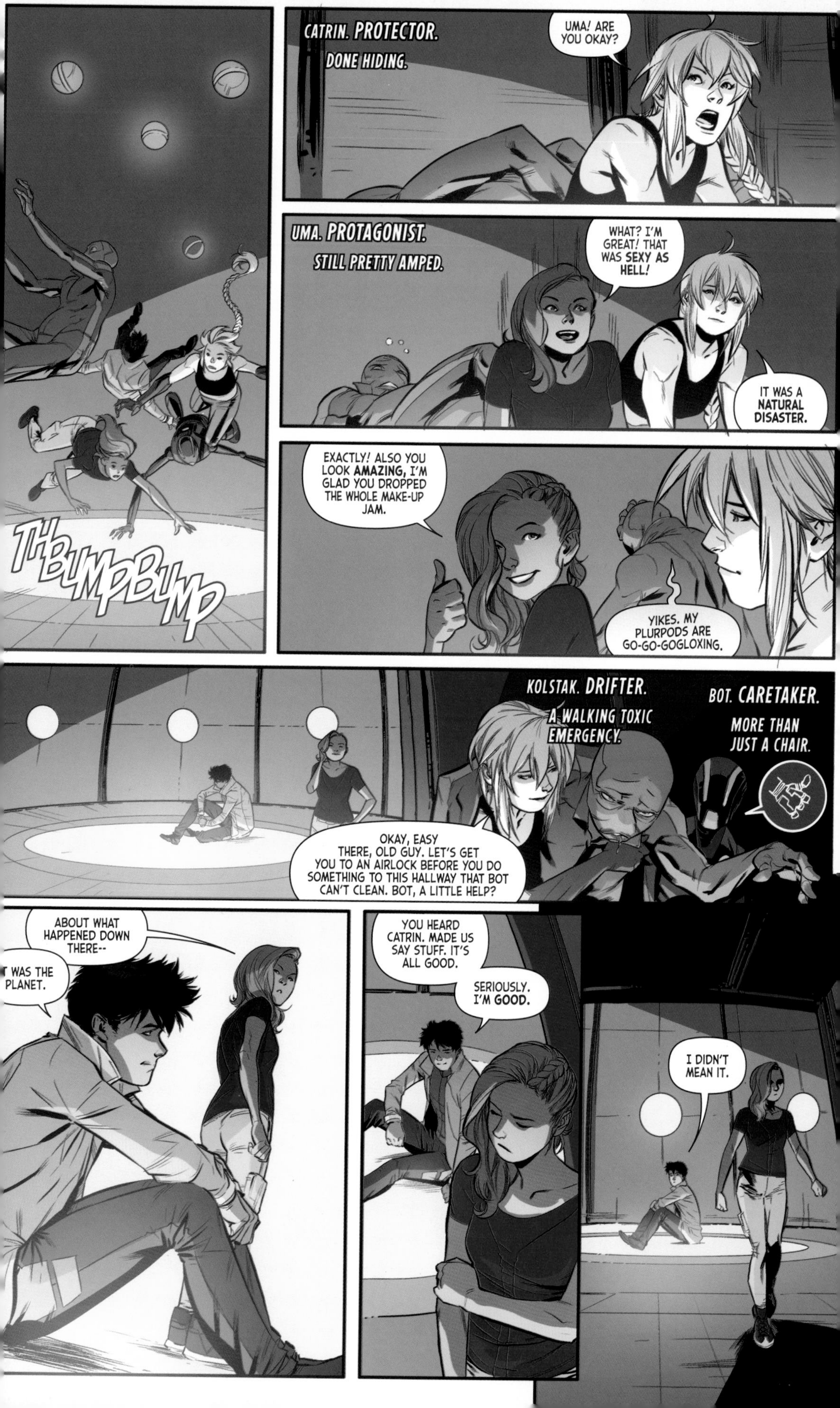

THBUMPBUMP
CATRIN. PROTECTOR.
DONE HIDING.
UMA! ARE YOU OKAY?
UMA. PROTAGONIST.
STILL PRETTY AMPED.
WHAT? I'M GREAT! THAT WAS SEXY AS HELL!
IT WAS A NATURAL DISASTER.
EXACTLY! ALSO YOU LOOK AMAZING, I'M GLAD YOU DROPPED THE WHOLE MAKE-UP JAM.
YIKES. MY PLURPODS ARE GO-GO-GOGLOXING.
KOLSTAK. DRIFTER.
A WALKING TOXIC EMERGENCY.
BOT. CARETAKER.
MORE THAN JUST A CHAIR.
OKAY, EASY THERE, OLD GUY. LET'S GET YOU TO AN AIRLOCK BEFORE YOU DO SOMETHING TO THIS HALLWAY THAT BOT CAN'T CLEAN. BOT, A LITTLE HELP?
ABOUT WHAT HAPPENED DOWN THERE--
T WAS THE PLANET.
YOU HEARD CATRIN. MADE US SAY STUFF. IT'S ALL GOOD.
SERIOUSLY. I'M GOOD.
I DIDN'T MEAN IT.

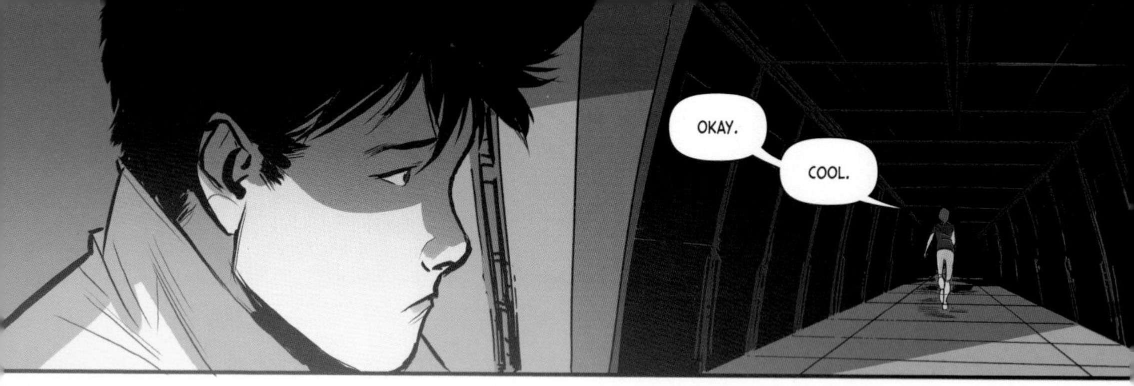
OKAY.
COOL.

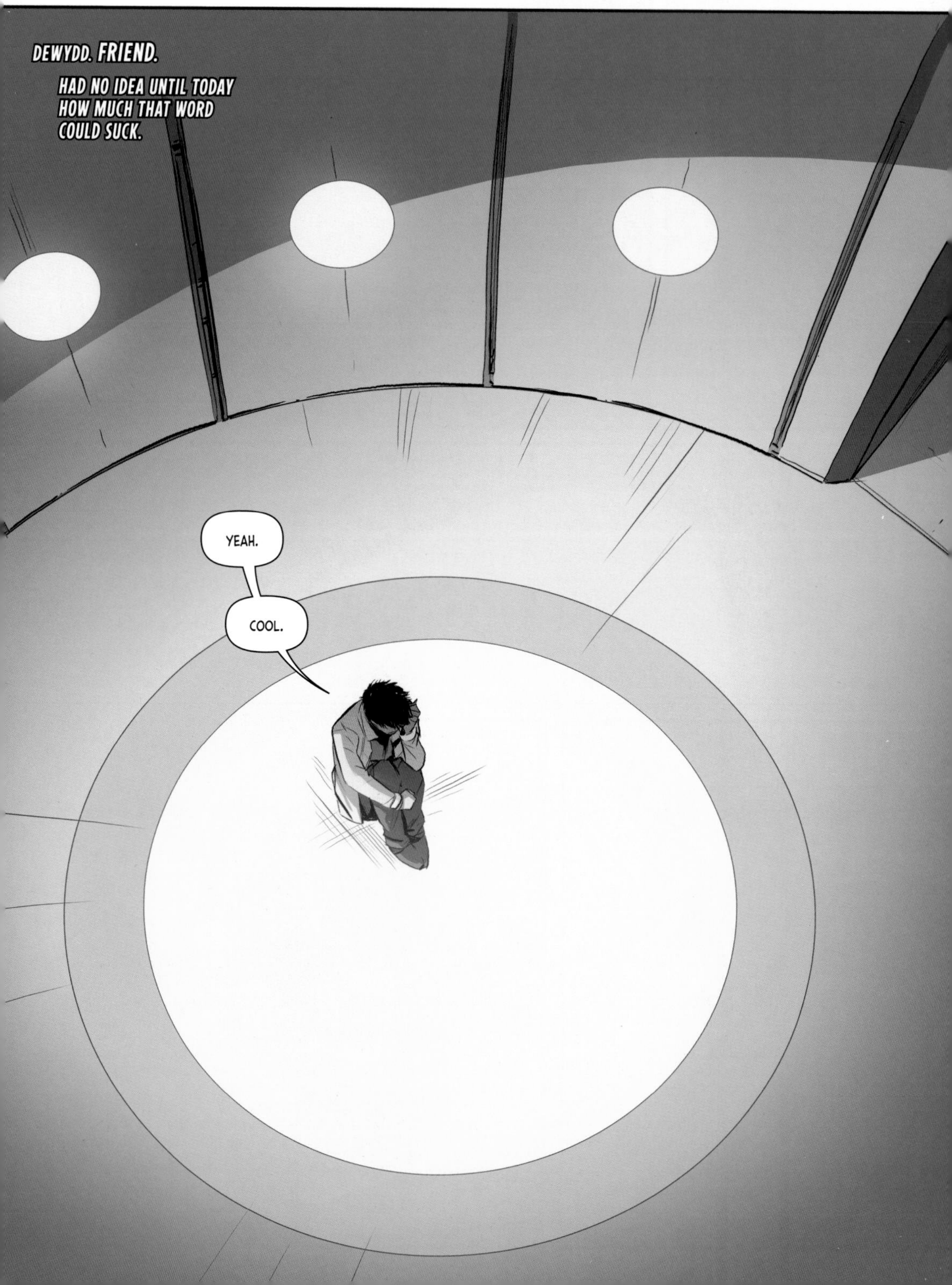
DEWYDD. FRIEND.
HAD NO IDEA UNTIL TODAY HOW MUCH THAT WORD COULD SUCK.
YEAH.
COOL.

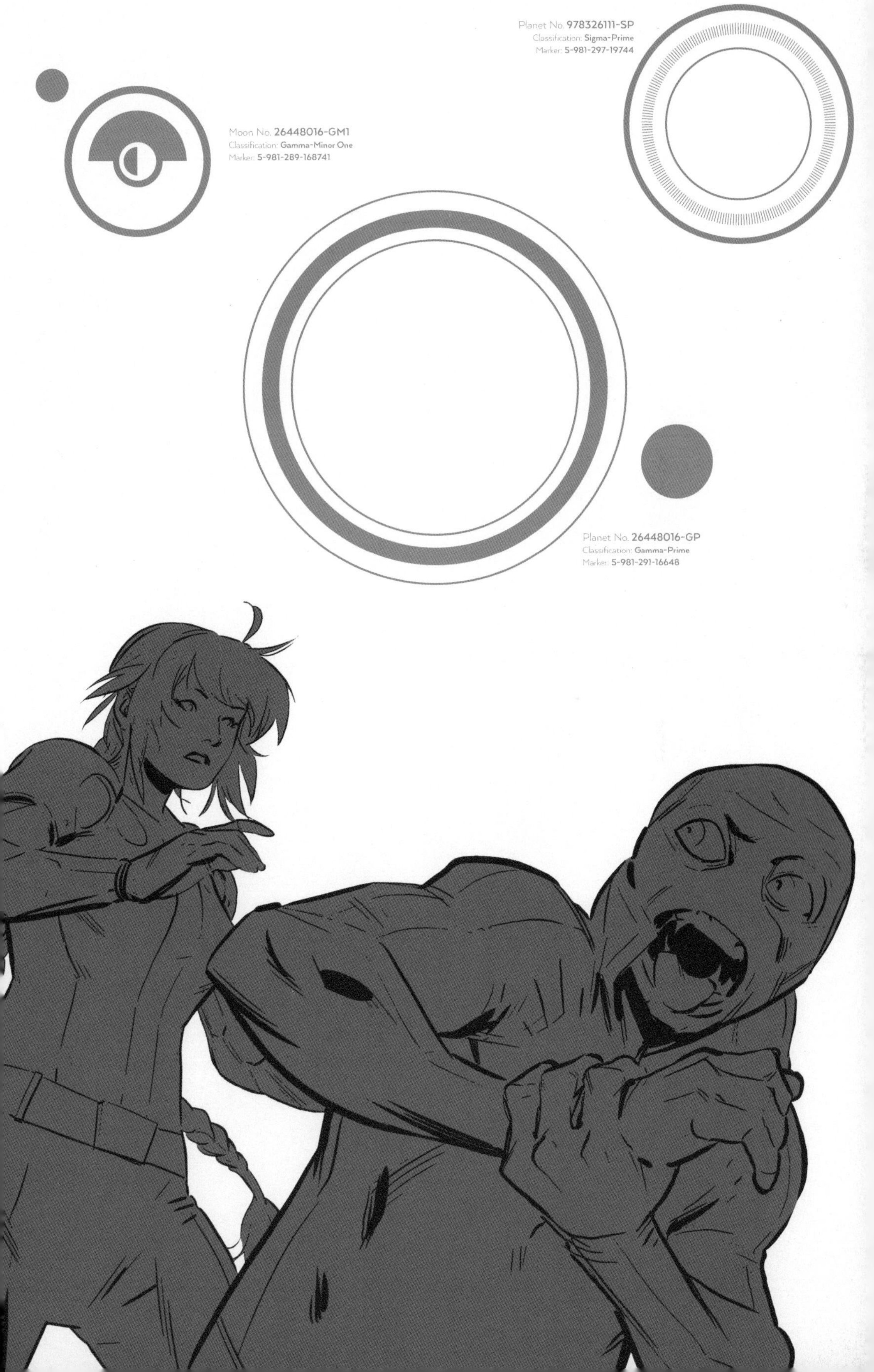
Planet No. 978326111-SP
Classification: Sigma-Prime
Marker: 5-981-297-19744
Moon No. 26448016-GM1
Classification: Gamma-Minor One
Marker: 5-981-289-168741
Planet No. 26448016-GP
Classification: Gamma-Prime
Marker: 5-981-291-16648

CHAPTER **SIX**

HOW IT WORKS

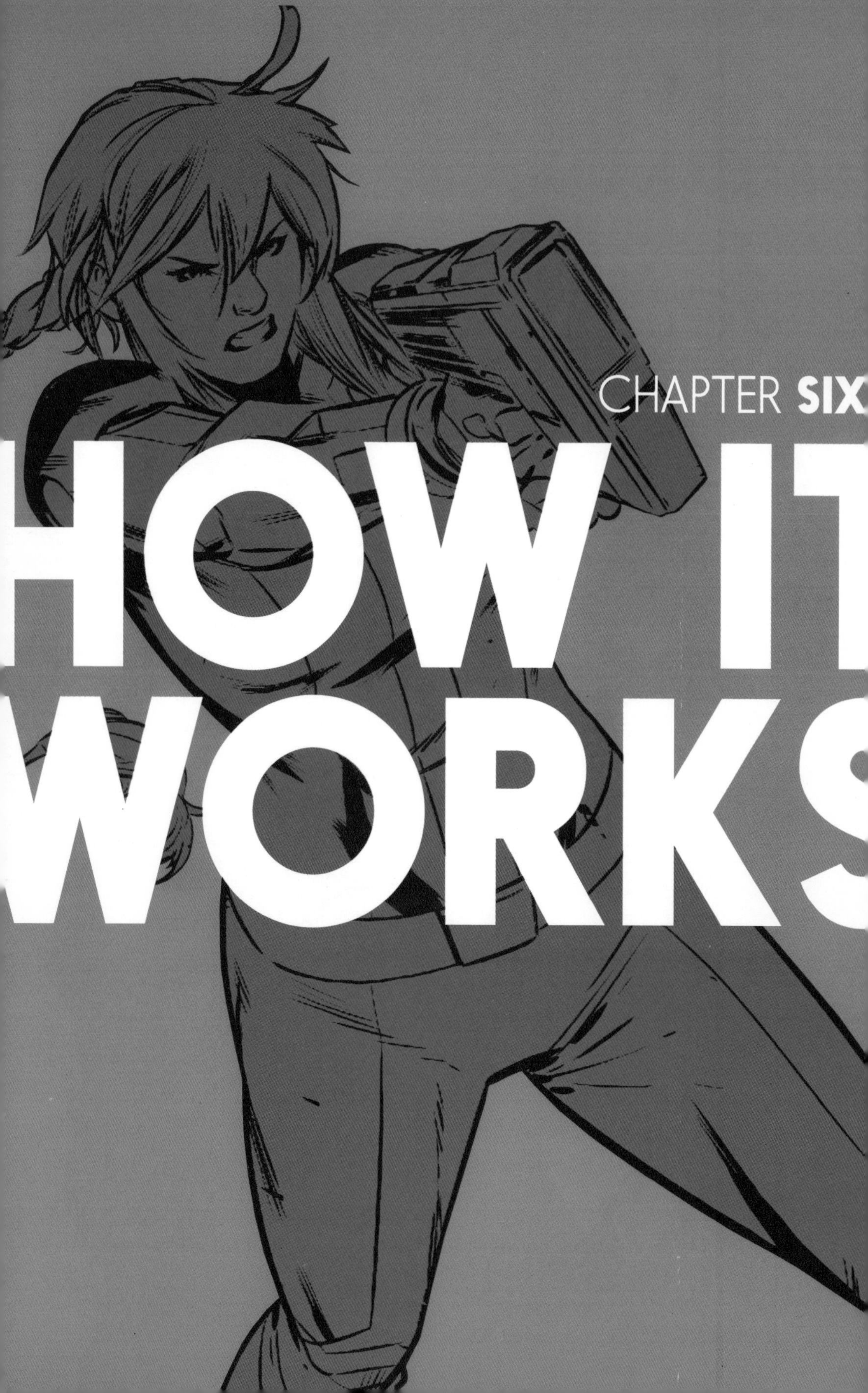

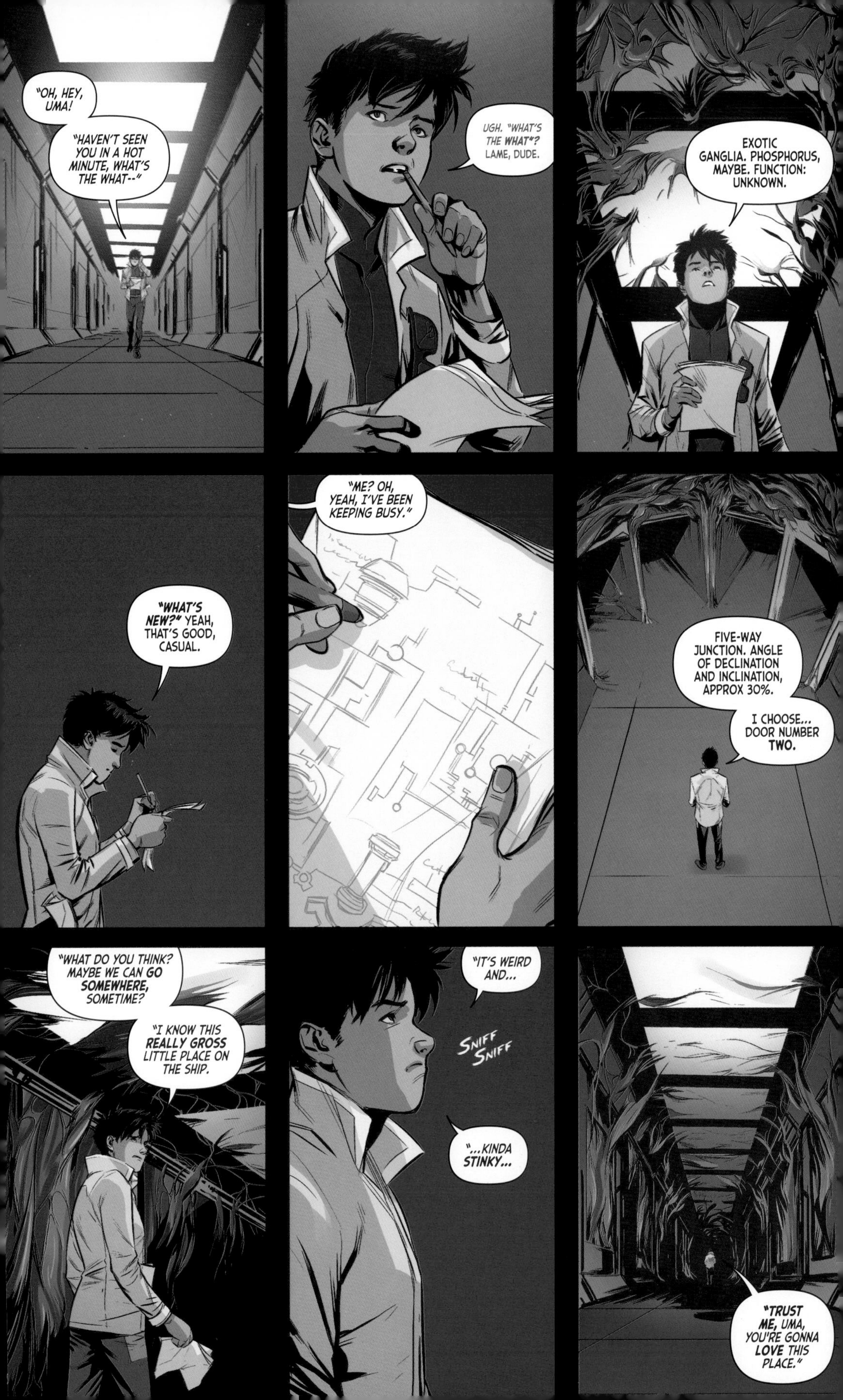
"OH, HEY, UMA!
"HAVEN'T SEEN YOU IN A HOT MINUTE, WHAT'S THE WHAT--"
UGH. "WHAT'S THE WHAT"? LAME, DUDE.
EXOTIC GANGLIA. PHOSPHORUS, MAYBE. FUNCTION: UNKNOWN.
"WHAT'S NEW?" YEAH, THAT'S GOOD, CASUAL.
"ME? OH, YEAH, I'VE BEEN KEEPING BUSY."
FIVE-WAY JUNCTION. ANGLE OF DECLINATION AND INCLINATION, APPROX 30%.
I CHOOSE... DOOR NUMBER TWO.
"WHAT DO YOU THINK? MAYBE WE CAN GO SOMEWHERE, SOMETIME?
"I KNOW THIS REALLY GROSS LITTLE PLACE ON THE SHIP.
"IT'S WEIRD AND...
SNIFF SNIFF
"...KINDA STINKY...
"TRUST ME, UMA, YOU'RE GONNA LOVE THIS PLACE."

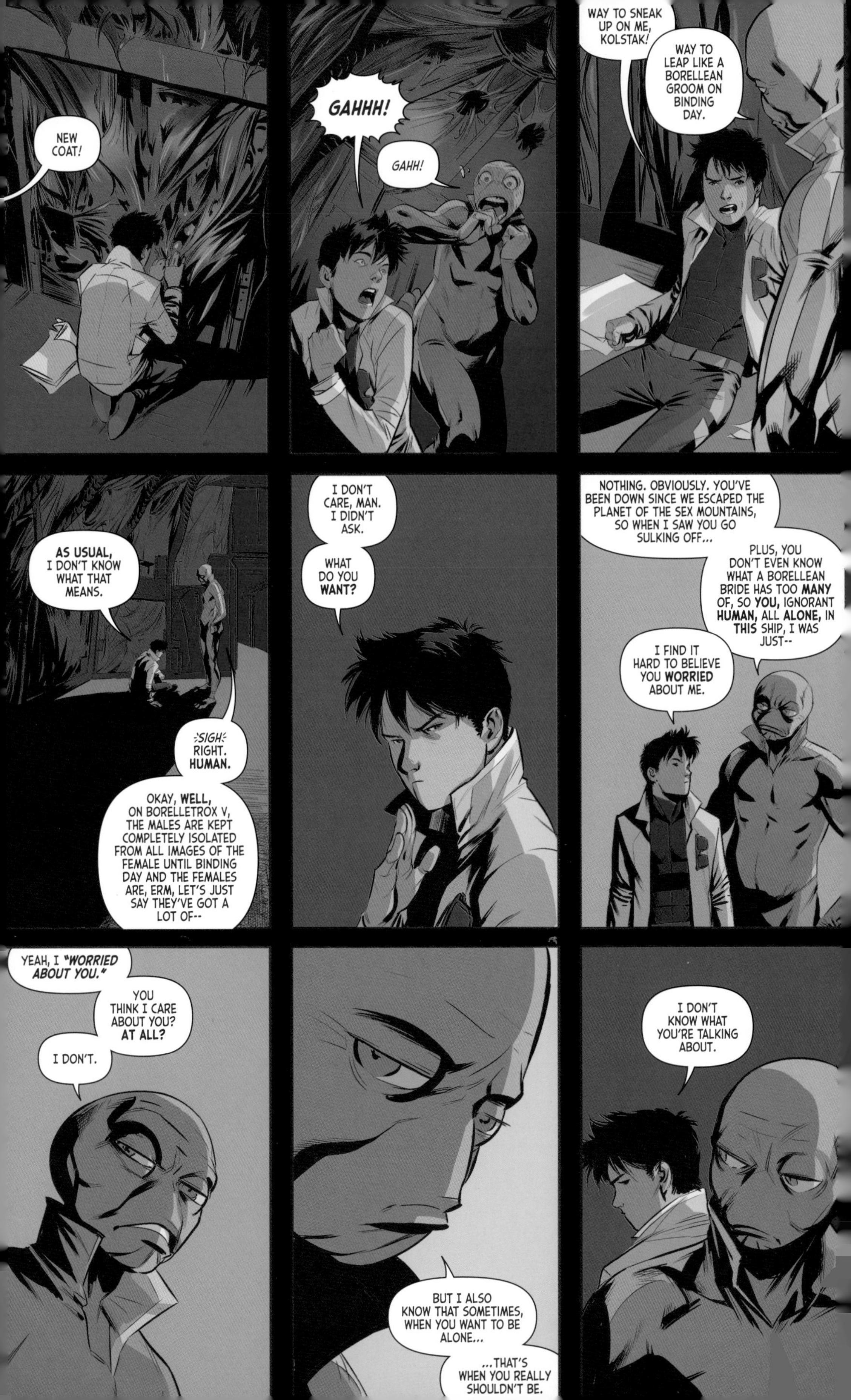
NEW COAT!
GAHHH!
GAHH!
WAY TO SNEAK UP ON ME, KOLSTAK!
WAY TO LEAP LIKE A BORELLEAN GROOM ON BINDING DAY.
AS USUAL, I DON'T KNOW WHAT THAT MEANS.
SIGH RIGHT. HUMAN.
OKAY, WELL, ON BORELLETROX V, THE MALES ARE KEPT COMPLETELY ISOLATED FROM ALL IMAGES OF THE FEMALE UNTIL BINDING DAY AND THE FEMALES ARE, ERM, LET'S JUST SAY THEY'VE GOT A LOT OF--
I DON'T CARE, MAN. I DIDN'T ASK.
WHAT DO YOU WANT?
NOTHING. OBVIOUSLY. YOU'VE BEEN DOWN SINCE WE ESCAPED THE PLANET OF THE SEX MOUNTAINS, SO WHEN I SAW YOU GO SULKING OFF...
PLUS, YOU DON'T EVEN KNOW WHAT A BORELLEAN BRIDE HAS TOO MANY OF, SO YOU, IGNORANT HUMAN, ALL ALONE, IN THIS SHIP, I WAS JUST--
I FIND IT HARD TO BELIEVE YOU WORRIED ABOUT ME.
YEAH, I "WORRIED ABOUT YOU."
YOU THINK I CARE ABOUT YOU? AT ALL?
I DON'T.
BUT I ALSO KNOW THAT SOMETIMES, WHEN YOU WANT TO BE ALONE...
...THAT'S WHEN YOU REALLY SHOULDN'T BE.
I DON'T KNOW WHAT YOU'RE TALKING ABOUT.

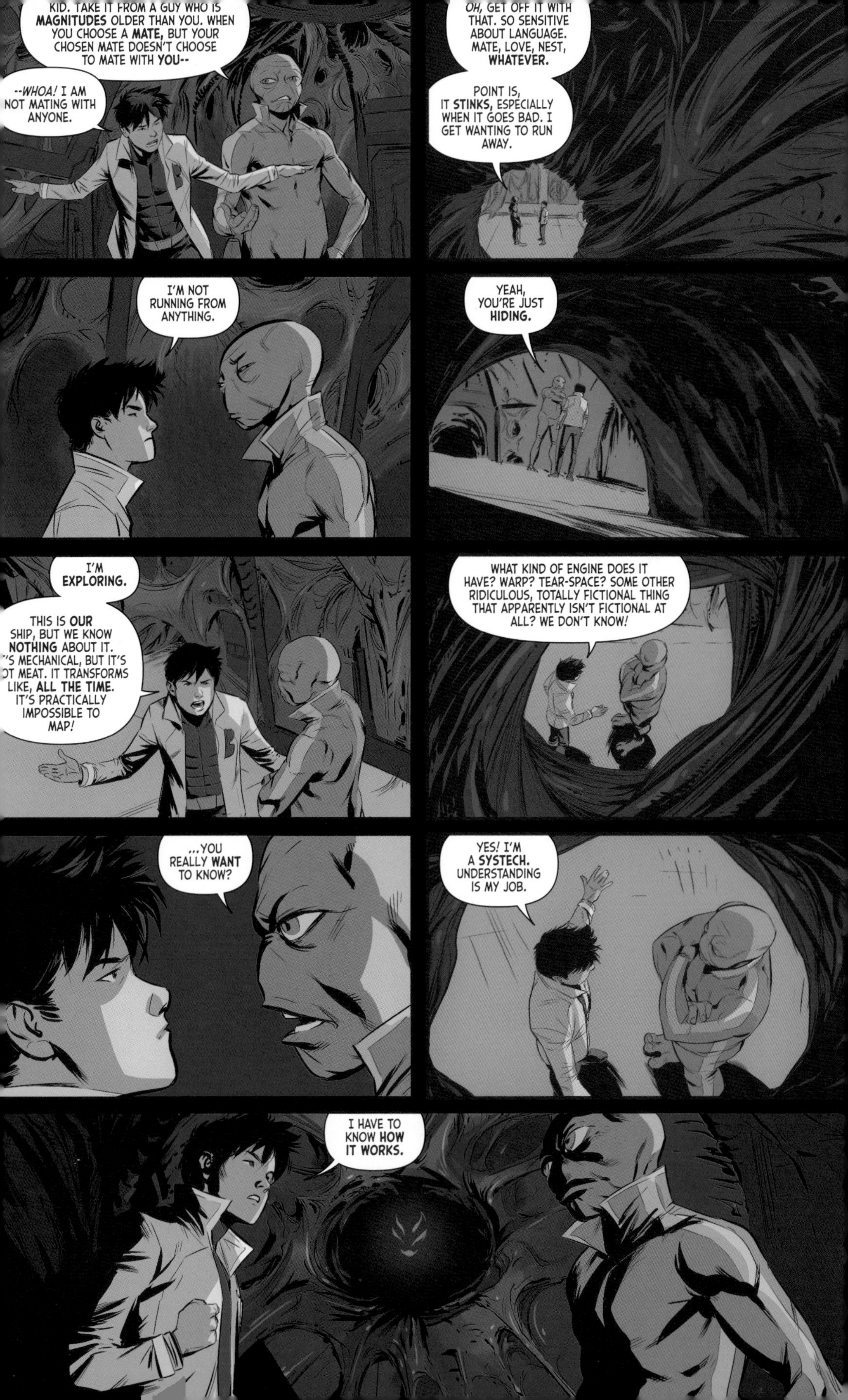
KID. TAKE IT FROM A GUY WHO IS MAGNITUDES OLDER THAN YOU. WHEN YOU CHOOSE A MATE, BUT YOUR CHOSEN MATE DOESN'T CHOOSE TO MATE WITH YOU--
--WHOA! I AM NOT MATING WITH ANYONE.
OH, GET OFF IT WITH THAT. SO SENSITIVE ABOUT LANGUAGE. MATE, LOVE, NEST, WHATEVER.
POINT IS, IT STINKS, ESPECIALLY WHEN IT GOES BAD. I GET WANTING TO RUN AWAY.
I'M NOT RUNNING FROM ANYTHING.
YEAH, YOU'RE JUST HIDING.
I'M EXPLORING.
THIS IS OUR SHIP, BUT WE KNOW NOTHING ABOUT IT. 'S MECHANICAL, BUT IT'S OT MEAT. IT TRANSFORMS LIKE, ALL THE TIME. IT'S PRACTICALLY IMPOSSIBLE TO MAP!
WHAT KIND OF ENGINE DOES IT HAVE? WARP? TEAR-SPACE? SOME OTHER RIDICULOUS, TOTALLY FICTIONAL THING THAT APPARENTLY ISN'T FICTIONAL AT ALL? WE DON'T KNOW!
...YOU REALLY WANT TO KNOW?
YES! I'M A SYSTECH. UNDERSTANDING IS MY JOB.
I HAVE TO KNOW HOW IT WORKS.

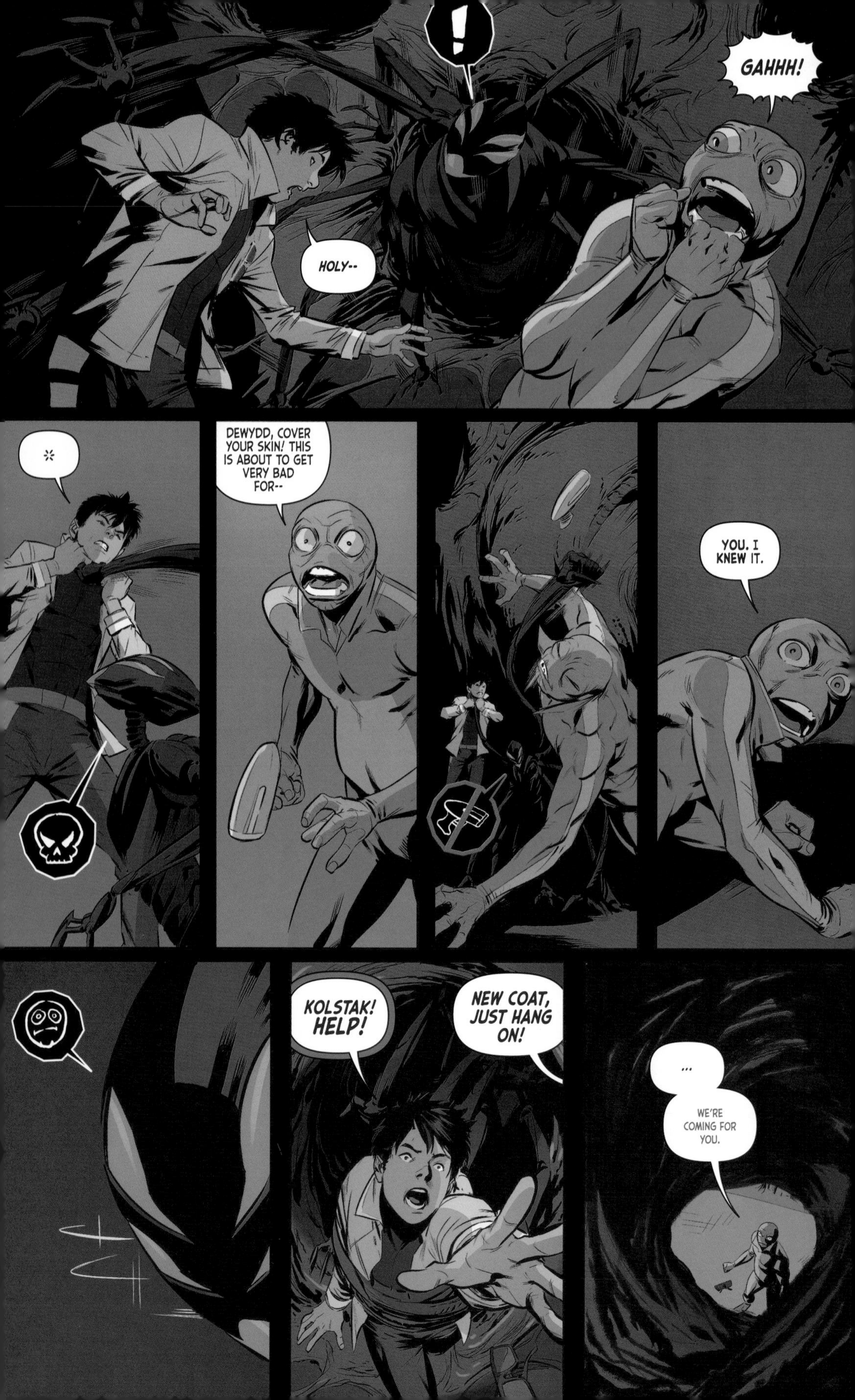
!
GAHHH!
HOLY--
DEWYDD, COVER YOUR SKIN! THIS IS ABOUT TO GET VERY BAD FOR--
YOU. I KNEW IT.
KOLSTAK! HELP!
NEW COAT, JUST HANG ON!
...
WE'RE COMING FOR YOU.

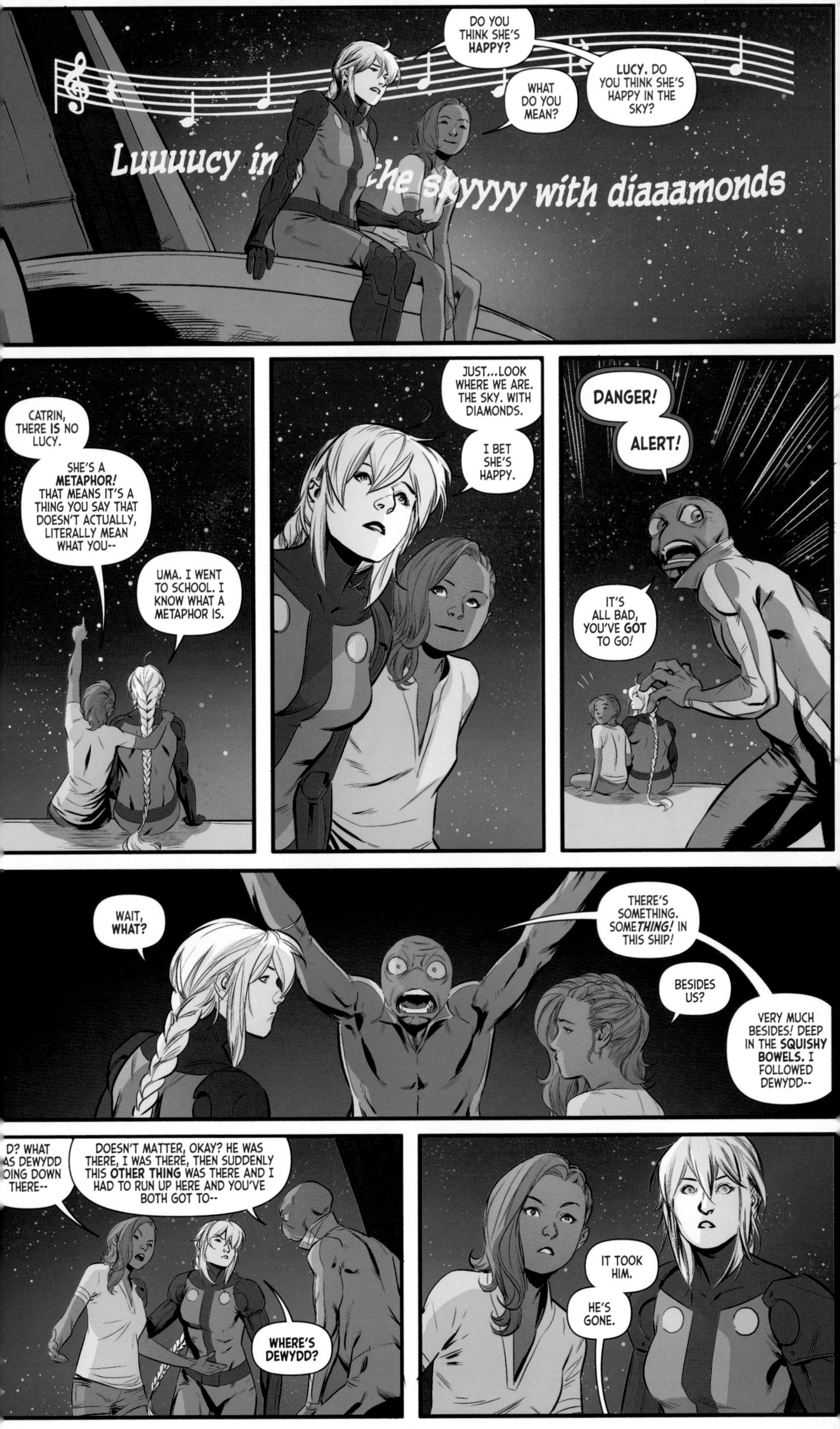
DO YOU THINK SHE'S HAPPY?
WHAT DO YOU MEAN?
LUCY. DO YOU THINK SHE'S HAPPY IN THE SKY?
Luuuucy in the skyyyy with diaaamonds
CATRIN, THERE IS NO LUCY.
SHE'S A METAPHOR! THAT MEANS IT'S A THING YOU SAY THAT DOESN'T ACTUALLY, LITERALLY MEAN WHAT YOU--
UMA. I WENT TO SCHOOL. I KNOW WHAT A METAPHOR IS.
JUST...LOOK WHERE WE ARE. THE SKY. WITH DIAMONDS.
I BET SHE'S HAPPY.
DANGER!
ALERT!
IT'S ALL BAD, YOU'VE GOT TO GO!
WAIT, WHAT?
THERE'S SOMETHING. SOMETHING! IN THIS SHIP!
BESIDES US?
VERY MUCH BESIDES! DEEP IN THE SQUISHY BOWELS. I FOLLOWED DEWYDD--
D? WHAT AS DEWYDD OING DOWN THERE--
DOESN'T MATTER, OKAY? HE WAS THERE, I WAS THERE, THEN SUDDENLY THIS OTHER THING WAS THERE AND I HAD TO RUN UP HERE AND YOU'VE BOTH GOT TO--
WHERE'S DEWYDD?
IT TOOK HIM.
HE'S GONE.

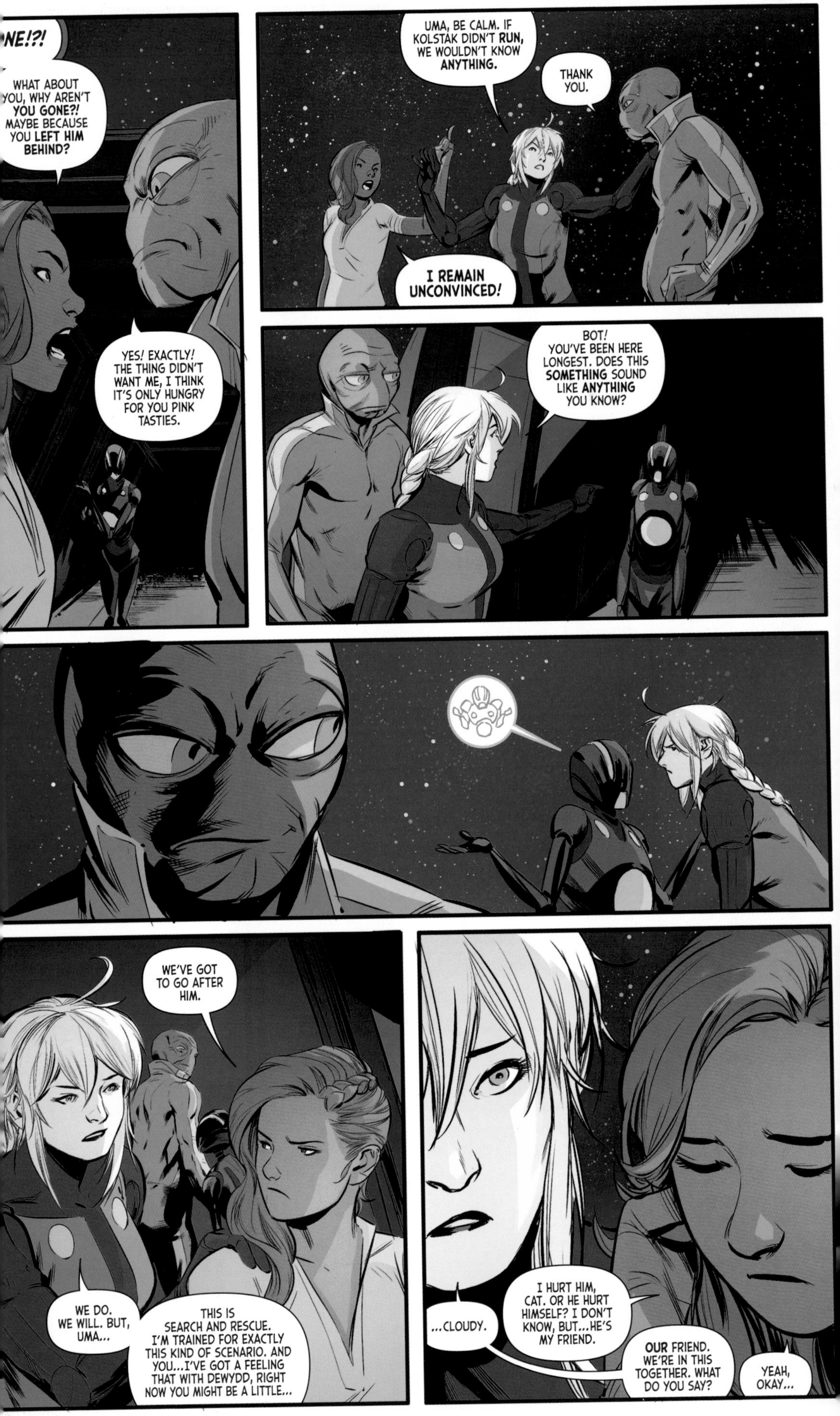

NE!?!
WHAT ABOUT YOU, WHY AREN'T **YOU GONE?!** MAYBE BECAUSE YOU **LEFT HIM BEHIND?**
YES! EXACTLY! THE THING DIDN'T WANT ME, I THINK IT'S ONLY HUNGRY FOR YOU PINK TASTIES.
UMA, BE CALM. IF KOLSTAK DIDN'T **RUN,** WE WOULDN'T KNOW **ANYTHING.**
THANK YOU.
I REMAIN UNCONVINCED!
BOT! YOU'VE BEEN HERE LONGEST. DOES THIS **SOMETHING** SOUND LIKE **ANYTHING** YOU KNOW?
WE'VE GOT TO GO AFTER HIM.
WE DO. WE WILL. BUT, UMA...
THIS IS SEARCH AND RESCUE. I'M TRAINED FOR EXACTLY THIS KIND OF SCENARIO. AND YOU...I'VE GOT A FEELING THAT WITH DEWYDD, RIGHT NOW YOU MIGHT BE A LITTLE...
...CLOUDY.
I HURT HIM, CAT. OR HE HURT HIMSELF? I DON'T KNOW, BUT...HE'S MY FRIEND.
OUR FRIEND. WE'RE IN THIS TOGETHER. WHAT DO YOU SAY?
YEAH, OKAY...

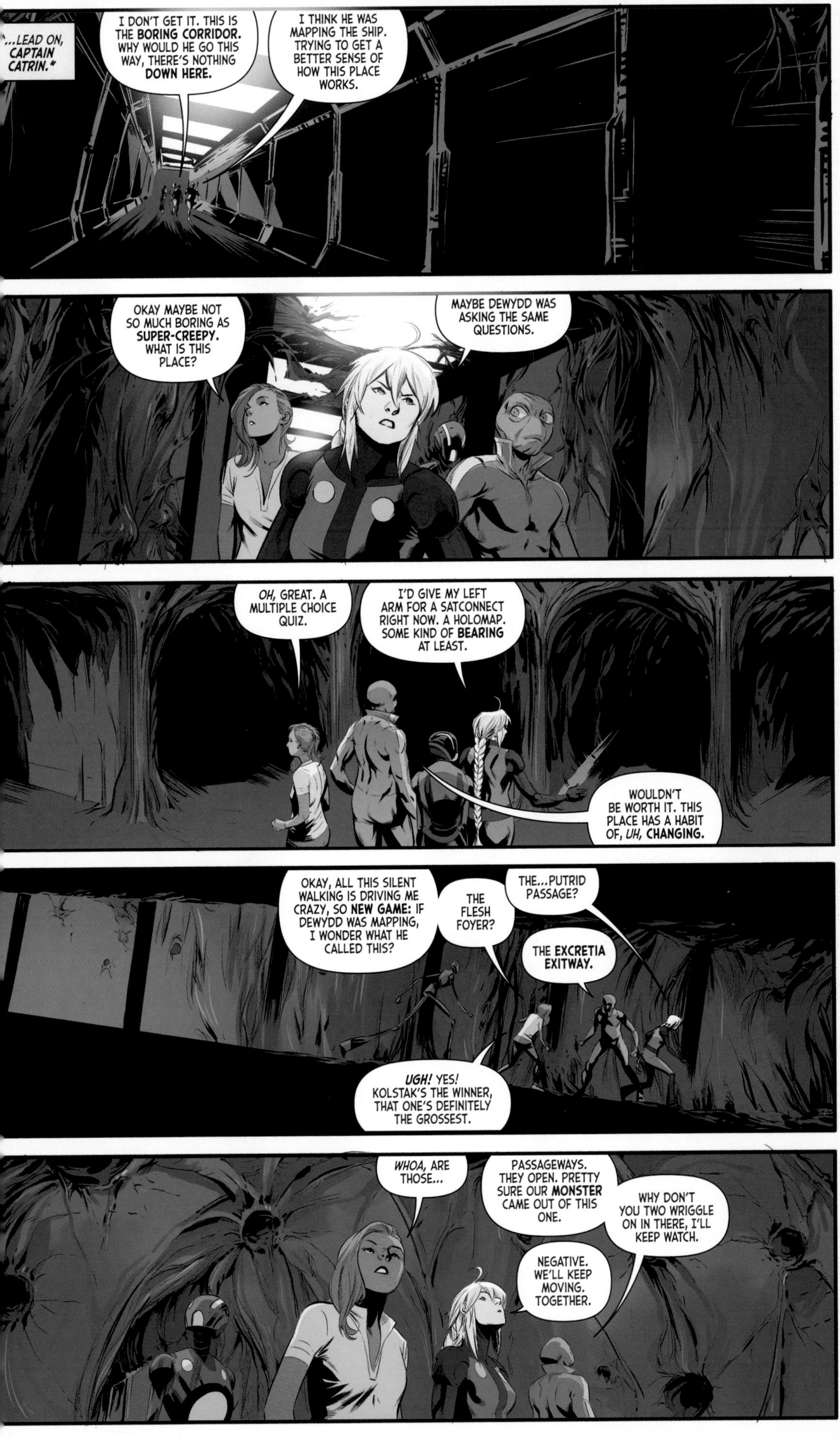
"...LEAD ON, CAPTAIN CATRIN."
I DON'T GET IT. THIS IS THE BORING CORRIDOR. WHY WOULD HE GO THIS WAY, THERE'S NOTHING DOWN HERE.
I THINK HE WAS MAPPING THE SHIP. TRYING TO GET A BETTER SENSE OF HOW THIS PLACE WORKS.
OKAY MAYBE NOT SO MUCH BORING AS SUPER-CREEPY. WHAT IS THIS PLACE?
MAYBE DEWYDD WAS ASKING THE SAME QUESTIONS.
OH, GREAT. A MULTIPLE CHOICE QUIZ.
I'D GIVE MY LEFT ARM FOR A SATCONNECT RIGHT NOW. A HOLOMAP. SOME KIND OF BEARING AT LEAST.
WOULDN'T BE WORTH IT. THIS PLACE HAS A HABIT OF, UH, CHANGING.
OKAY, ALL THIS SILENT WALKING IS DRIVING ME CRAZY, SO NEW GAME: IF DEWYDD WAS MAPPING, I WONDER WHAT HE CALLED THIS?
THE FLESH FOYER?
THE...PUTRID PASSAGE?
THE EXCRETIA EXITWAY.
UGH! YES! KOLSTAK'S THE WINNER, THAT ONE'S DEFINITELY THE GROSSEST.
WHOA, ARE THOSE...
PASSAGEWAYS. THEY OPEN. PRETTY SURE OUR MONSTER CAME OUT OF THIS ONE.
WHY DON'T YOU TWO WRIGGLE ON IN THERE, I'LL KEEP WATCH.
NEGATIVE. WE'LL KEEP MOVING. TOGETHER.

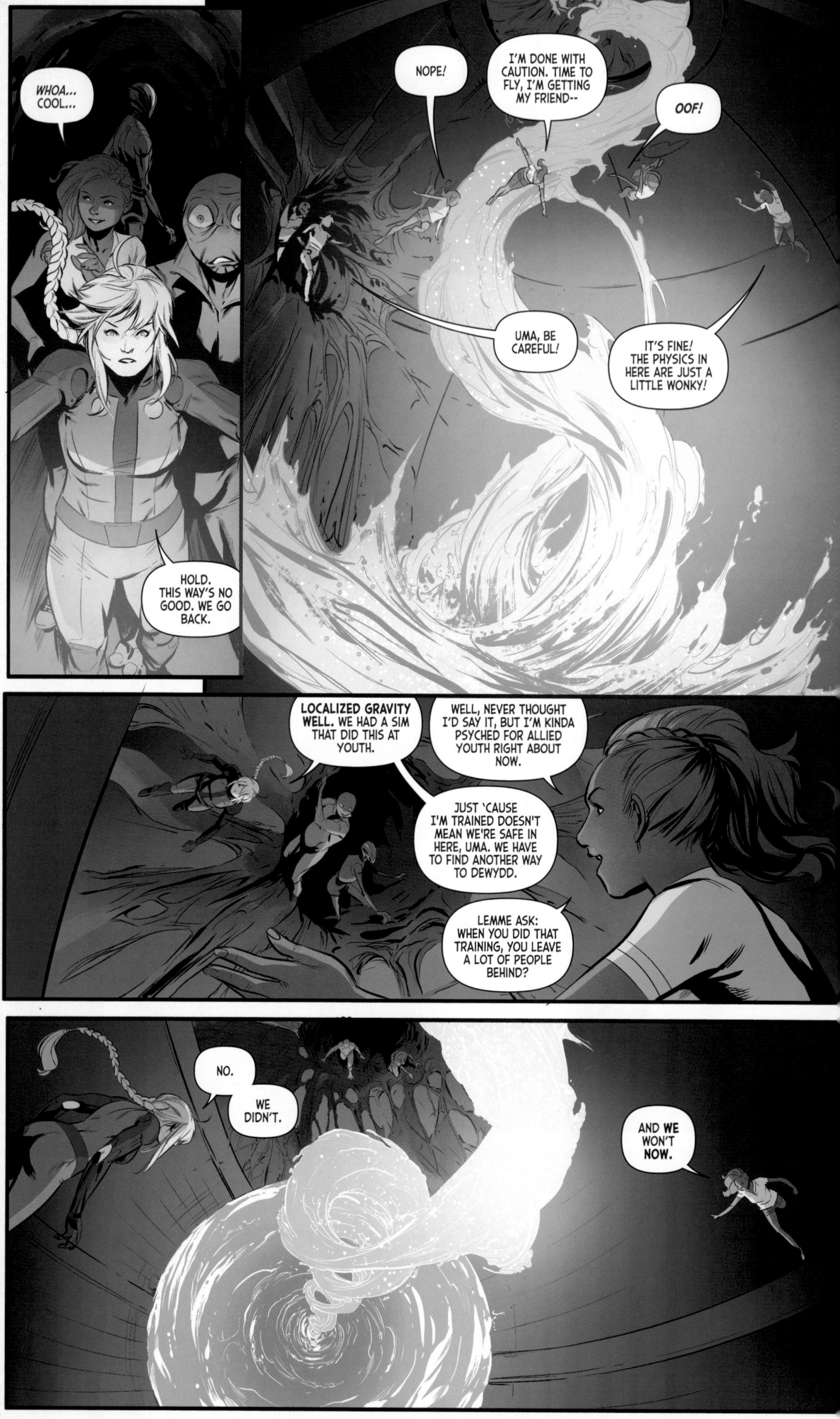
WHOA... COOL...
HOLD. THIS WAY'S NO GOOD. WE GO BACK.
NOPE!
I'M DONE WITH CAUTION. TIME TO FLY, I'M GETTING MY FRIEND--
OOF!
UMA, BE CAREFUL!
IT'S FINE! THE PHYSICS IN HERE ARE JUST A LITTLE WONKY!
LOCALIZED GRAVITY WELL. WE HAD A SIM THAT DID THIS AT YOUTH.
WELL, NEVER THOUGHT I'D SAY IT, BUT I'M KINDA PSYCHED FOR ALLIED YOUTH RIGHT ABOUT NOW.
JUST 'CAUSE I'M TRAINED DOESN'T MEAN WE'RE SAFE IN HERE, UMA. WE HAVE TO FIND ANOTHER WAY TO DEWYDD.
LEMME ASK: WHEN YOU DID THAT TRAINING, YOU LEAVE A LOT OF PEOPLE BEHIND?
NO.
WE DIDN'T.
AND WE WON'T NOW.

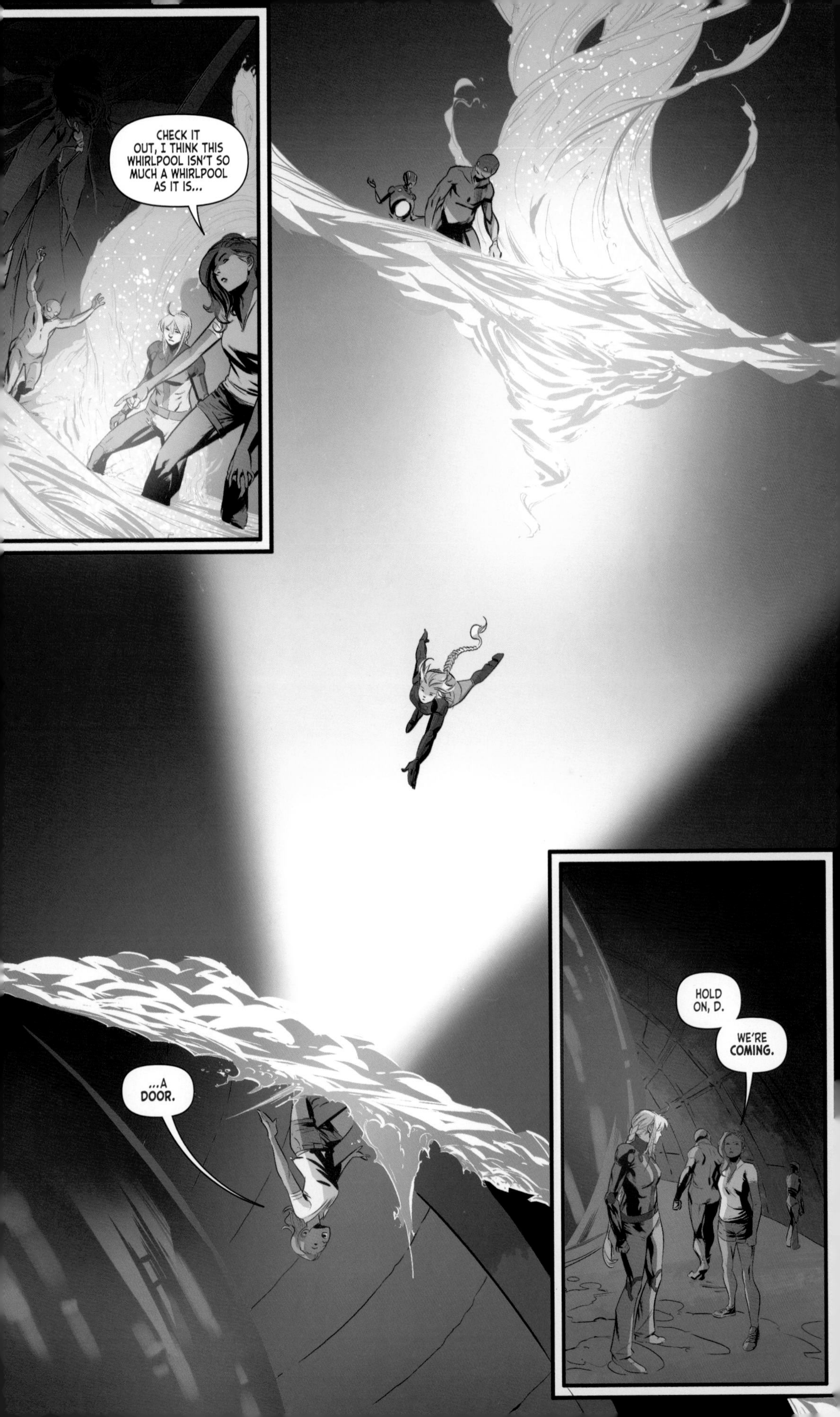

CHECK IT OUT, I THINK THIS WHIRLPOOL ISN'T SO MUCH A WHIRLPOOL AS IT IS...
...A DOOR.
HOLD ON, D.
WE'RE COMING.

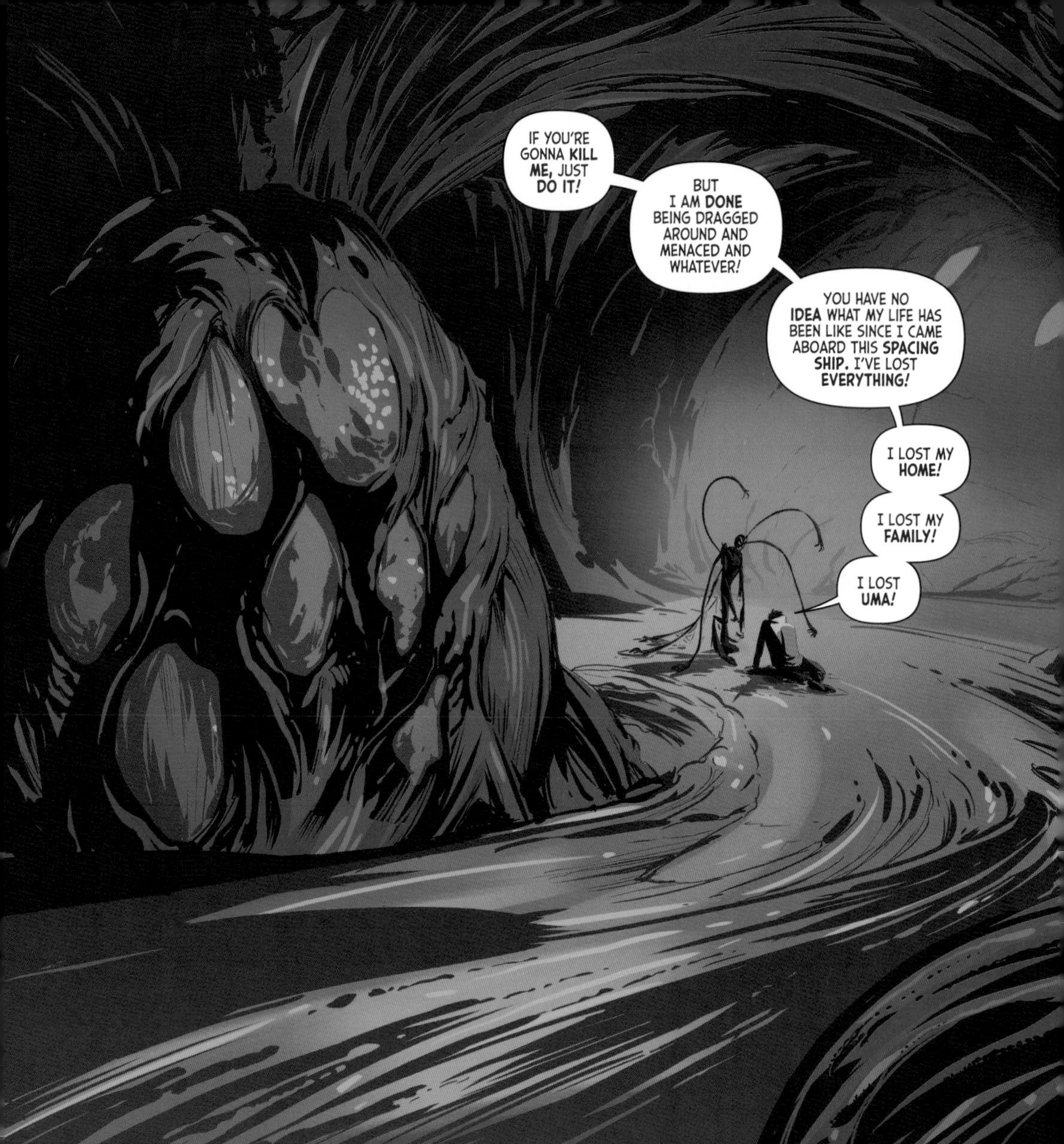
IF YOU'RE GONNA **KILL ME,** JUST **DO IT!**
BUT I AM **DONE** BEING DRAGGED AROUND AND MENACED AND WHATEVER!
YOU HAVE NO **IDEA** WHAT MY LIFE HAS BEEN LIKE SINCE I CAME ABOARD THIS **SPACING SHIP.** I'VE LOST **EVERYTHING!**
I LOST MY **HOME!**
I LOST MY **FAMILY!**
I LOST **UMA!**

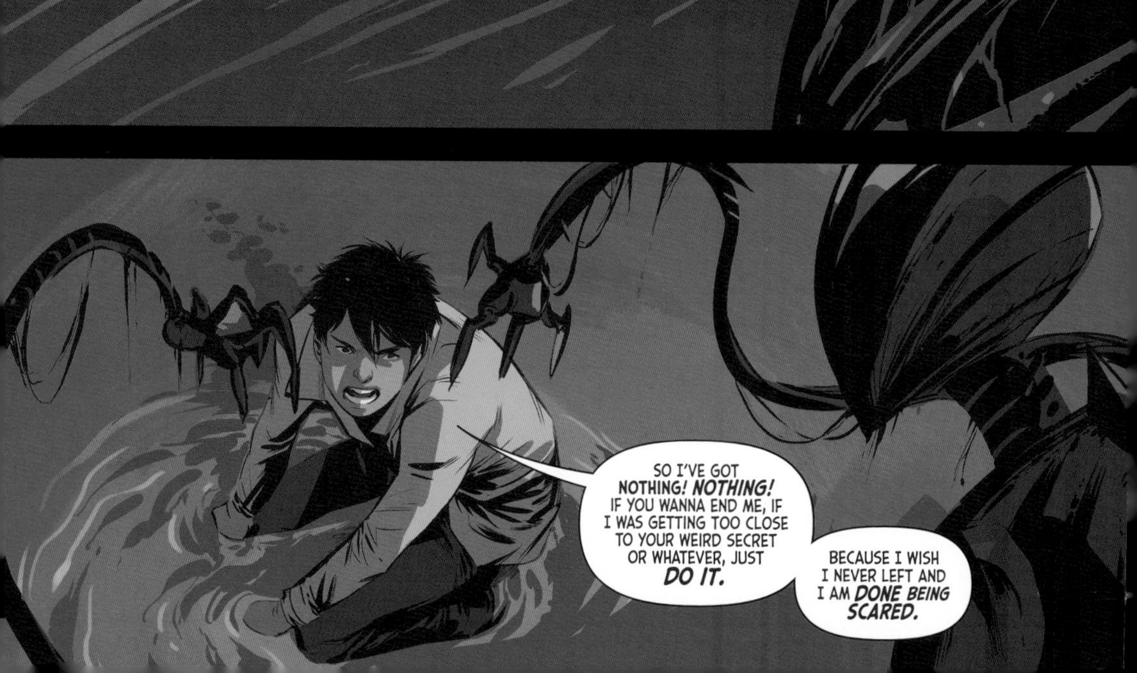
SO I'VE GOT **NOTHING! *NOTHING!*** IF YOU WANNA END ME, IF I WAS GETTING TOO CLOSE TO YOUR WEIRD SECRET OR WHATEVER, JUST ***DO IT.***
BECAUSE I WISH I NEVER LEFT AND I AM ***DONE BEING SCARED.***

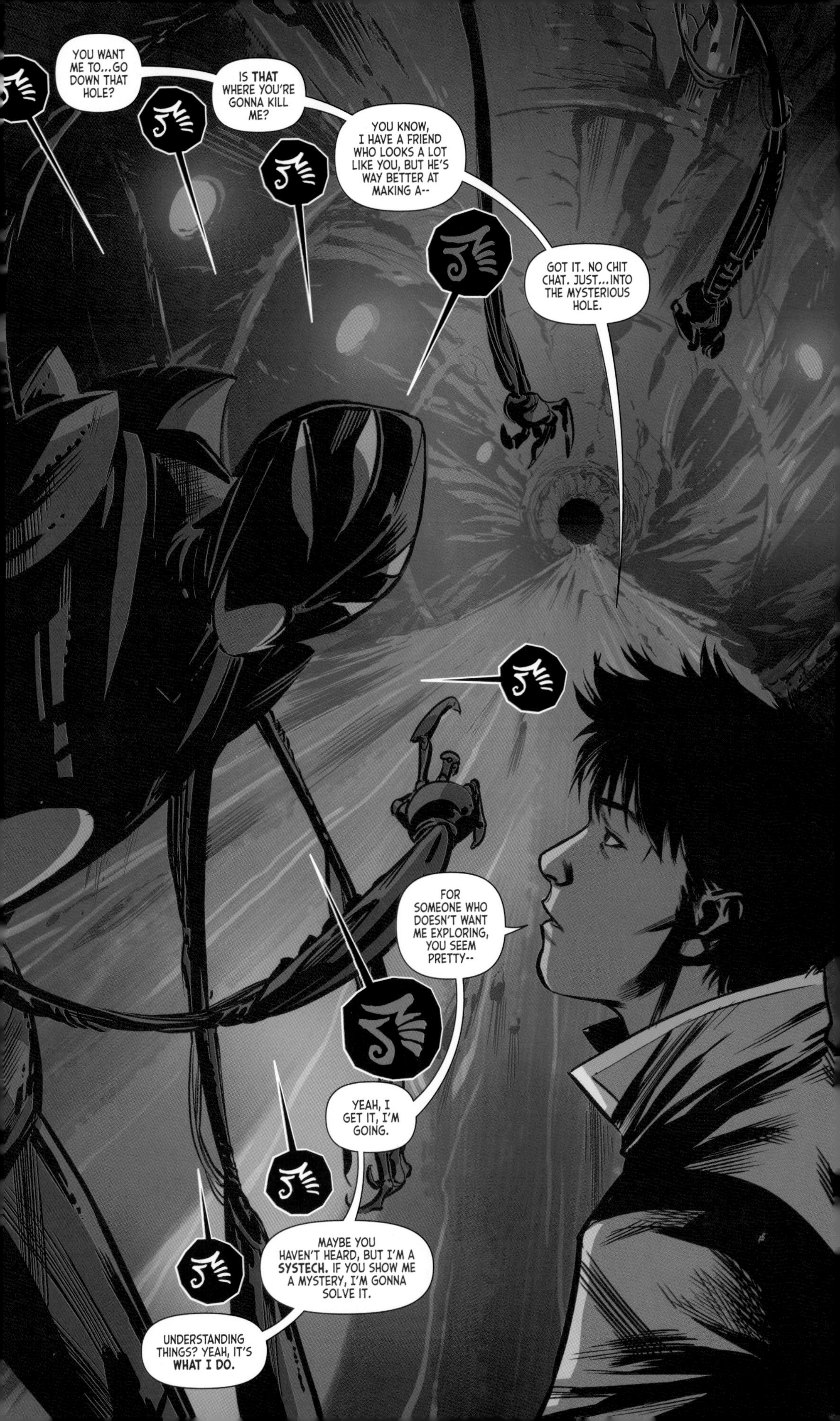

YOU WANT ME TO...GO DOWN THAT HOLE?
IS **THAT** WHERE YOU'RE GONNA KILL ME?
YOU KNOW, I HAVE A FRIEND WHO LOOKS A LOT LIKE YOU, BUT HE'S WAY BETTER AT MAKING A--
GOT IT. NO CHIT CHAT. JUST...INTO THE MYSTERIOUS HOLE.
FOR SOMEONE WHO DOESN'T WANT ME EXPLORING, YOU SEEM PRETTY--
YEAH, I GET IT, I'M GOING.
MAYBE YOU HAVEN'T HEARD, BUT I'M A **SYSTECH.** IF YOU SHOW ME A MYSTERY, I'M GONNA SOLVE IT.
UNDERSTANDING THINGS? YEAH, IT'S **WHAT I DO.**

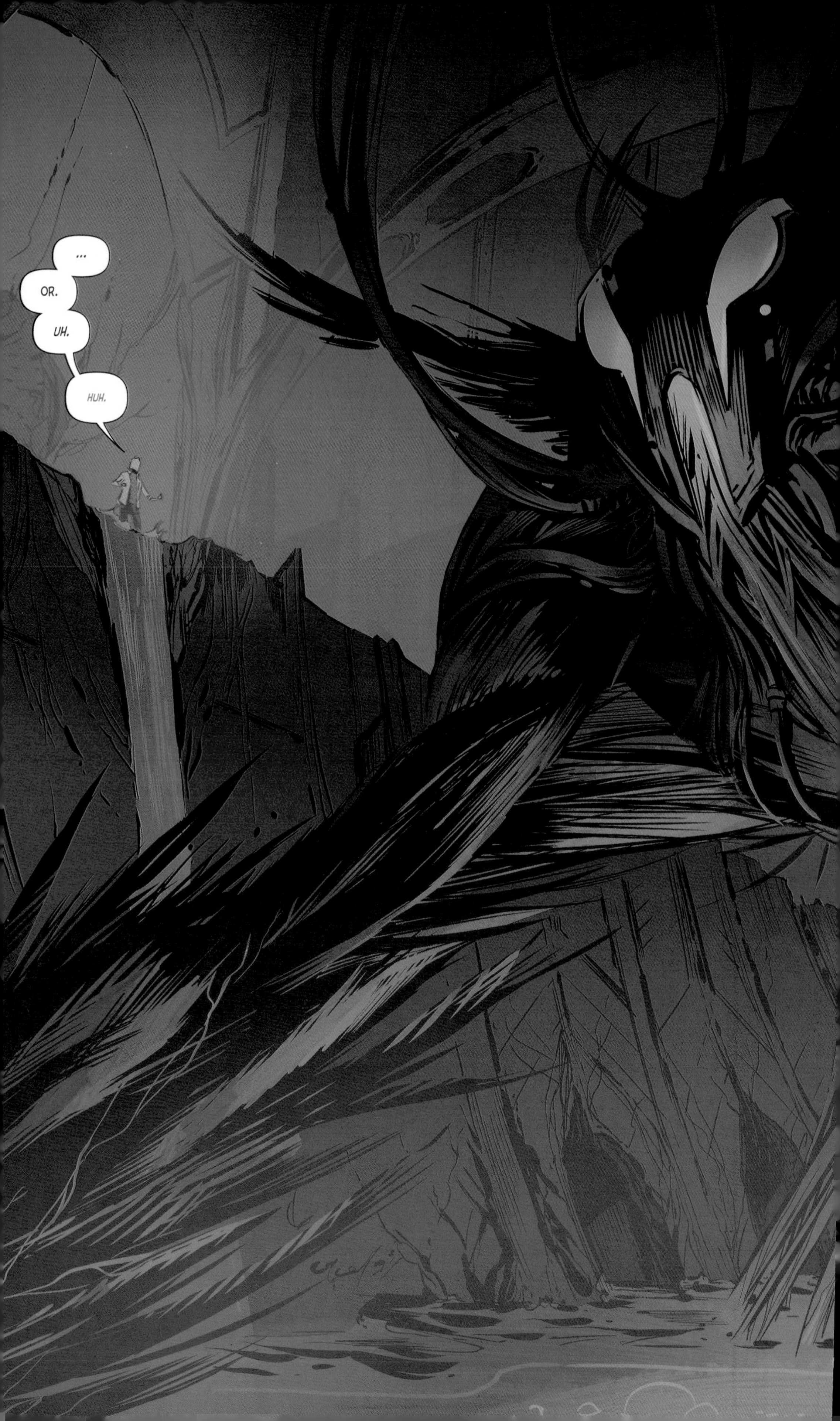
...
OR.
UH.
HUH.

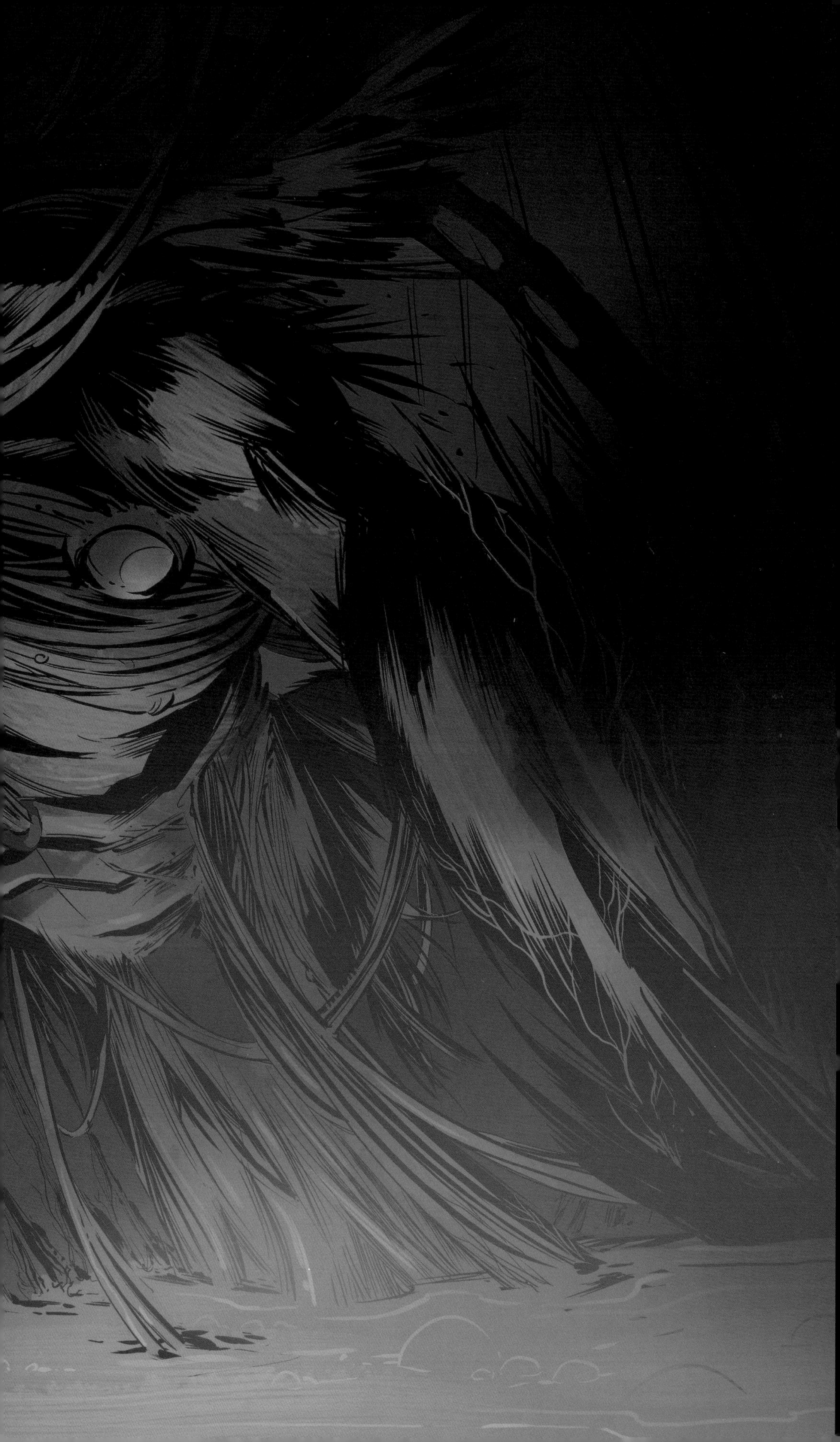

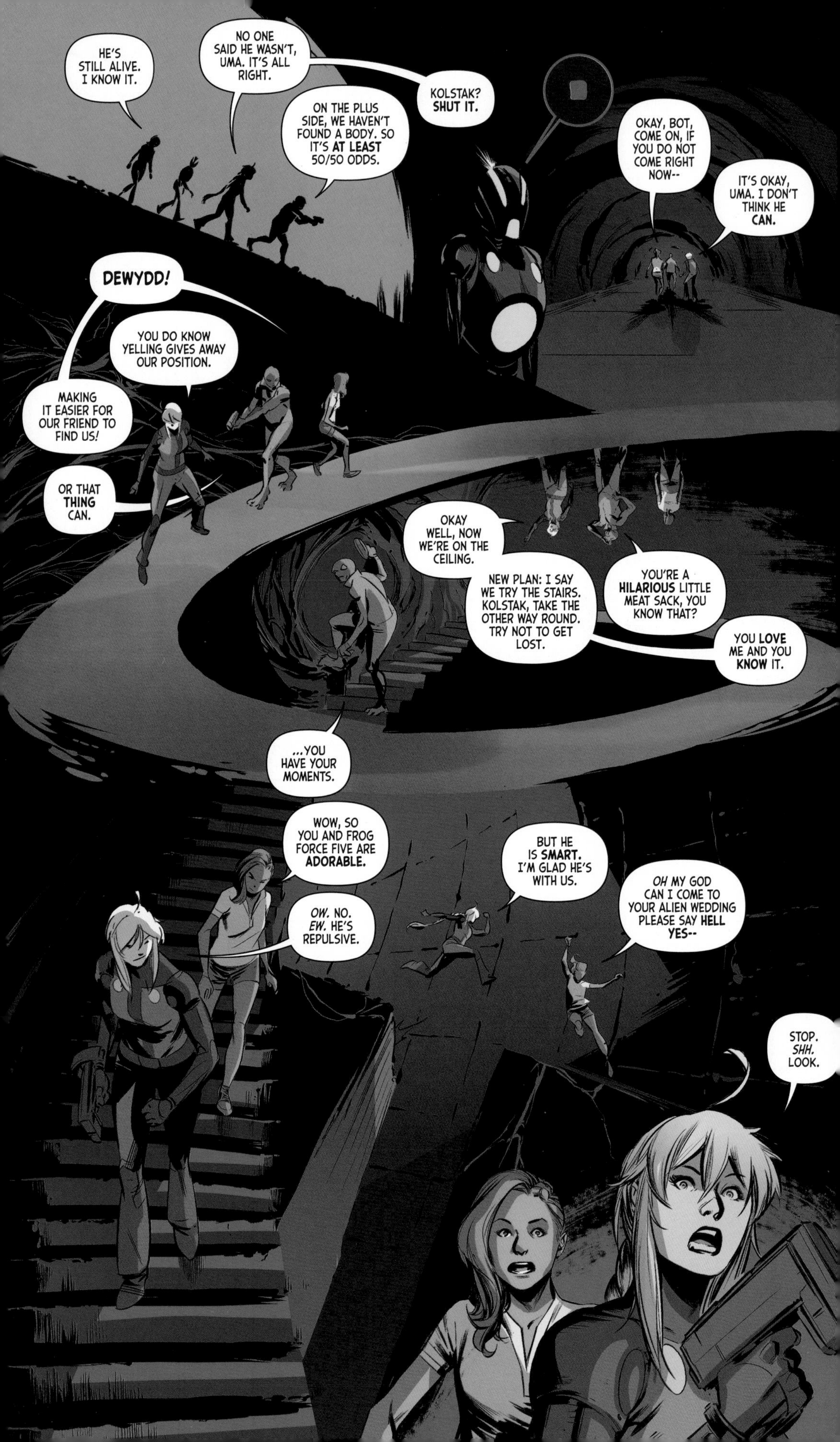

HE'S STILL ALIVE. I KNOW IT.
NO ONE SAID HE WASN'T, UMA. IT'S ALL RIGHT.
KOLSTAK? **SHUT IT.**
ON THE PLUS SIDE, WE HAVEN'T FOUND A BODY. SO IT'S **AT LEAST** 50/50 ODDS.
OKAY, BOT, COME ON, IF YOU DO NOT COME RIGHT NOW--
IT'S OKAY, UMA. I DON'T THINK HE **CAN.**
DEWYDD!
YOU DO KNOW YELLING GIVES AWAY OUR POSITION.
MAKING IT EASIER FOR OUR FRIEND TO FIND US!
OR THAT **THING** CAN.
OKAY WELL, NOW WE'RE ON THE CEILING.
NEW PLAN: I SAY WE TRY THE STAIRS. KOLSTAK, TAKE THE OTHER WAY ROUND. TRY NOT TO GET LOST.
YOU'RE A **HILARIOUS** LITTLE MEAT SACK, YOU KNOW THAT?
YOU **LOVE** ME AND YOU **KNOW** IT.
...YOU HAVE YOUR MOMENTS.
WOW, SO YOU AND FROG FORCE FIVE ARE **ADORABLE.**
OW. NO. *EW.* HE'S REPULSIVE.
BUT HE IS **SMART.** I'M GLAD HE'S WITH US.
OH MY GOD CAN I COME TO YOUR ALIEN WEDDING PLEASE SAY **HELL YES--**
STOP. *SHH.* LOOK.

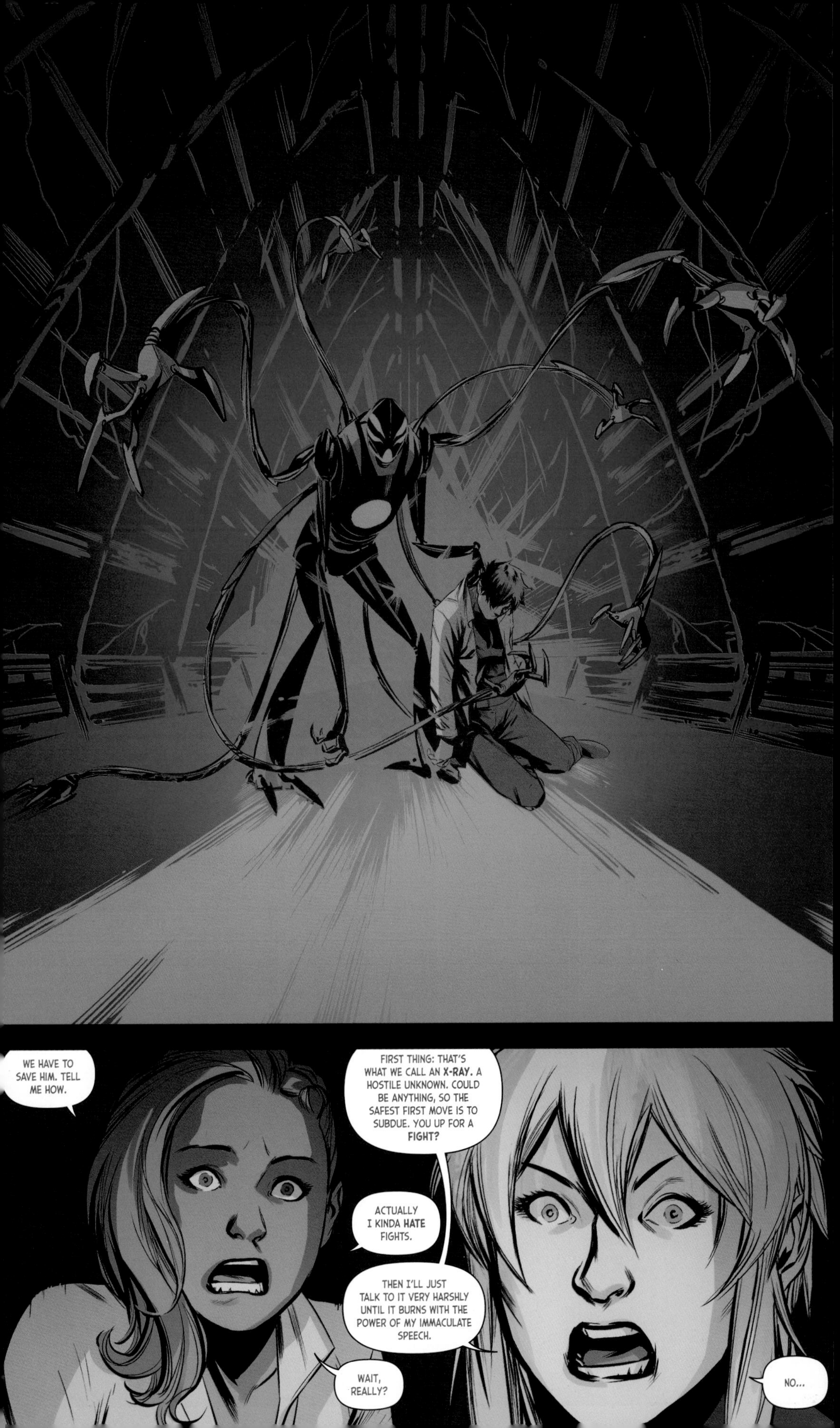

WE HAVE TO SAVE HIM. TELL ME HOW.
FIRST THING: THAT'S WHAT WE CALL AN **X-RAY.** A HOSTILE UNKNOWN. COULD BE ANYTHING, SO THE SAFEST FIRST MOVE IS TO SUBDUE. YOU UP FOR A **FIGHT?**
ACTUALLY I KINDA **HATE** FIGHTS.
THEN I'LL JUST TALK TO IT VERY HARSHLY UNTIL IT BURNS WITH THE POWER OF MY IMMACULATE SPEECH.
WAIT, REALLY?
NO...

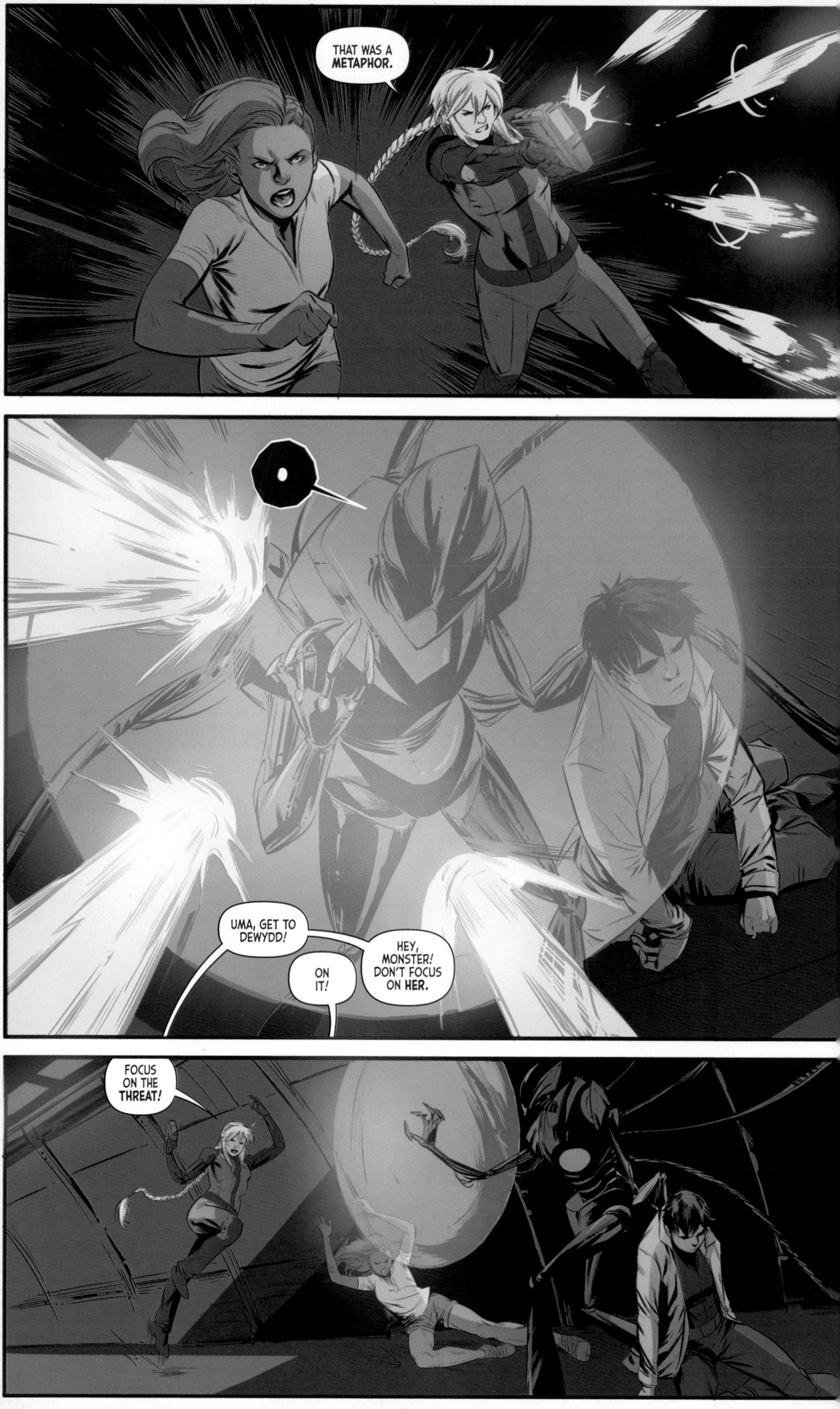
THAT WAS A METAPHOR.
UMA, GET TO DEWYDD!
ON IT!
HEY, MONSTER! DON'T FOCUS ON HER.
FOCUS ON THE THREAT!

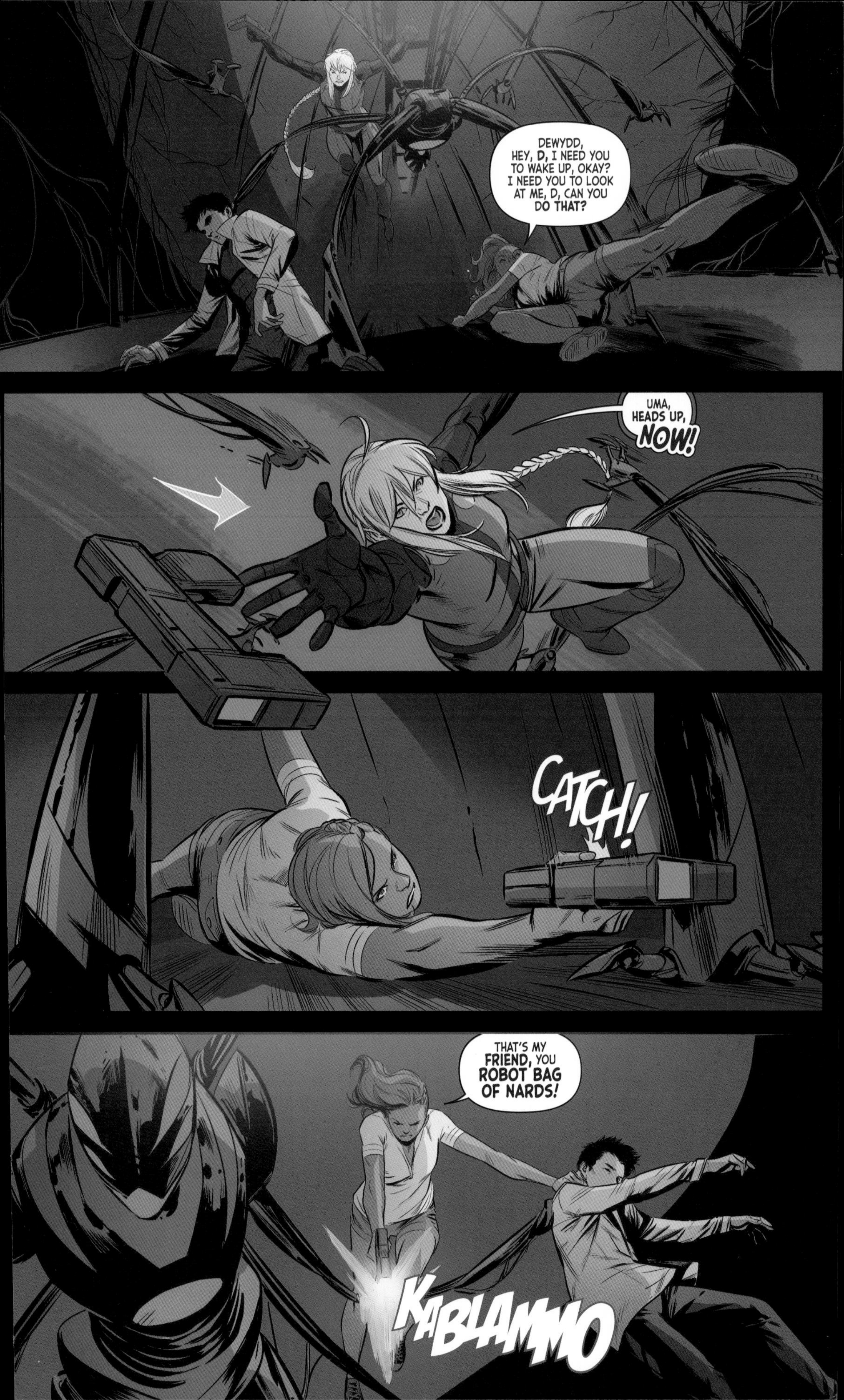
DEWYDD, HEY, D, I NEED YOU TO WAKE UP, OKAY? I NEED YOU TO LOOK AT ME, D, CAN YOU DO THAT?
UMA, HEADS UP, NOW!
CATCH!
THAT'S MY FRIEND, YOU ROBOT BAG OF NARDS!
KABLAMMO

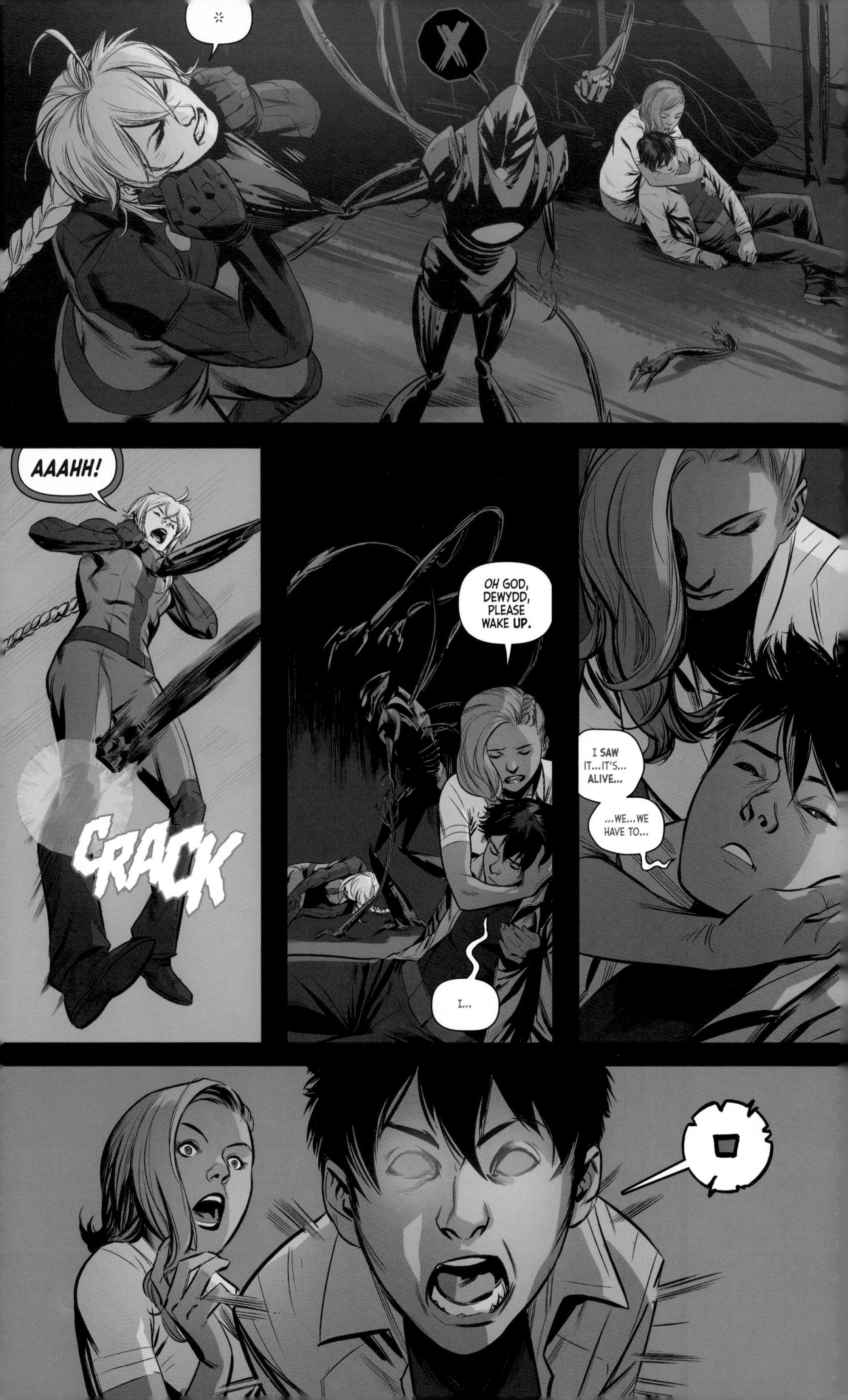
AAAHH!
CRACK
OH GOD, DEWYDD, PLEASE WAKE UP.
I...
I SAW IT...IT'S... ALIVE...
...WE...WE HAVE TO...

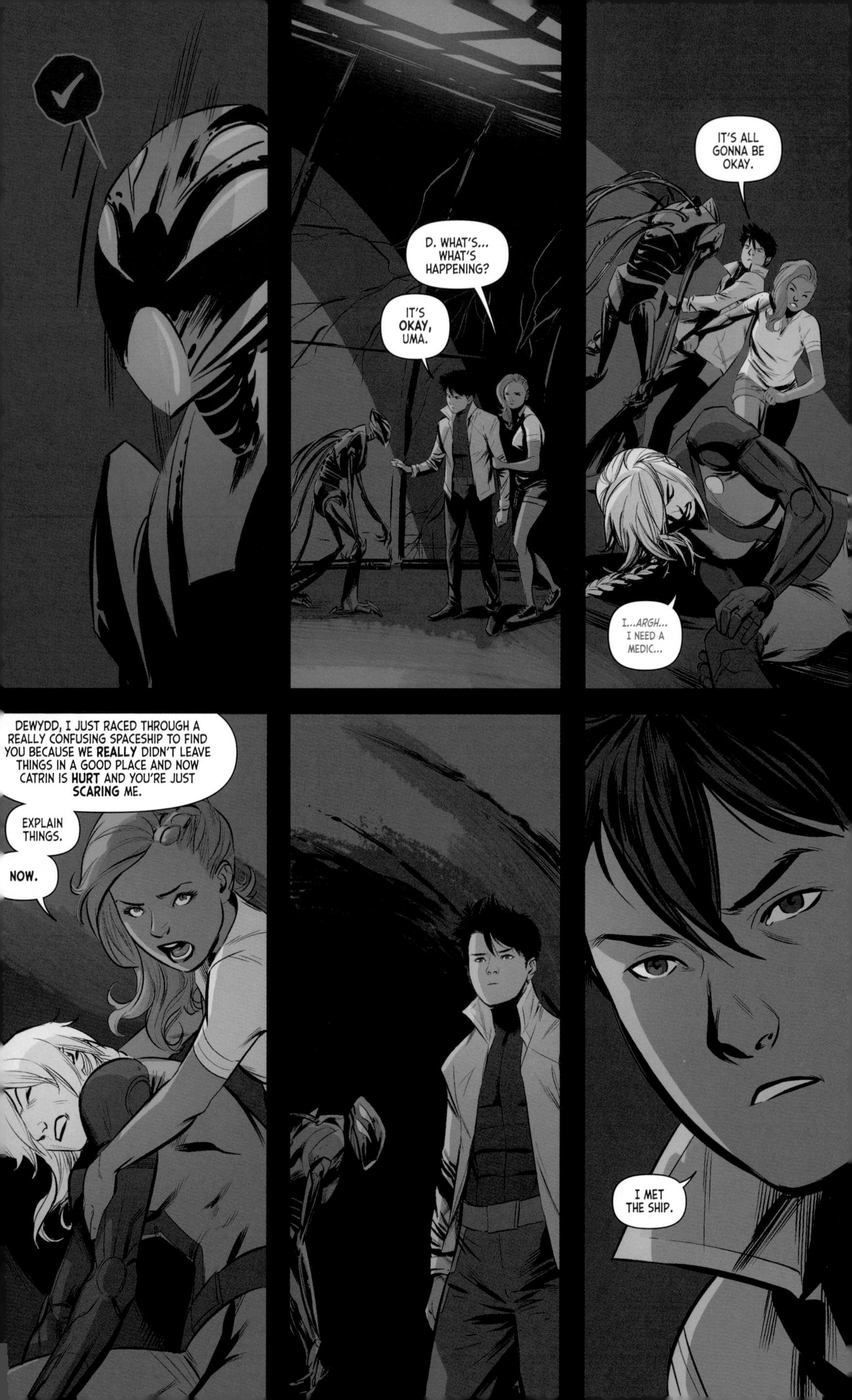

D. WHAT'S... WHAT'S HAPPENING?
IT'S OKAY, UMA.
IT'S ALL GONNA BE OKAY.
I...ARGH... I NEED A MEDIC...
DEWYDD, I JUST RACED THROUGH A REALLY CONFUSING SPACESHIP TO FIND YOU BECAUSE WE REALLY DIDN'T LEAVE THINGS IN A GOOD PLACE AND NOW CATRIN IS HURT AND YOU'RE JUST SCARING ME.
EXPLAIN THINGS.
NOW.
I MET THE SHIP.

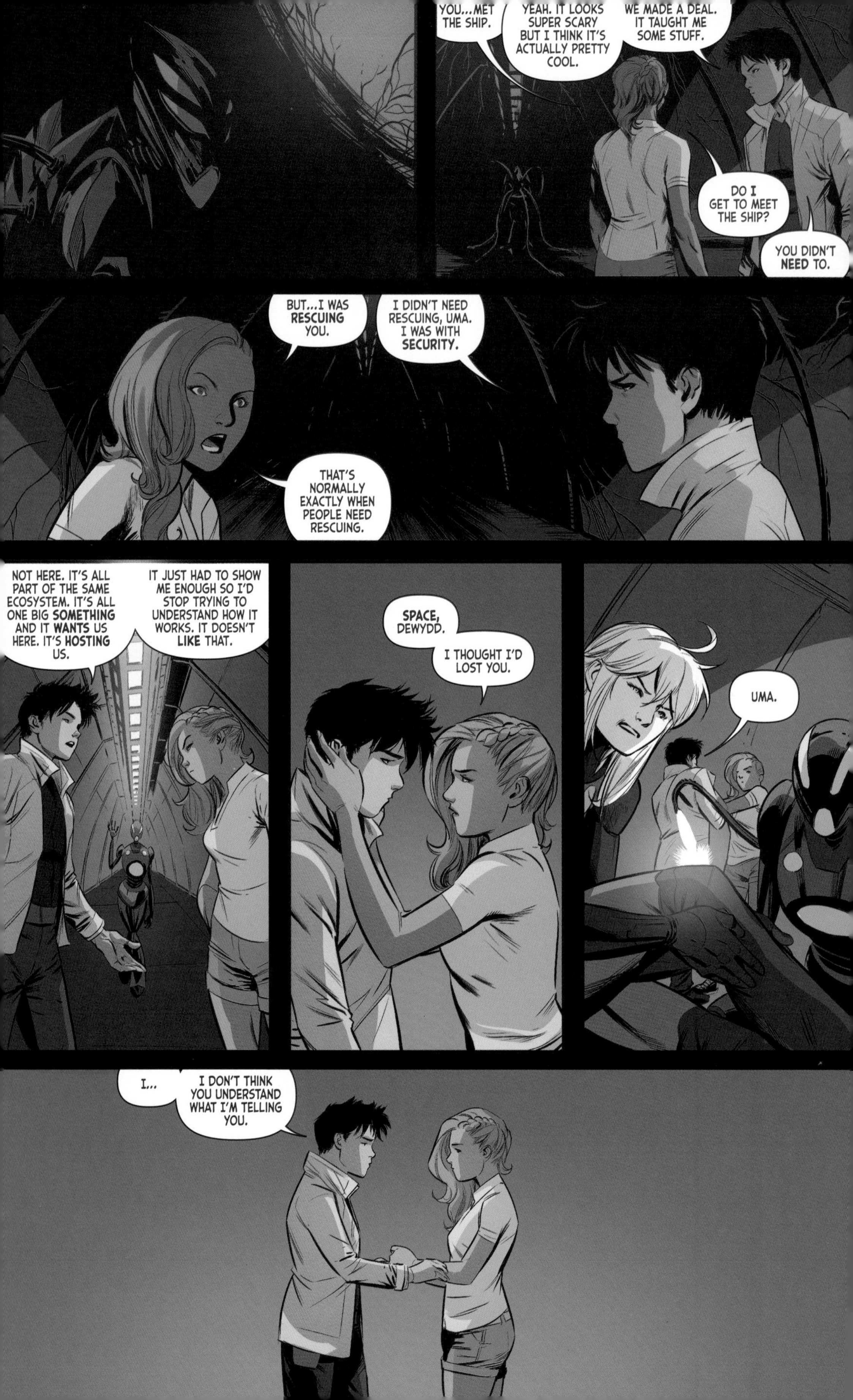
YOU...MET THE SHIP.
YEAH. IT LOOKS SUPER SCARY BUT I THINK IT'S ACTUALLY PRETTY COOL.
WE MADE A DEAL. IT TAUGHT ME SOME STUFF.
DO I GET TO MEET THE SHIP?
YOU DIDN'T NEED TO.
BUT...I WAS RESCUING YOU.
I DIDN'T NEED RESCUING, UMA. I WAS WITH SECURITY.
THAT'S NORMALLY EXACTLY WHEN PEOPLE NEED RESCUING.
NOT HERE. IT'S ALL PART OF THE SAME ECOSYSTEM. IT'S ALL ONE BIG SOMETHING AND IT WANTS US HERE. IT'S HOSTING US.
IT JUST HAD TO SHOW ME ENOUGH SO I'D STOP TRYING TO UNDERSTAND HOW IT WORKS. IT DOESN'T LIKE THAT.
SPACE, DEWYDD.
I THOUGHT I'D LOST YOU.
UMA.
I...
I DON'T THINK YOU UNDERSTAND WHAT I'M TELLING YOU.

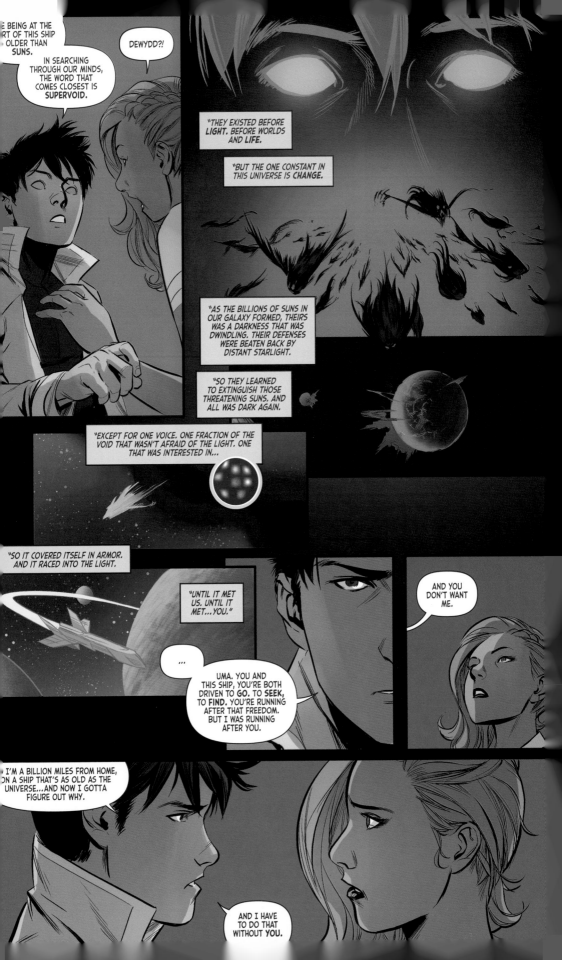

...E BEING AT THE ...RT OF THIS SHIP ... OLDER THAN SUNS.

IN SEARCHING THROUGH OUR MINDS, THE WORD THAT COMES CLOSEST IS SUPERVOID.

DEWYDD?!

"THEY EXISTED BEFORE LIGHT. BEFORE WORLDS AND LIFE.

"BUT THE ONE CONSTANT IN THIS UNIVERSE IS CHANGE.

"AS THE BILLIONS OF SUNS IN OUR GALAXY FORMED, THEIRS WAS A DARKNESS THAT WAS DWINDLING. THEIR DEFENSES WERE BEATEN BACK BY DISTANT STARLIGHT.

"SO THEY LEARNED TO EXTINGUISH THOSE THREATENING SUNS. AND ALL WAS DARK AGAIN.

"EXCEPT FOR ONE VOICE. ONE FRACTION OF THE VOID THAT WASN'T AFRAID OF THE LIGHT. ONE THAT WAS INTERESTED IN...

"SO IT COVERED ITSELF IN ARMOR. AND IT RACED INTO THE LIGHT.

"UNTIL IT MET US. UNTIL IT MET...YOU."

AND YOU DON'T WANT ME.

...

UMA. YOU AND THIS SHIP, YOU'RE BOTH DRIVEN TO GO. TO SEEK, TO FIND. YOU'RE RUNNING AFTER THAT FREEDOM. BUT I WAS RUNNING AFTER YOU.

I'M A BILLION MILES FROM HOME, ...N A SHIP THAT'S AS OLD AS THE UNIVERSE...AND NOW I GOTTA FIGURE OUT WHY.

AND I HAVE TO DO THAT WITHOUT YOU.

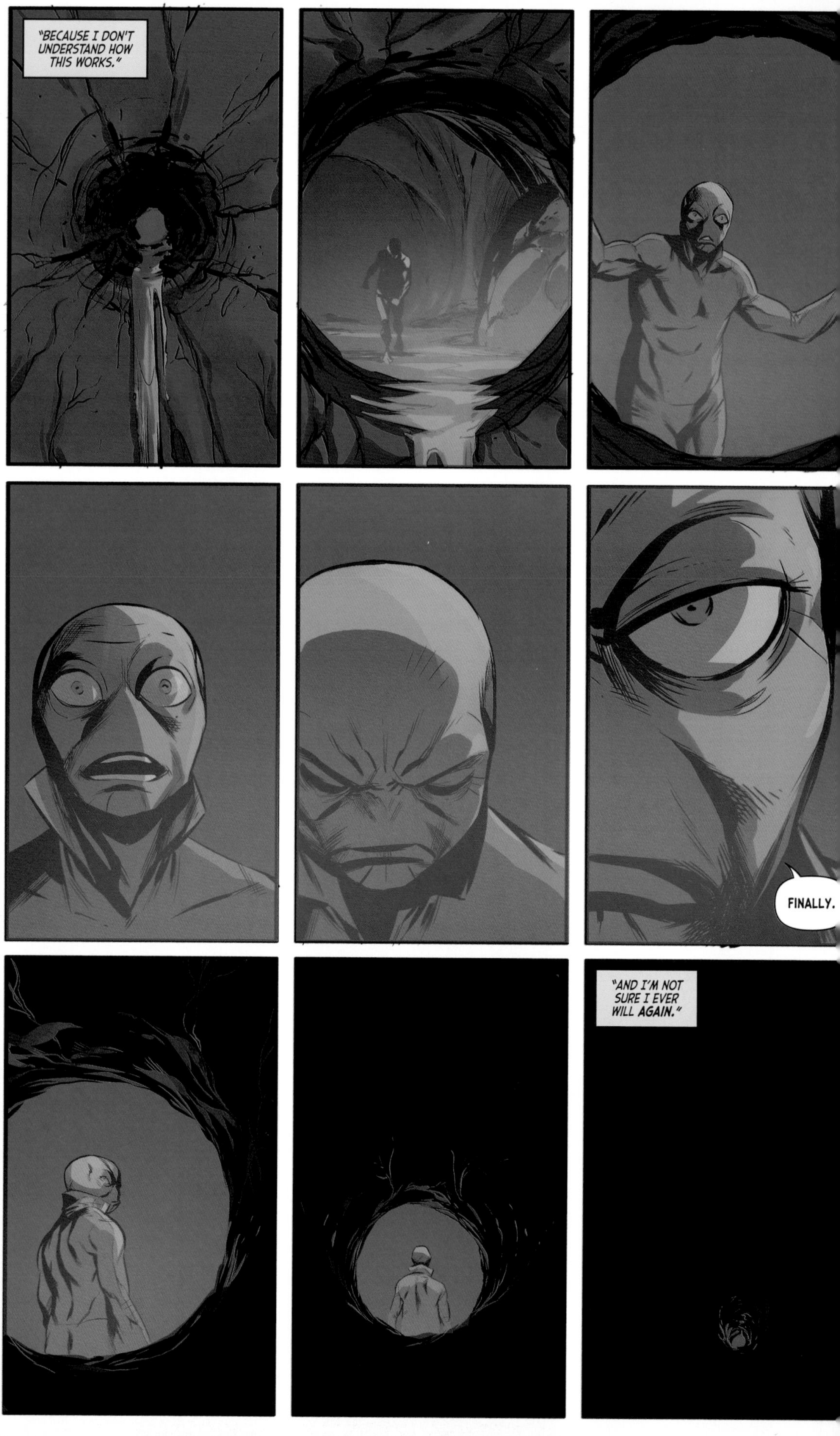
"BECAUSE I DON'T UNDERSTAND HOW THIS WORKS."
FINALLY.
"AND I'M NOT SURE I EVER WILL AGAIN."

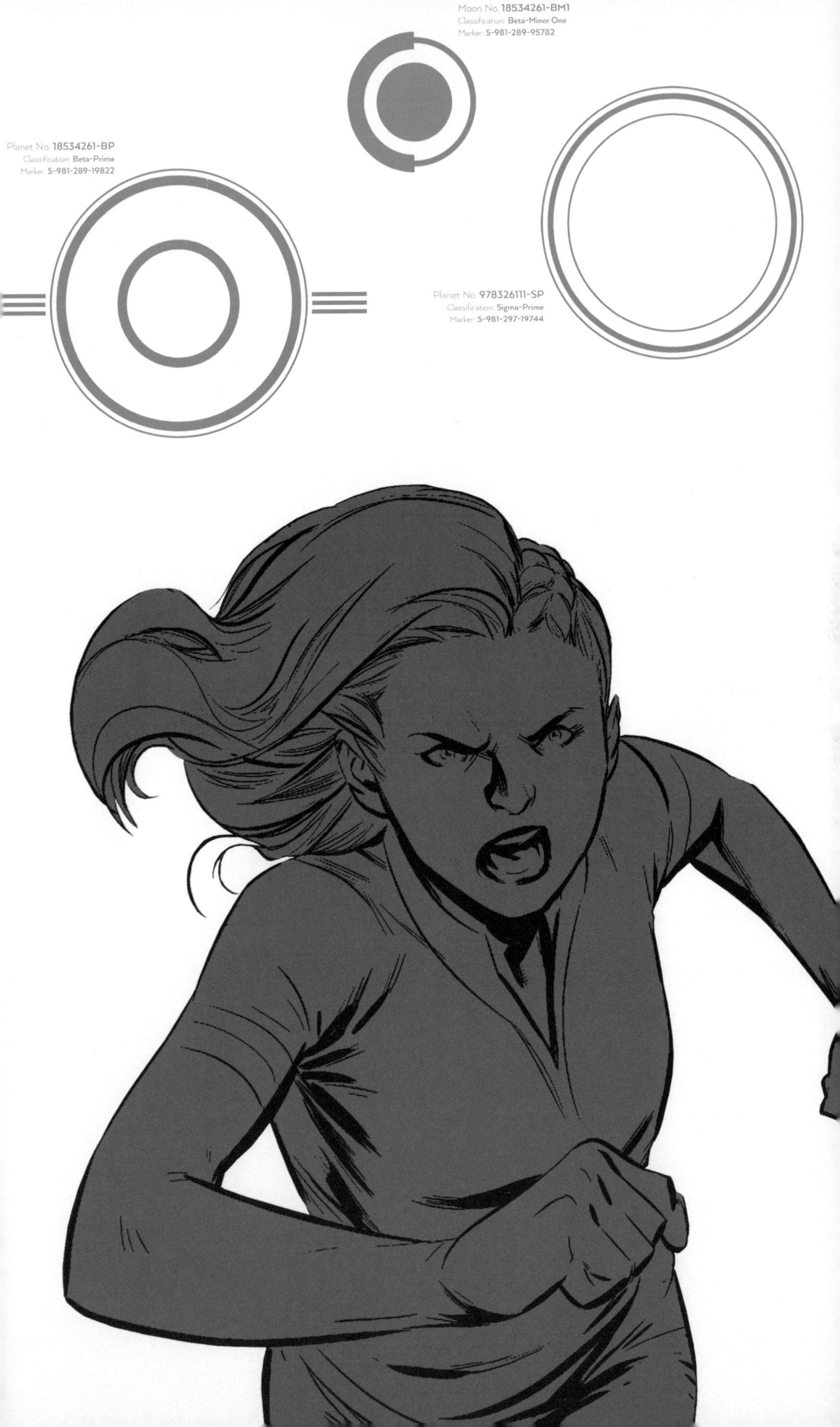
Moon No. 18534261-BM1
Classification: Beta-Minor One
Marker: 5-981-289-95782
Planet No. 18534261-BP
Classification: Beta-Prime
Marker: 5-981-289-19822
Planet No. 978326111-SP
Classification: Sigma-Prime
Marker: 5-981-297-19744

CHAPTER **SEVEN**

THE GOD PARTY

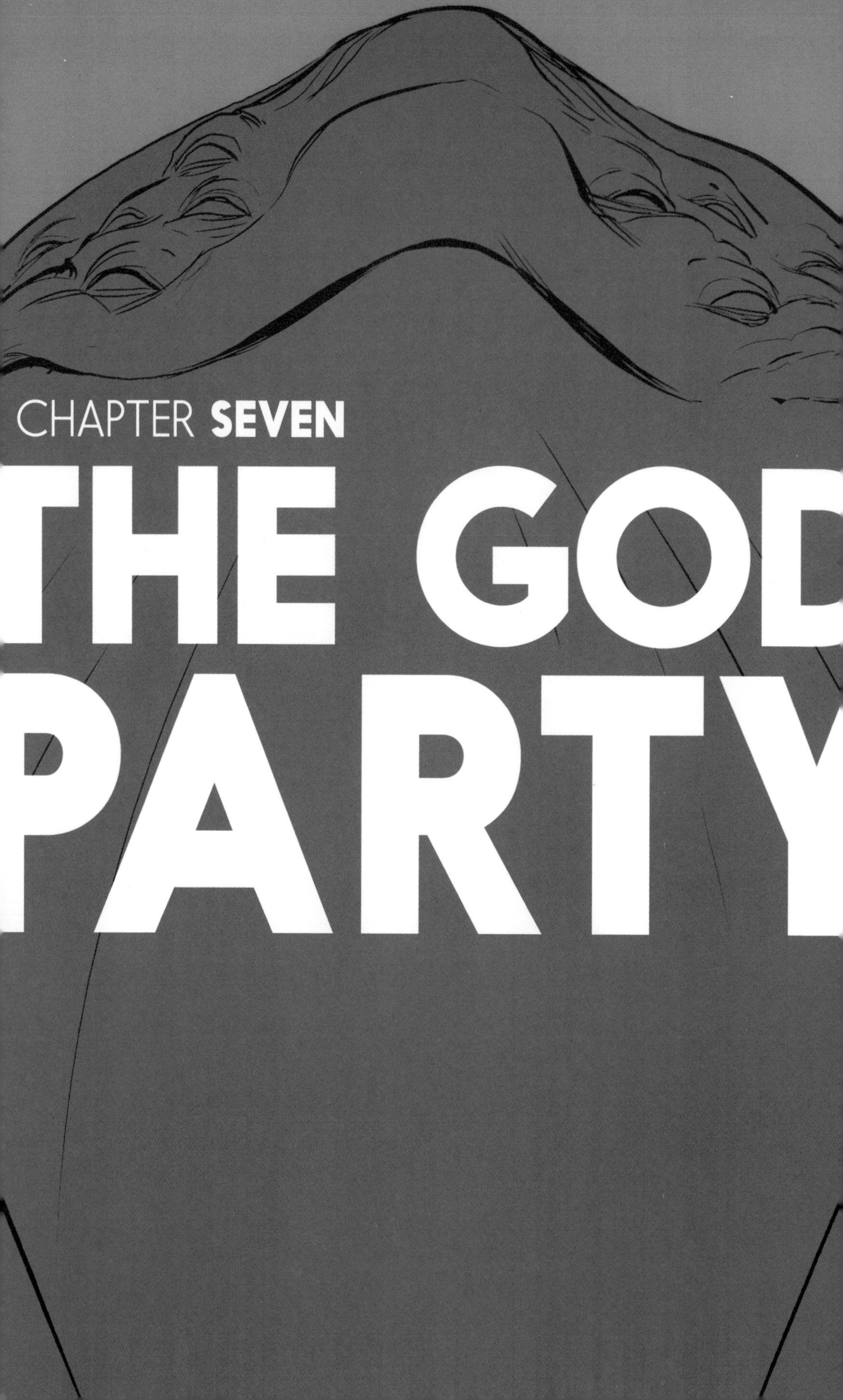

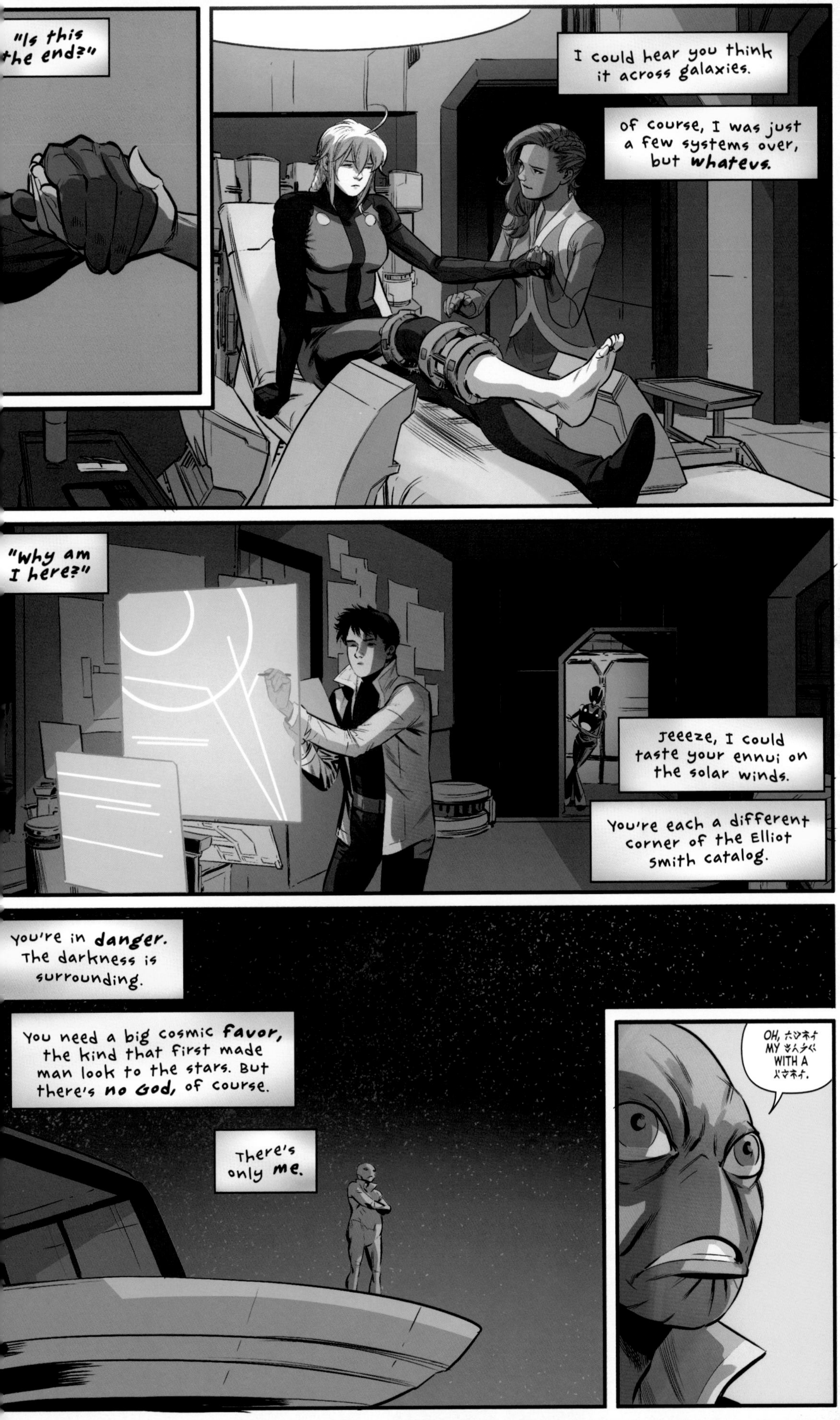
"Is this the end?"
I could hear you think it across galaxies.
Of course, I was just a few systems over, but **whatevs.**
"Why am I here?"
Jeeeze, I could taste your ennui on the solar winds.
You're each a different corner of the Elliot Smith catalog.
You're in **danger.** The darkness is surrounding.
You need a big cosmic **favor,** the kind that first made man look to the stars. But there's **no God,** of course.
There's only **me.**
OH,
MY
WITH A

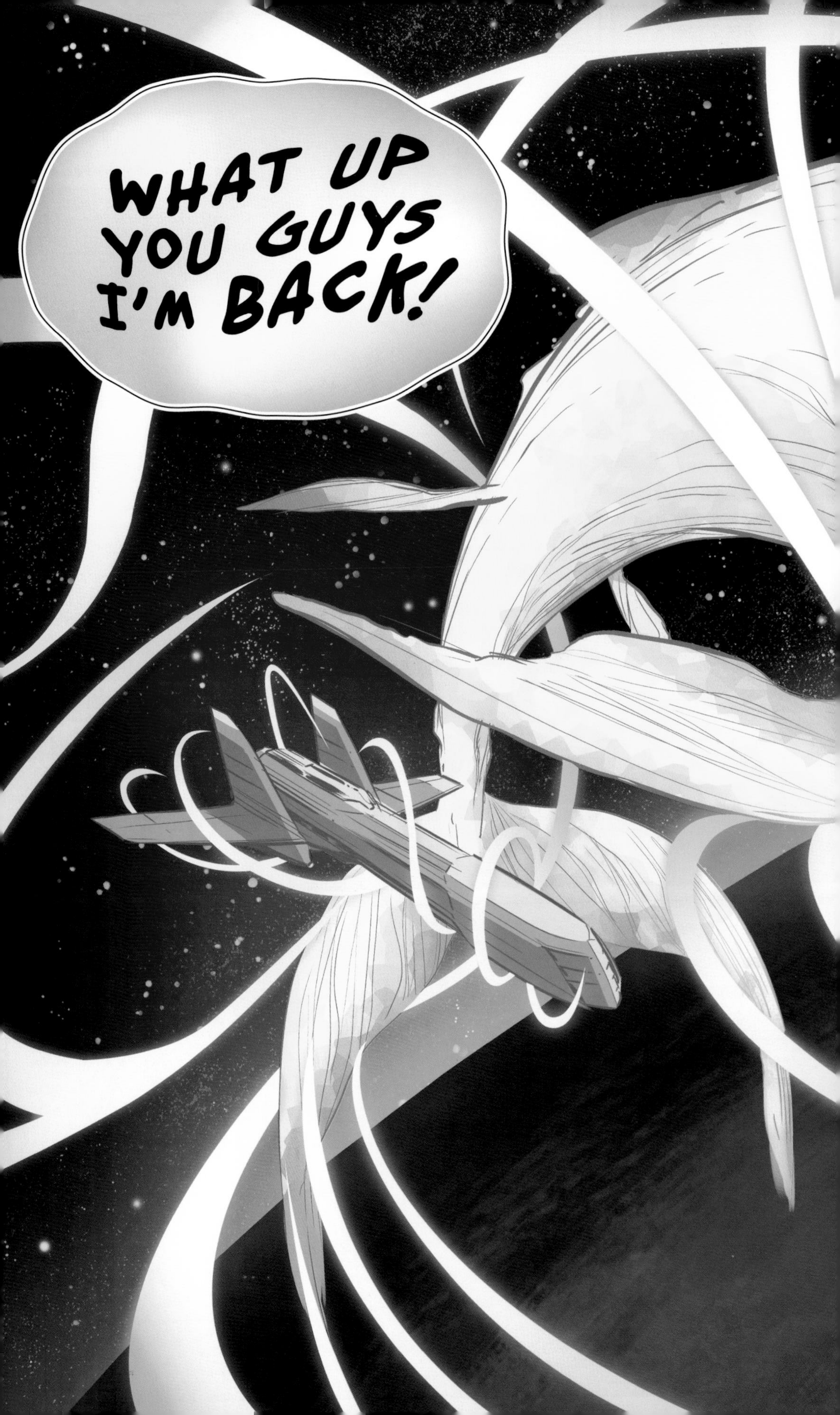
WHAT UP YOU GUYS I'M BACK!

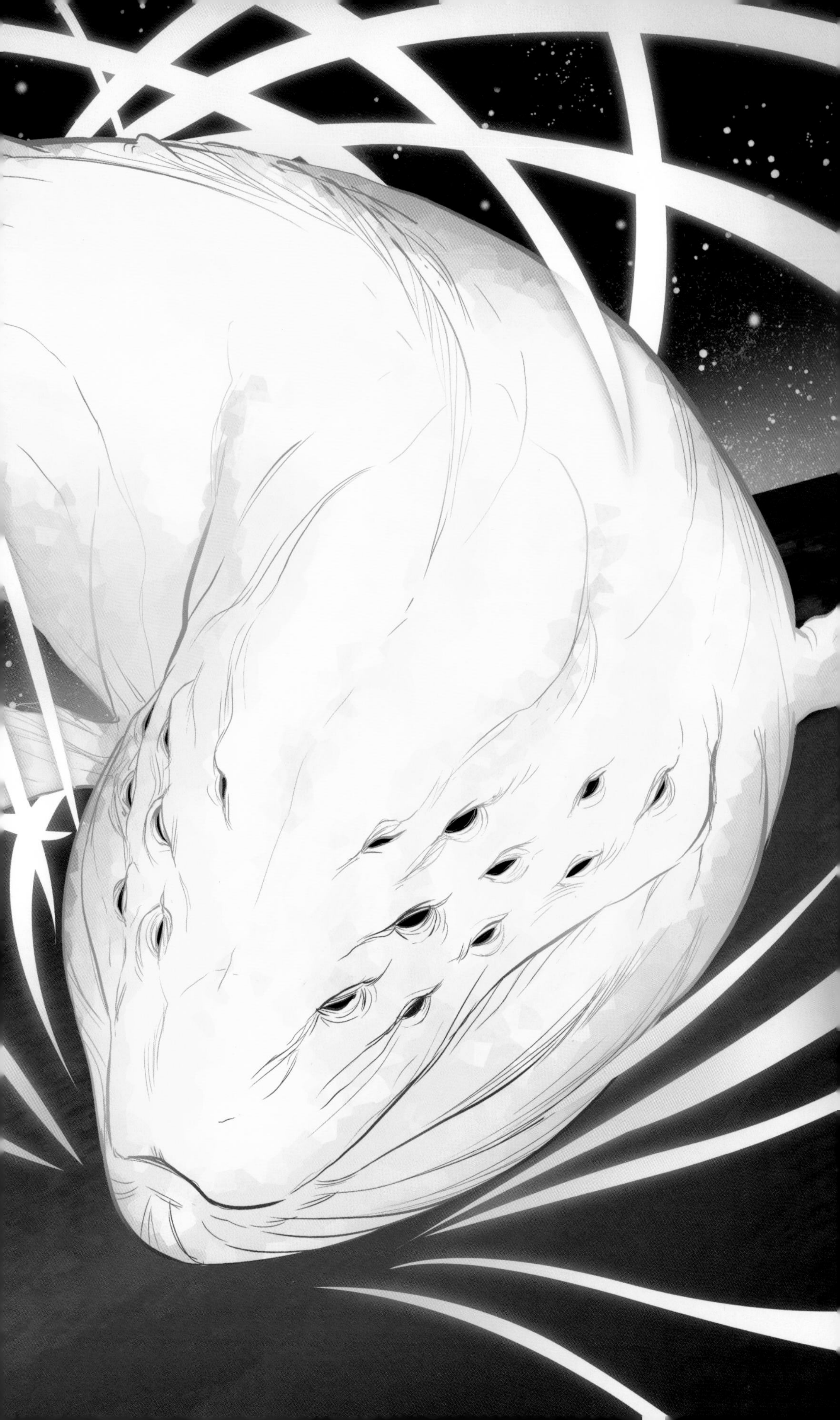

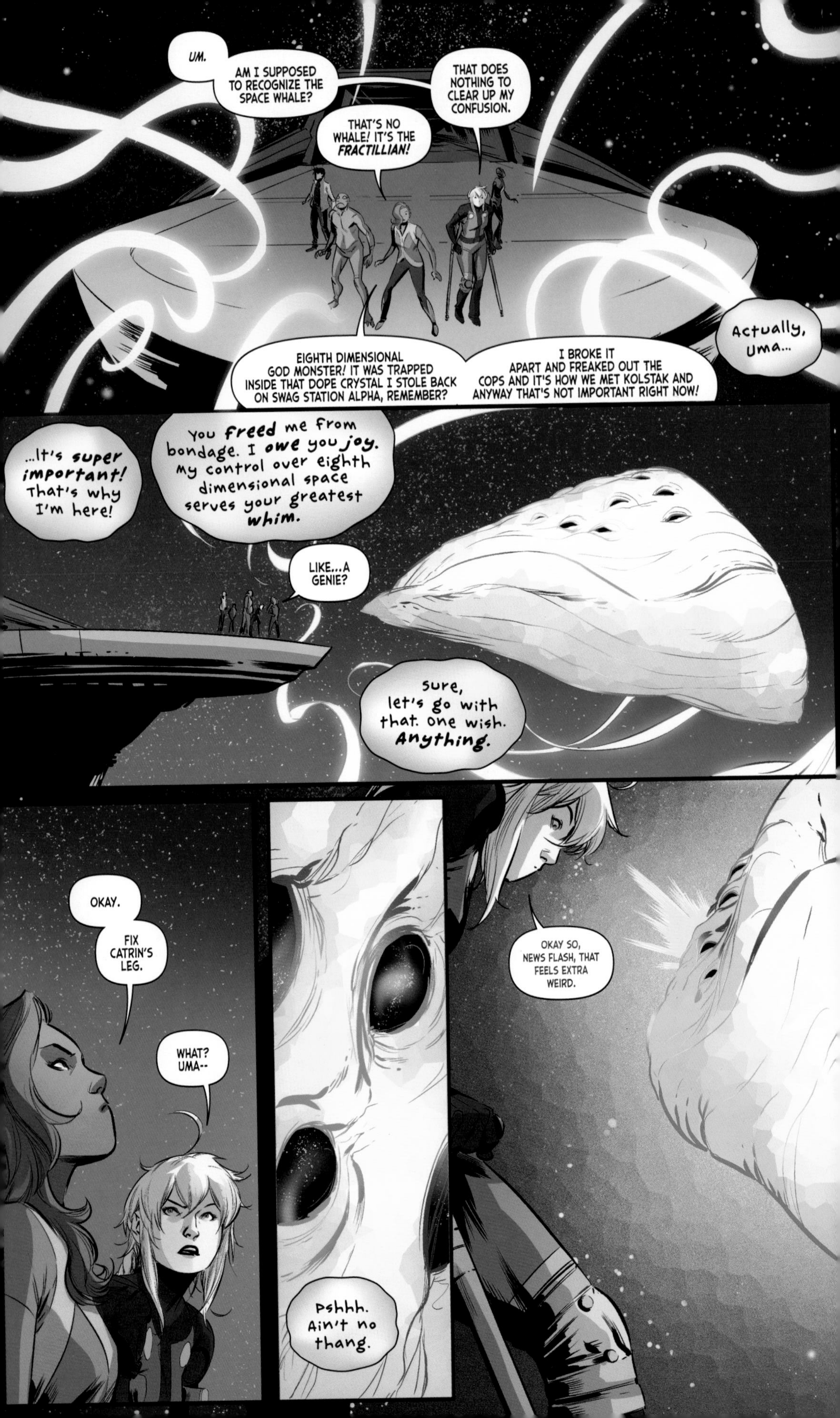
UM.
AM I SUPPOSED TO RECOGNIZE THE SPACE WHALE?
THAT DOES NOTHING TO CLEAR UP MY CONFUSION.
THAT'S NO WHALE! IT'S THE *FRACTILLIAN!*
EIGHTH DIMENSIONAL GOD MONSTER! IT WAS TRAPPED INSIDE THAT DOPE CRYSTAL I STOLE BACK ON SWAG STATION ALPHA, REMEMBER?
I BROKE IT APART AND FREAKED OUT THE COPS AND IT'S HOW WE MET KOLSTAK AND ANYWAY THAT'S NOT IMPORTANT RIGHT NOW!
Actually, Uma...
...It's **super important!** That's why I'm here!
You **freed** me from bondage. I **owe you joy.** My control over eighth dimensional space serves your greatest **whim.**
LIKE...A GENIE?
Sure, let's go with that. One wish. **Anything.**
OKAY.
FIX CATRIN'S LEG.
WHAT? UMA--
Pshhh. Ain't no thang.
OKAY SO, NEWS FLASH, THAT FEELS EXTRA WEIRD.

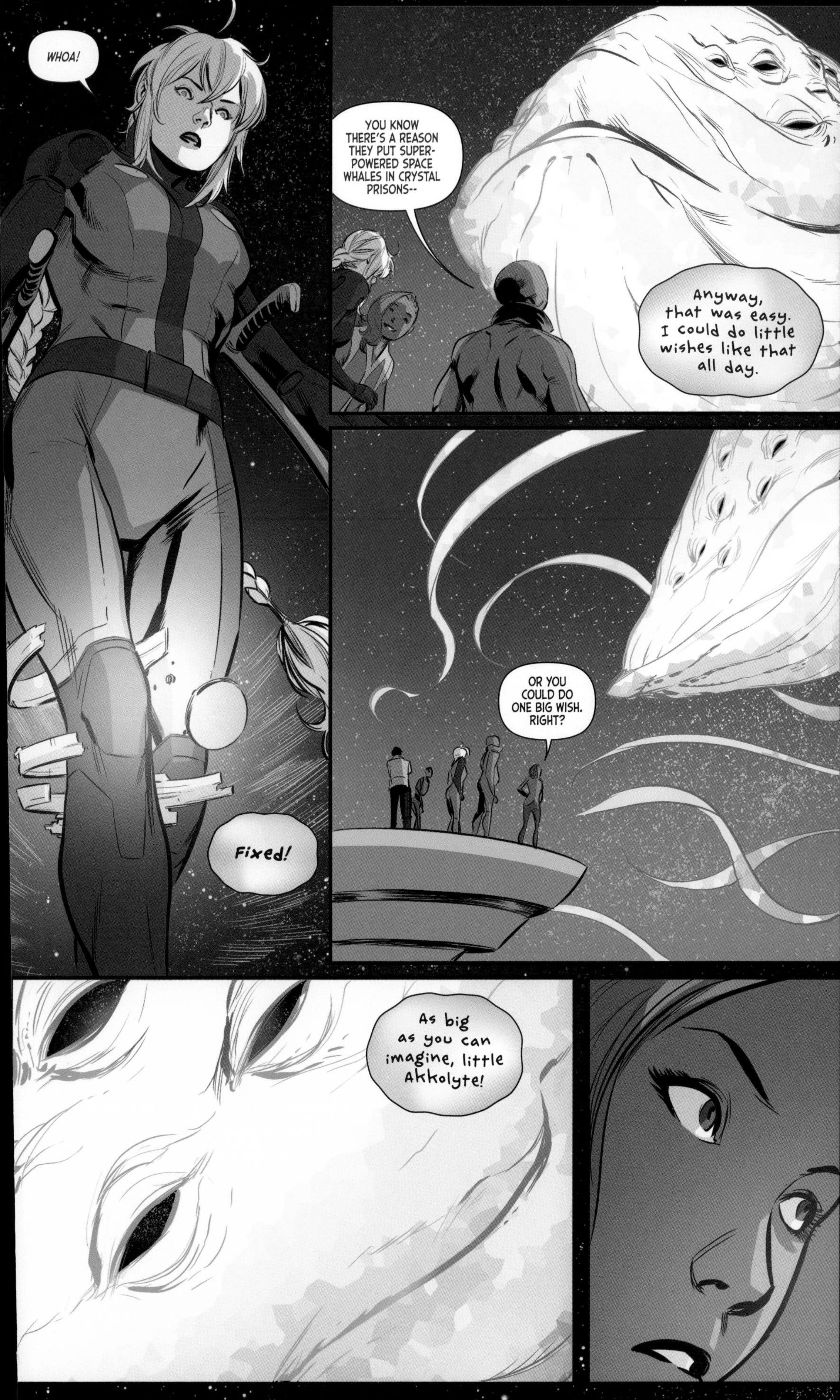
WHOA!
Fixed!
YOU KNOW THERE'S A REASON THEY PUT SUPER-POWERED SPACE WHALES IN CRYSTAL PRISONS--
Anyway, that was easy. I could do little wishes like that all day.
OR YOU COULD DO ONE BIG WISH. RIGHT?
As big as you can imagine, little Akkolyte!

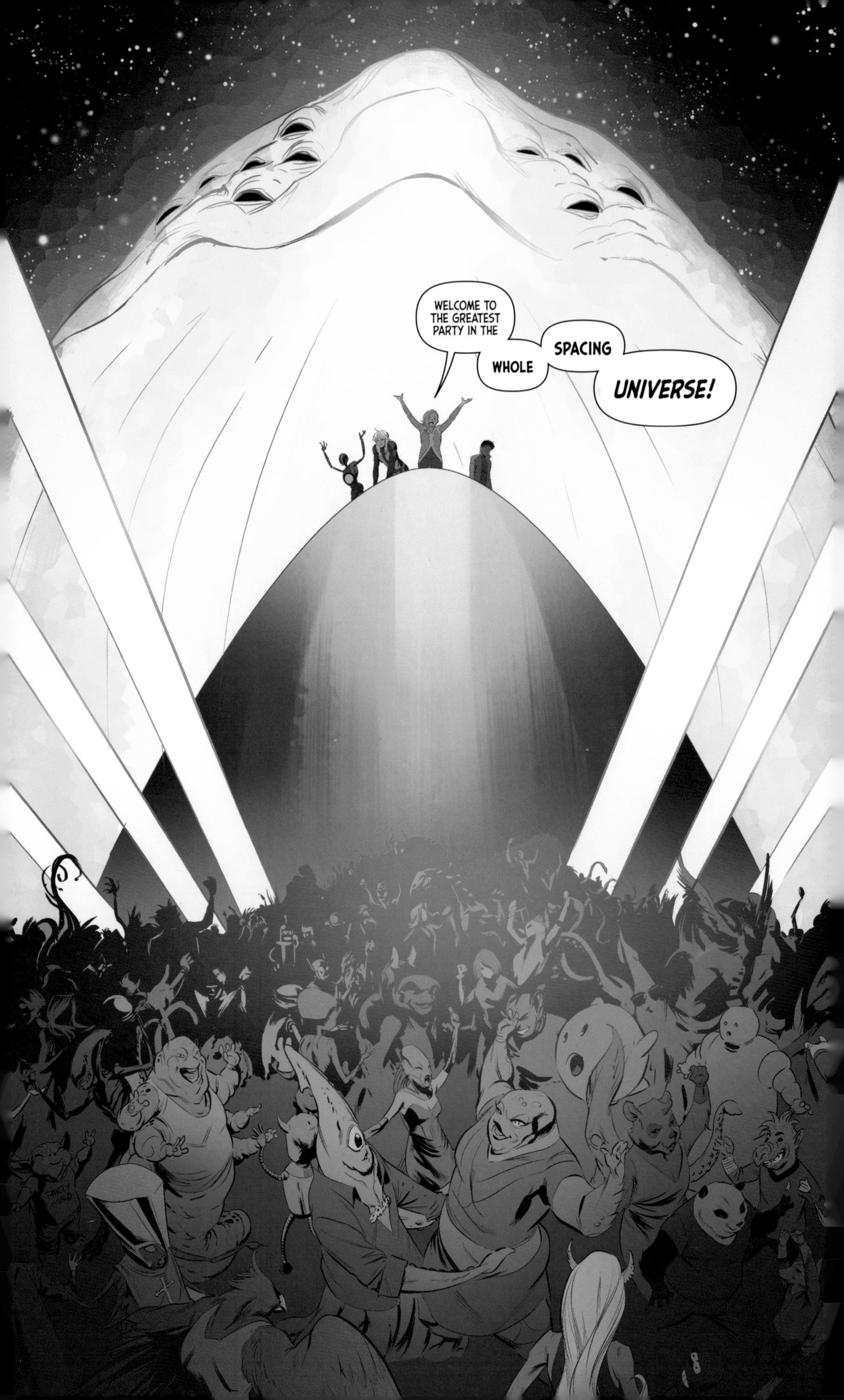
WELCOME TO THE GREATEST PARTY IN THE
WHOLE
SPACING
UNIVERSE!

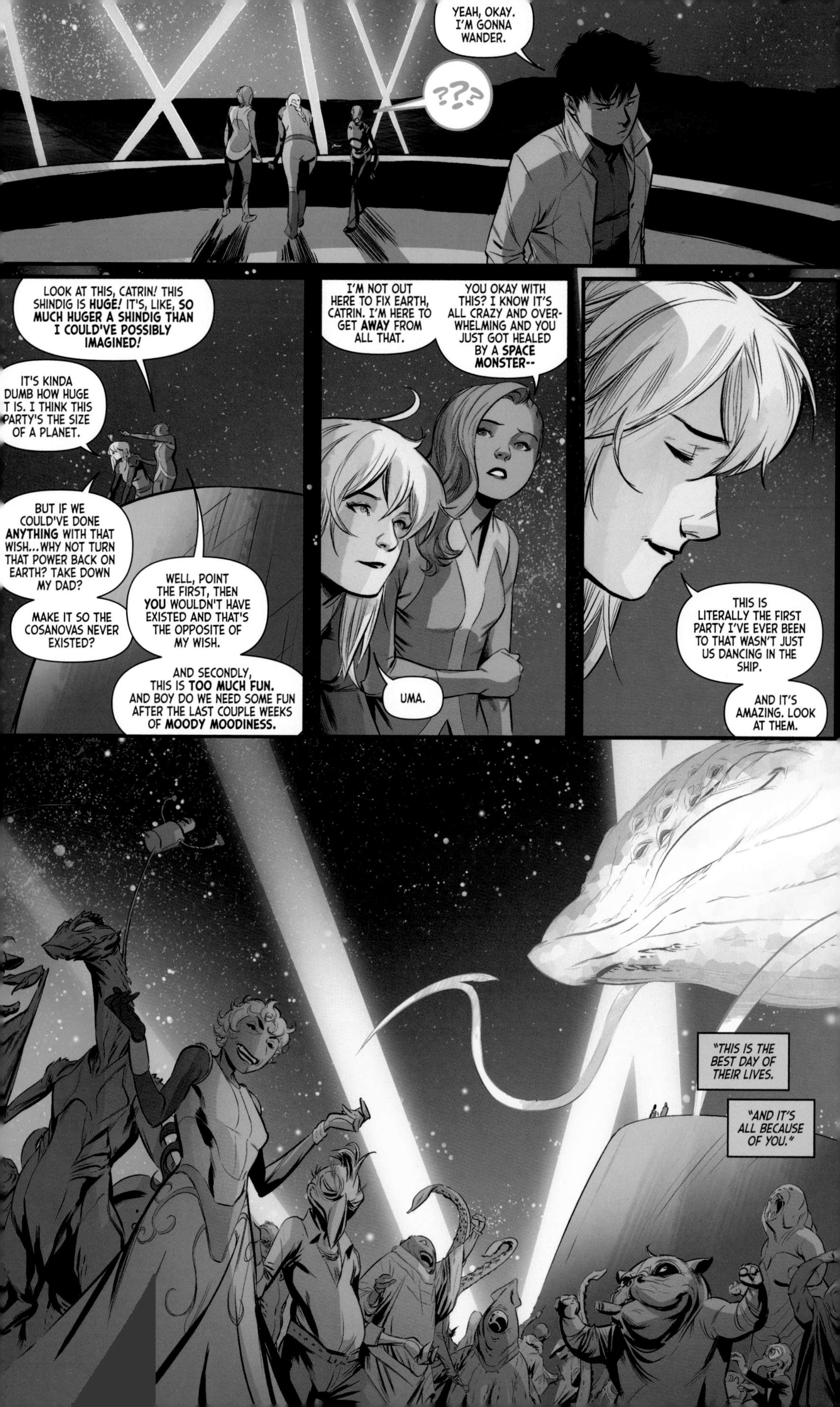
YEAH, OKAY. I'M GONNA WANDER.
???
LOOK AT THIS, CATRIN! THIS SHINDIG IS HUGE! IT'S, LIKE, SO MUCH HUGER A SHINDIG THAN I COULD'VE POSSIBLY IMAGINED!
IT'S KINDA DUMB HOW HUGE T IS. I THINK THIS PARTY'S THE SIZE OF A PLANET.
BUT IF WE COULD'VE DONE ANYTHING WITH THAT WISH...WHY NOT TURN THAT POWER BACK ON EARTH? TAKE DOWN MY DAD?
MAKE IT SO THE COSANOVAS NEVER EXISTED?
WELL, POINT THE FIRST, THEN YOU WOULDN'T HAVE EXISTED AND THAT'S THE OPPOSITE OF MY WISH.
AND SECONDLY, THIS IS TOO MUCH FUN. AND BOY DO WE NEED SOME FUN AFTER THE LAST COUPLE WEEKS OF MOODY MOODINESS.
YOU OKAY WITH THIS? I KNOW IT'S ALL CRAZY AND OVERWHELMING AND YOU JUST GOT HEALED BY A SPACE MONSTER--
I'M NOT OUT HERE TO FIX EARTH, CATRIN. I'M HERE TO GET AWAY FROM ALL THAT.
UMA.
THIS IS LITERALLY THE FIRST PARTY I'VE EVER BEEN TO THAT WASN'T JUST US DANCING IN THE SHIP.
AND IT'S AMAZING. LOOK AT THEM.
"THIS IS THE BEST DAY OF THEIR LIVES.
"AND IT'S ALL BECAUSE OF YOU."

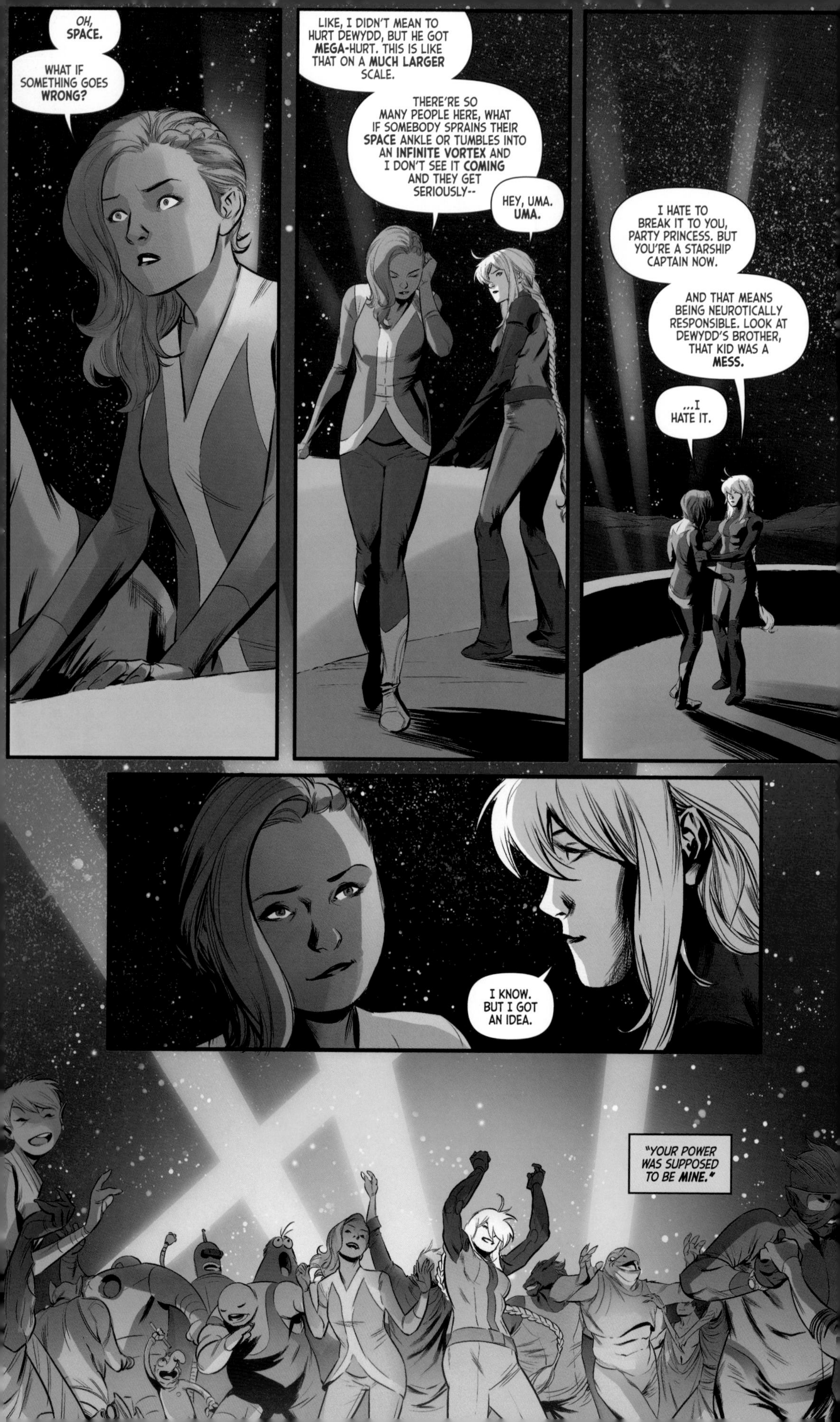
OH, SPACE.
WHAT IF SOMETHING GOES WRONG?
LIKE, I DIDN'T MEAN TO HURT DEWYDD, BUT HE GOT MEGA-HURT. THIS IS LIKE THAT ON A MUCH LARGER SCALE.
THERE'RE SO MANY PEOPLE HERE, WHAT IF SOMEBODY SPRAINS THEIR SPACE ANKLE OR TUMBLES INTO AN INFINITE VORTEX AND I DON'T SEE IT COMING AND THEY GET SERIOUSLY--
HEY, UMA. UMA.
I HATE TO BREAK IT TO YOU, PARTY PRINCESS. BUT YOU'RE A STARSHIP CAPTAIN NOW.
AND THAT MEANS BEING NEUROTICALLY RESPONSIBLE. LOOK AT DEWYDD'S BROTHER, THAT KID WAS A MESS.
...I HATE IT.
I KNOW. BUT I GOT AN IDEA.
"YOUR POWER WAS SUPPOSED TO BE MINE."

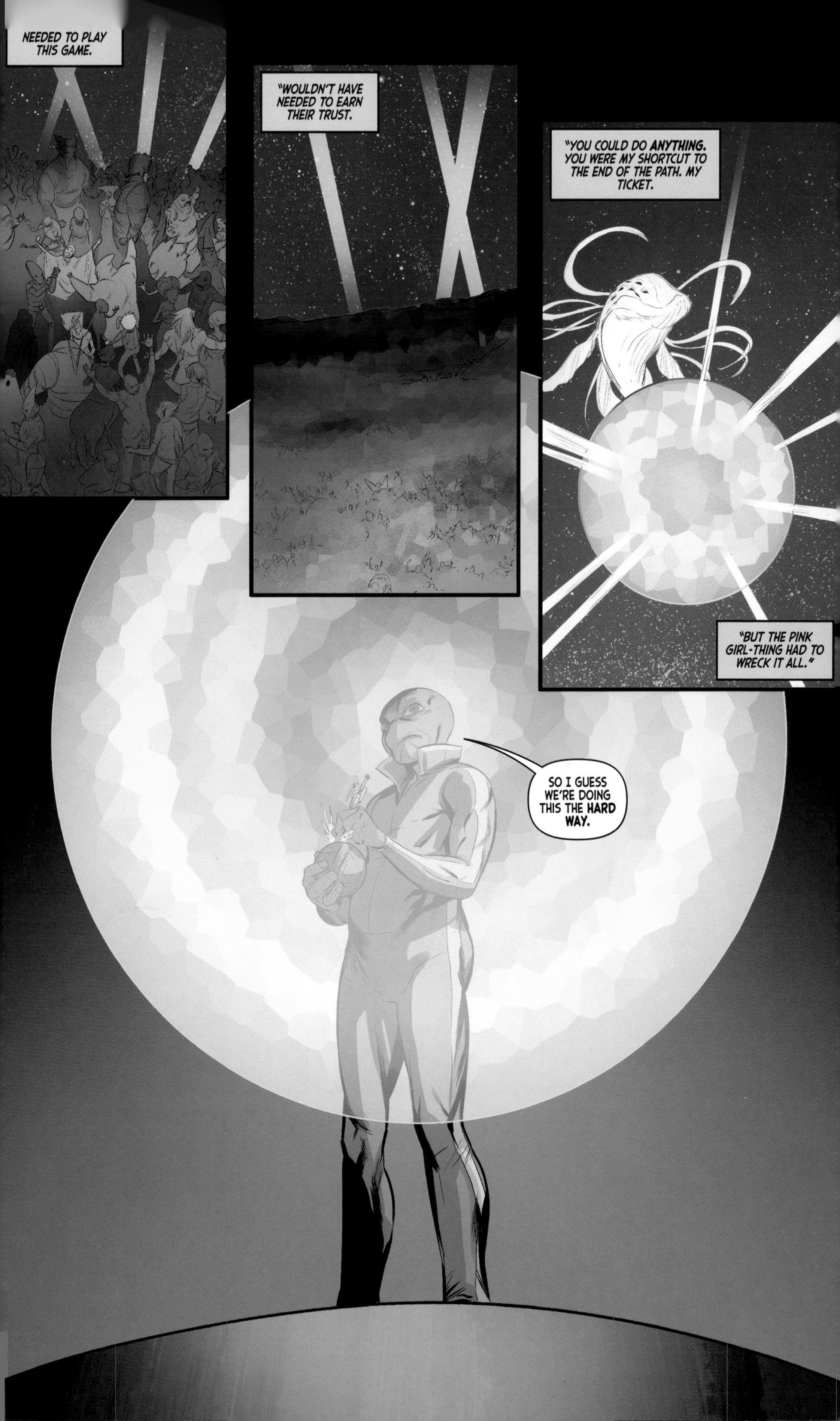
NEEDED TO PLAY THIS GAME.
"WOULDN'T HAVE NEEDED TO EARN THEIR TRUST.
"YOU COULD DO ANYTHING. YOU WERE MY SHORTCUT TO THE END OF THE PATH. MY TICKET.
"BUT THE PINK GIRL-THING HAD TO WRECK IT ALL."
SO I GUESS WE'RE DOING THIS THE HARD WAY.

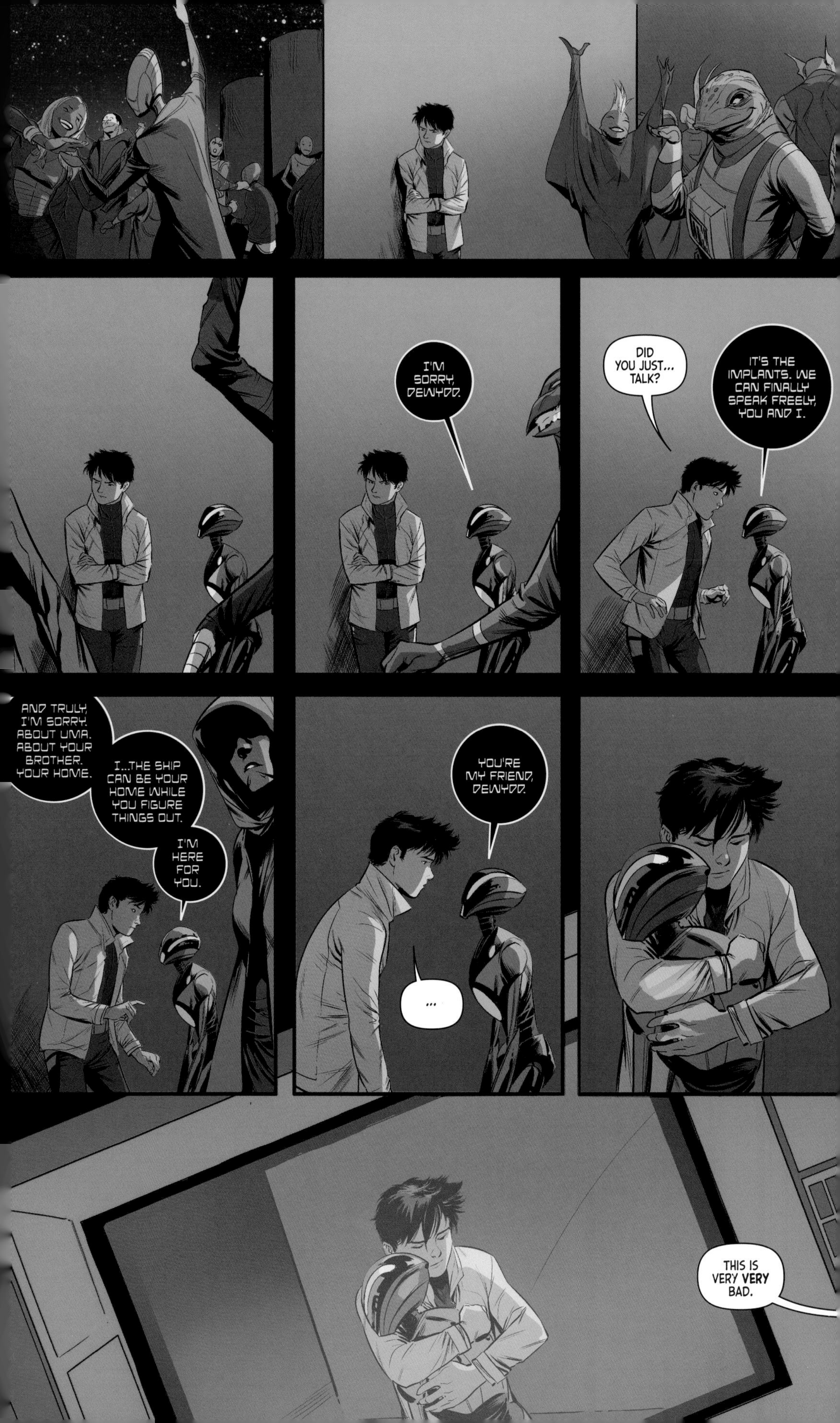
I'M SORRY, DEWYDD.
DID YOU JUST... TALK?
IT'S THE IMPLANTS. WE CAN FINALLY SPEAK FREELY, YOU AND I.
AND TRULY, I'M SORRY. ABOUT UMA. ABOUT YOUR BROTHER. YOUR HOME.
I...THE SHIP CAN BE YOUR HOME WHILE YOU FIGURE THINGS OUT.
I'M HERE FOR YOU.
YOU'RE MY FRIEND, DEWYDD.
...
THIS IS VERY **VERY** BAD.

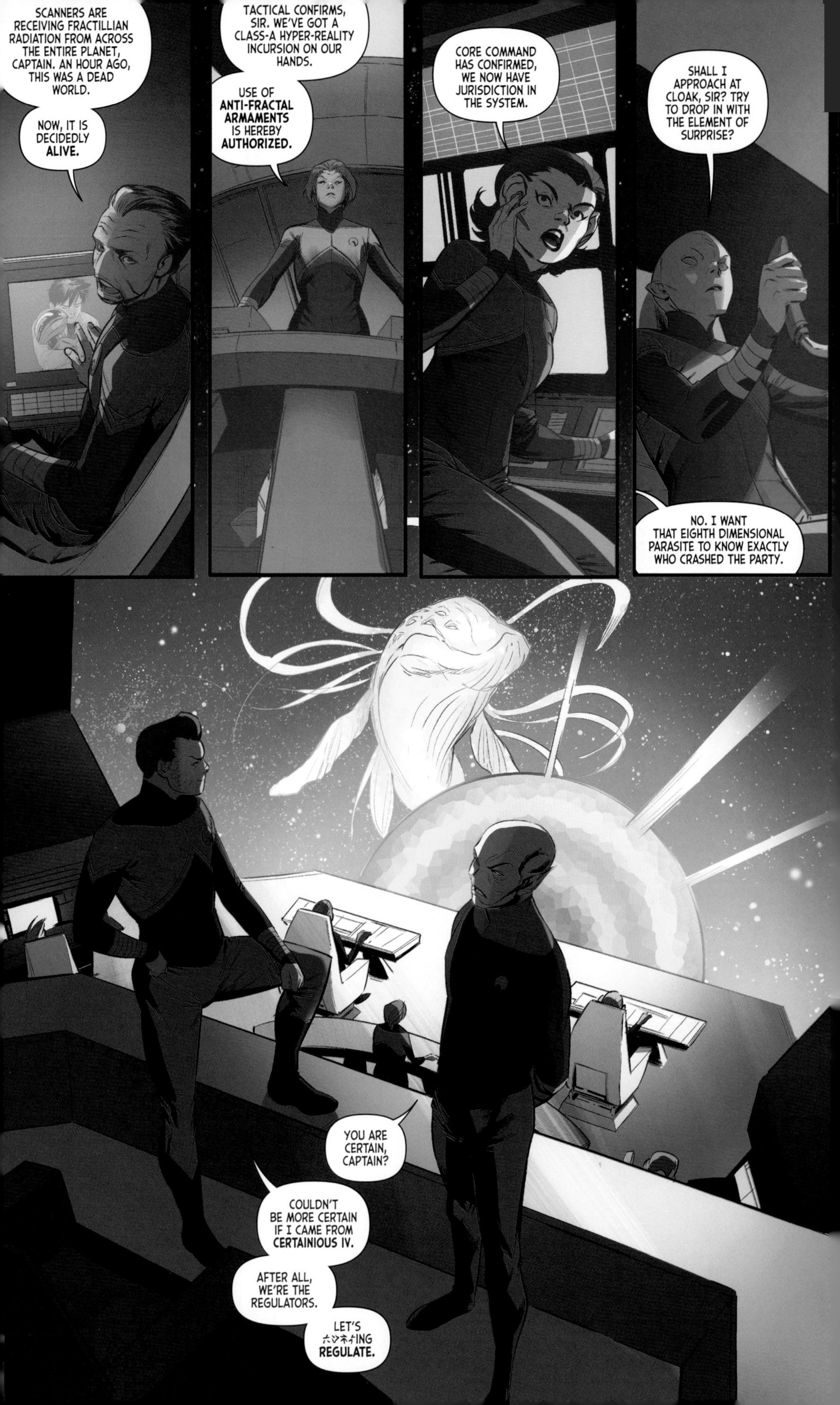

SCANNERS ARE RECEIVING FRACTILLIAN RADIATION FROM ACROSS THE ENTIRE PLANET, CAPTAIN. AN HOUR AGO, THIS WAS A DEAD WORLD.
NOW, IT IS DECIDEDLY **ALIVE.**
TACTICAL CONFIRMS, SIR. WE'VE GOT A CLASS-A HYPER-REALITY INCURSION ON OUR HANDS.
USE OF **ANTI-FRACTAL ARMAMENTS** IS HEREBY **AUTHORIZED.**
CORE COMMAND HAS CONFIRMED, WE NOW HAVE JURISDICTION IN THE SYSTEM.
SHALL I APPROACH AT CLOAK, SIR? TRY TO DROP IN WITH THE ELEMENT OF SURPRISE?
NO. I WANT THAT EIGHTH DIMENSIONAL PARASITE TO KNOW EXACTLY WHO CRASHED THE PARTY.
YOU ARE CERTAIN, CAPTAIN?
COULDN'T BE MORE CERTAIN IF I CAME FROM **CERTAINIOUS IV.**
AFTER ALL, WE'RE THE REGULATORS.
LET'S ING **REGULATE.**

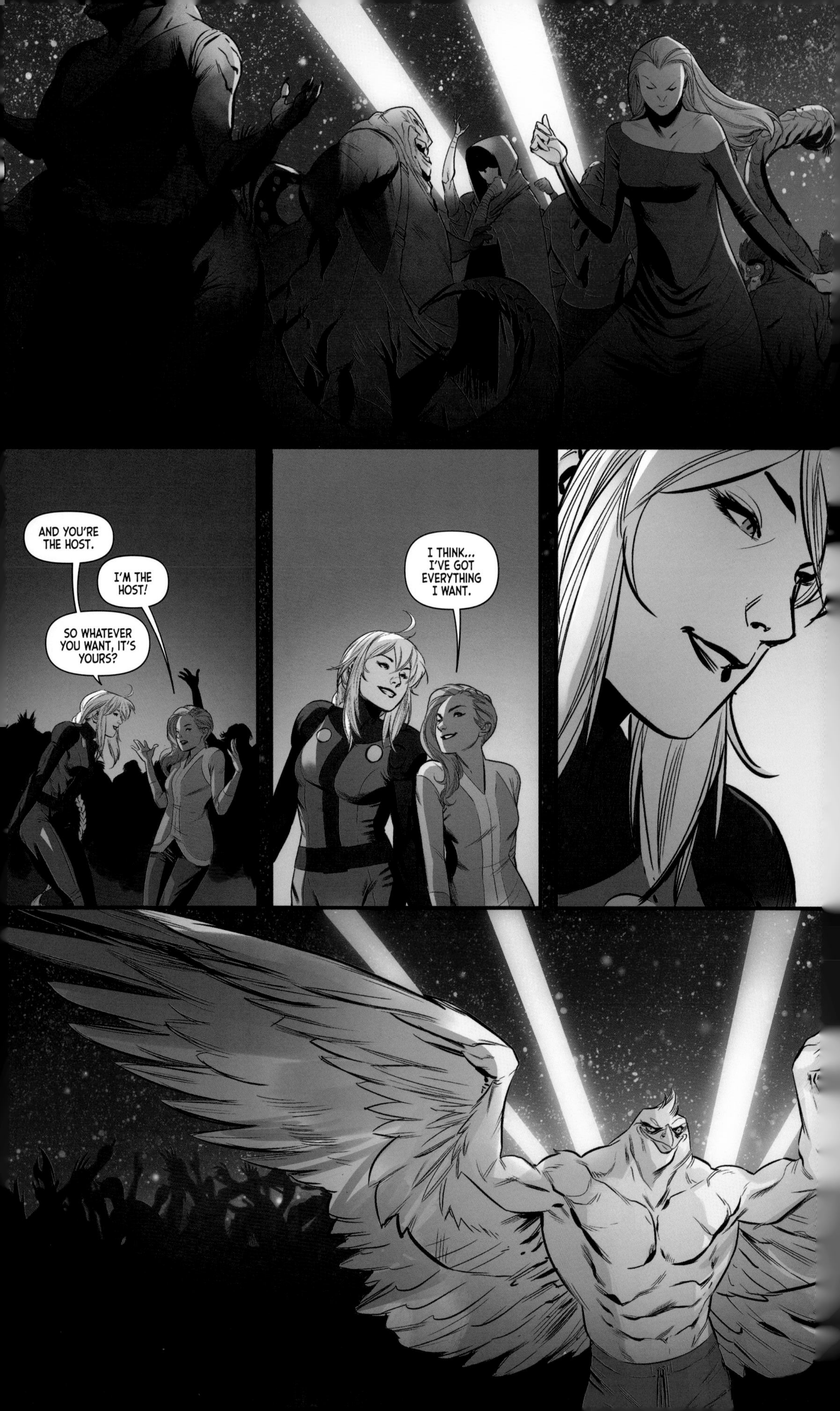
AND YOU'RE THE HOST.
I'M THE HOST!
SO WHATEVER YOU WANT, IT'S YOURS?
I THINK... I'VE GOT EVERYTHING I WANT.

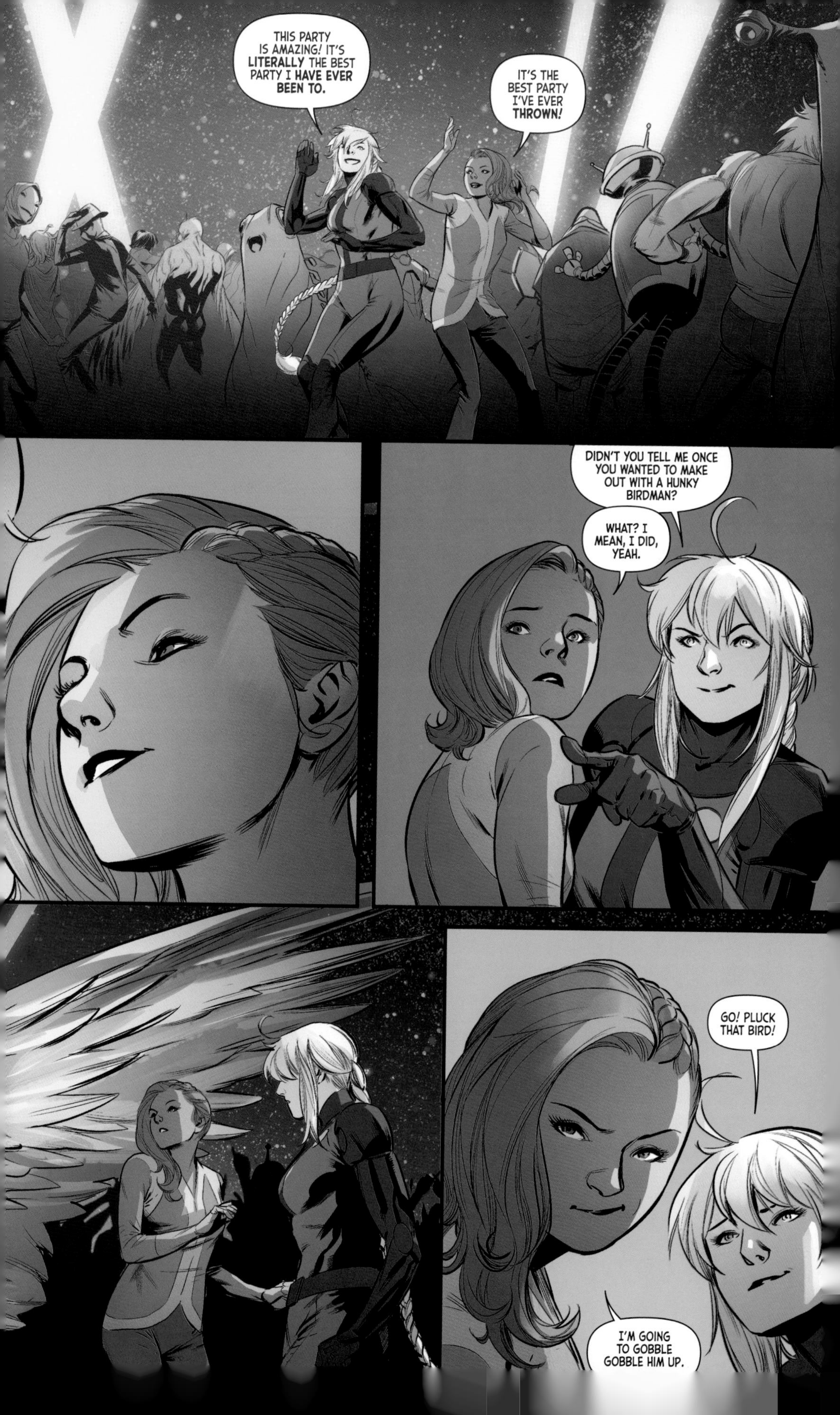
THIS PARTY IS AMAZING! IT'S LITERALLY THE BEST PARTY I HAVE EVER BEEN TO.
IT'S THE BEST PARTY I'VE EVER THROWN!
DIDN'T YOU TELL ME ONCE YOU WANTED TO MAKE OUT WITH A HUNKY BIRDMAN?
WHAT? I MEAN, I DID, YEAH.
GO! PLUCK THAT BIRD!
I'M GOING TO GOBBLE GOBBLE HIM UP.

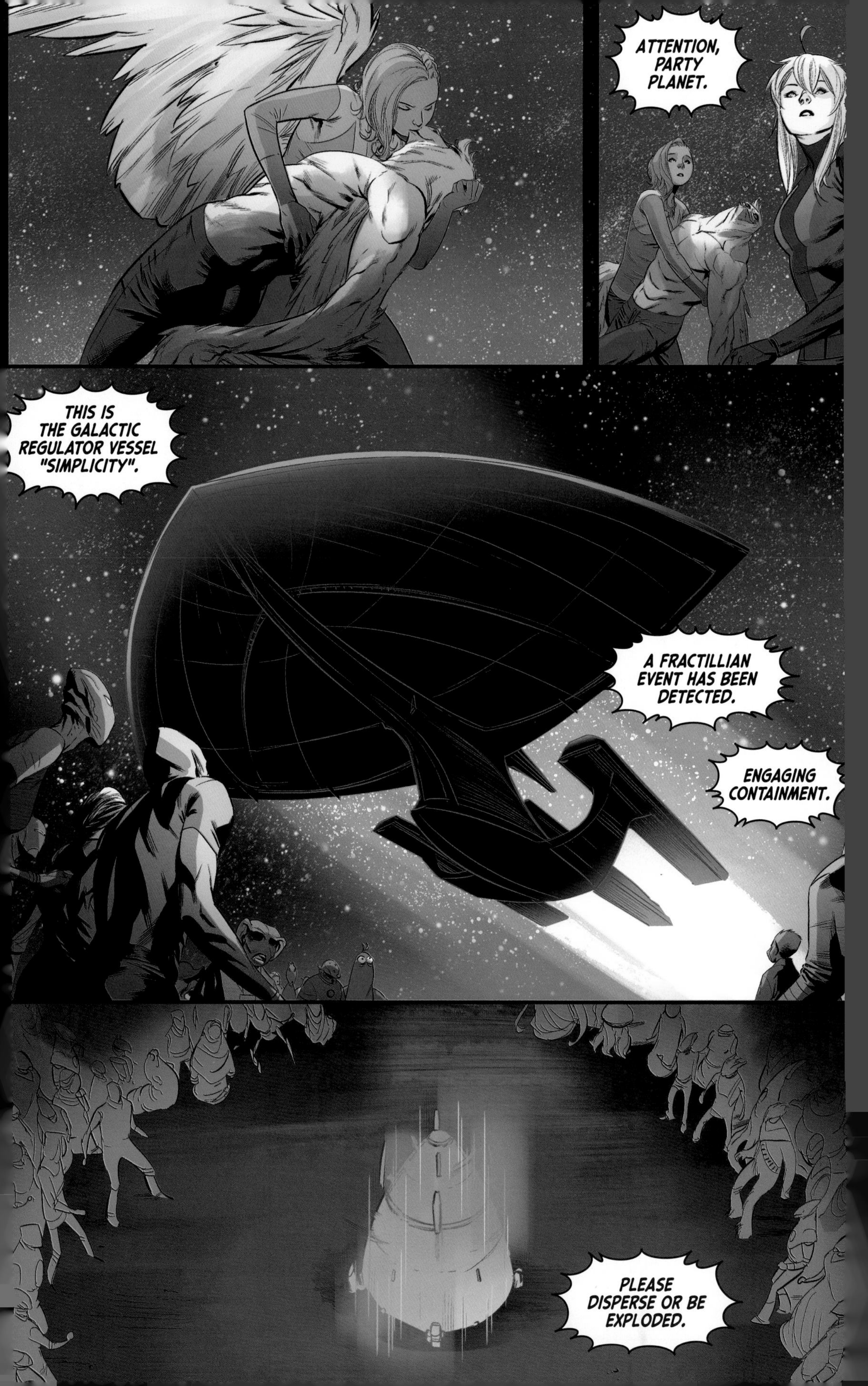

ATTENTION, PARTY PLANET.
THIS IS THE GALACTIC REGULATOR VESSEL "SIMPLICITY".
A FRACTILLIAN EVENT HAS BEEN DETECTED.
ENGAGING CONTAINMENT.
PLEASE DISPERSE OR BE EXPLODED.

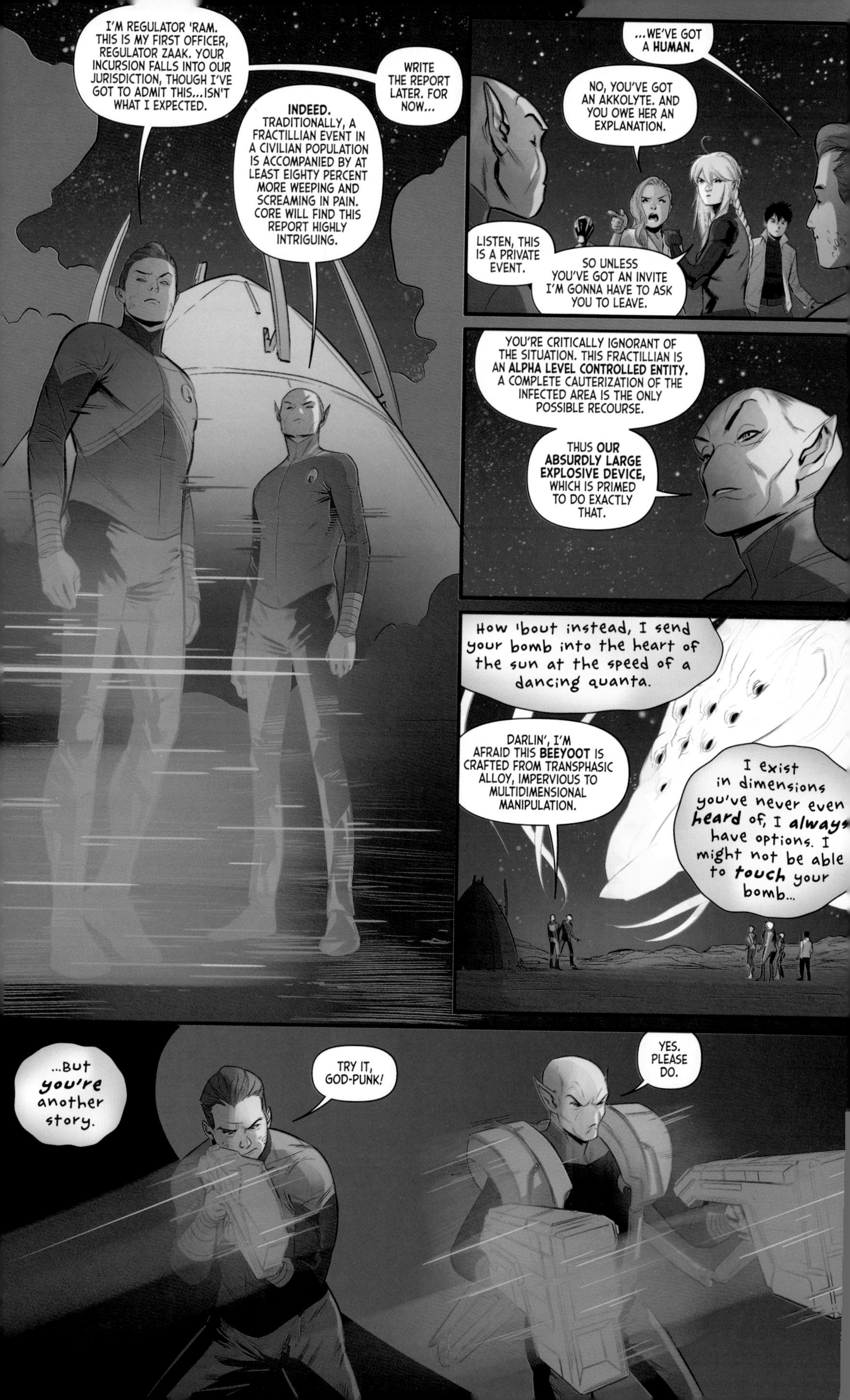
I'M REGULATOR 'RAM. THIS IS MY FIRST OFFICER, REGULATOR ZAAK. YOUR INCURSION FALLS INTO OUR JURISDICTION, THOUGH I'VE GOT TO ADMIT THIS...ISN'T WHAT I EXPECTED.
WRITE THE REPORT LATER. FOR NOW...
INDEED. TRADITIONALLY, A FRACTILLIAN EVENT IN A CIVILIAN POPULATION IS ACCOMPANIED BY AT LEAST EIGHTY PERCENT MORE WEEPING AND SCREAMING IN PAIN. CORE WILL FIND THIS REPORT HIGHLY INTRIGUING.
...WE'VE GOT A HUMAN.
NO, YOU'VE GOT AN AKKOLYTE. AND YOU OWE HER AN EXPLANATION.
LISTEN, THIS IS A PRIVATE EVENT.
SO UNLESS YOU'VE GOT AN INVITE I'M GONNA HAVE TO ASK YOU TO LEAVE.
YOU'RE CRITICALLY IGNORANT OF THE SITUATION. THIS FRACTILLIAN IS AN ALPHA LEVEL CONTROLLED ENTITY. A COMPLETE CAUTERIZATION OF THE INFECTED AREA IS THE ONLY POSSIBLE RECOURSE.
THUS OUR ABSURDLY LARGE EXPLOSIVE DEVICE, WHICH IS PRIMED TO DO EXACTLY THAT.
How 'bout instead, I send your bomb into the heart of the sun at the speed of a dancing quanta.
DARLIN', I'M AFRAID THIS BEEYOOT IS CRAFTED FROM TRANSPHASIC ALLOY, IMPERVIOUS TO MULTIDIMENSIONAL MANIPULATION.
I exist in dimensions you've never even heard of, I always have options. I might not be able to touch your bomb...
...But you're another story.
TRY IT, GOD-PUNK!
YES. PLEASE DO.

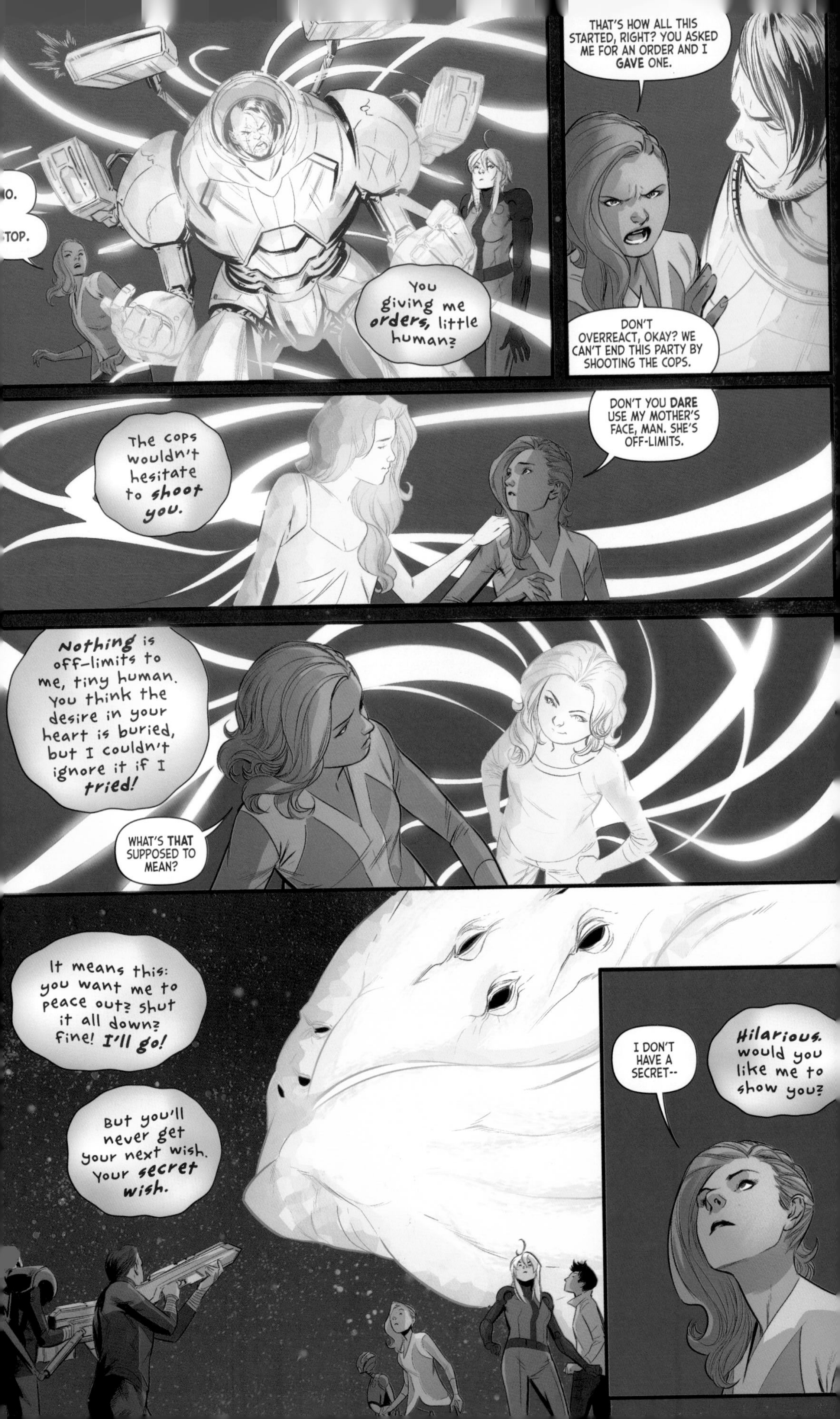

NO.
STOP.
You giving me orders, little human?
THAT'S HOW ALL THIS STARTED, RIGHT? YOU ASKED ME FOR AN ORDER AND I GAVE ONE.
DON'T OVERREACT, OKAY? WE CAN'T END THIS PARTY BY SHOOTING THE COPS.
The cops wouldn't hesitate to shoot you.
DON'T YOU DARE USE MY MOTHER'S FACE, MAN. SHE'S OFF-LIMITS.
Nothing is off-limits to me, tiny human. You think the desire in your heart is buried, but I couldn't ignore it if I tried!
WHAT'S THAT SUPPOSED TO MEAN?
It means this: you want me to peace out? shut it all down? fine! I'll go!
But you'll never get your next wish. Your secret wish.
I DON'T HAVE A SECRET--
Hilarious. would you like me to show you?

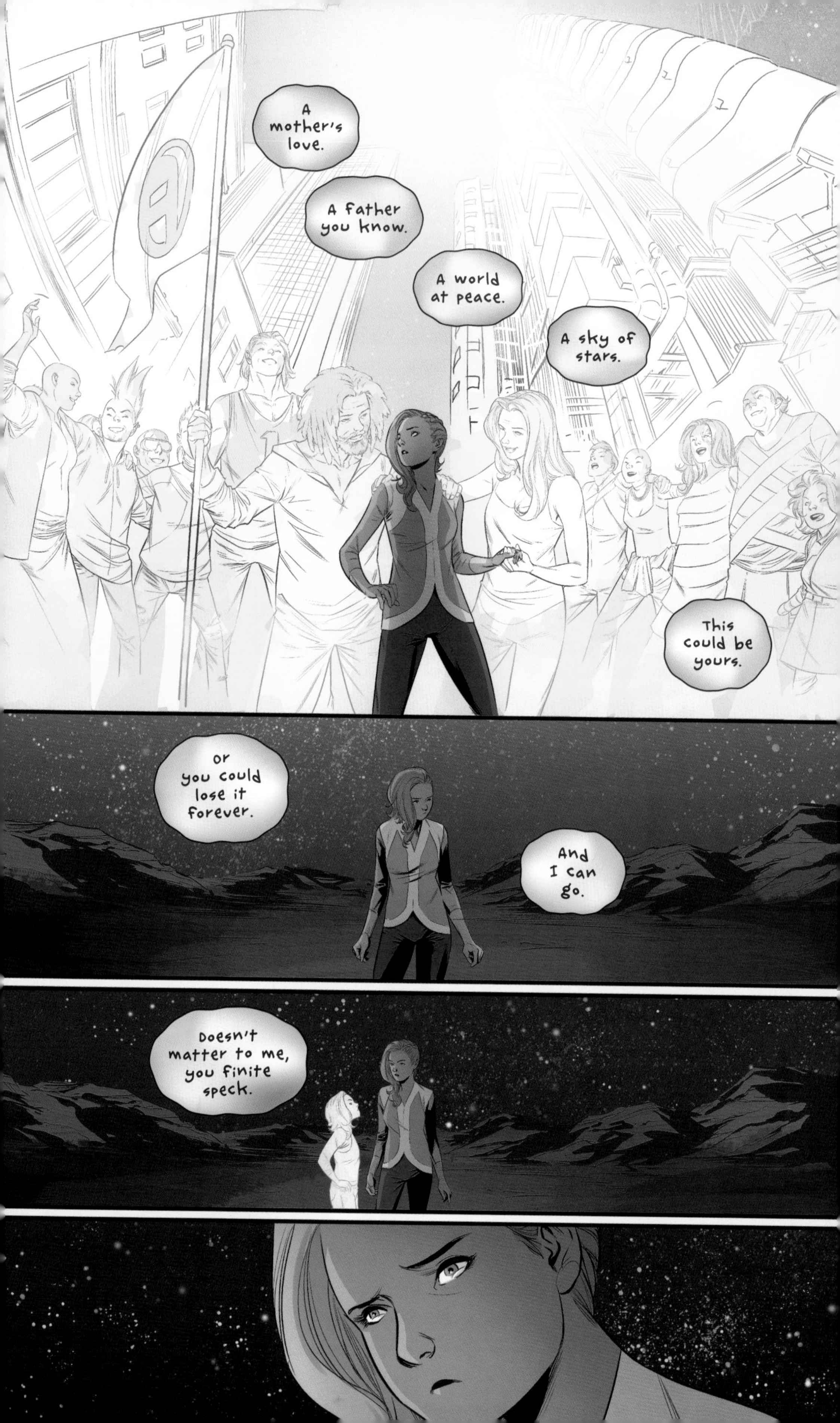
A mother's love.
A father you know.
A world at peace.
A sky of stars.
This could be yours.
Or you could lose it forever.
And I can go.
Doesn't matter to me, you finite speck.

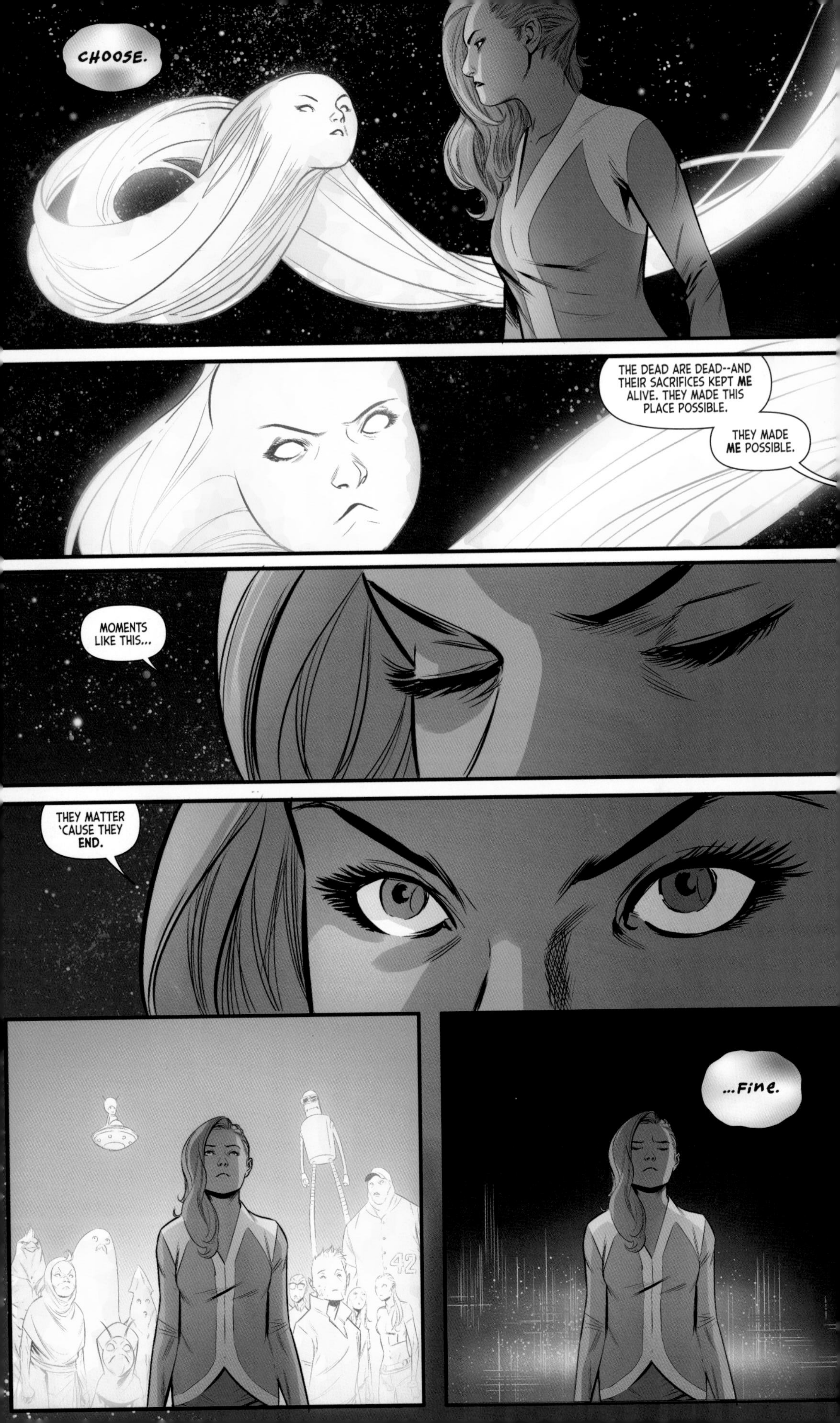
CHOOSE.
THE DEAD ARE DEAD--AND THEIR SACRIFICES KEPT ME ALIVE. THEY MADE THIS PLACE POSSIBLE.
THEY MADE ME POSSIBLE.
MOMENTS LIKE THIS...
THEY MATTER 'CAUSE THEY END.
42
...Fine.

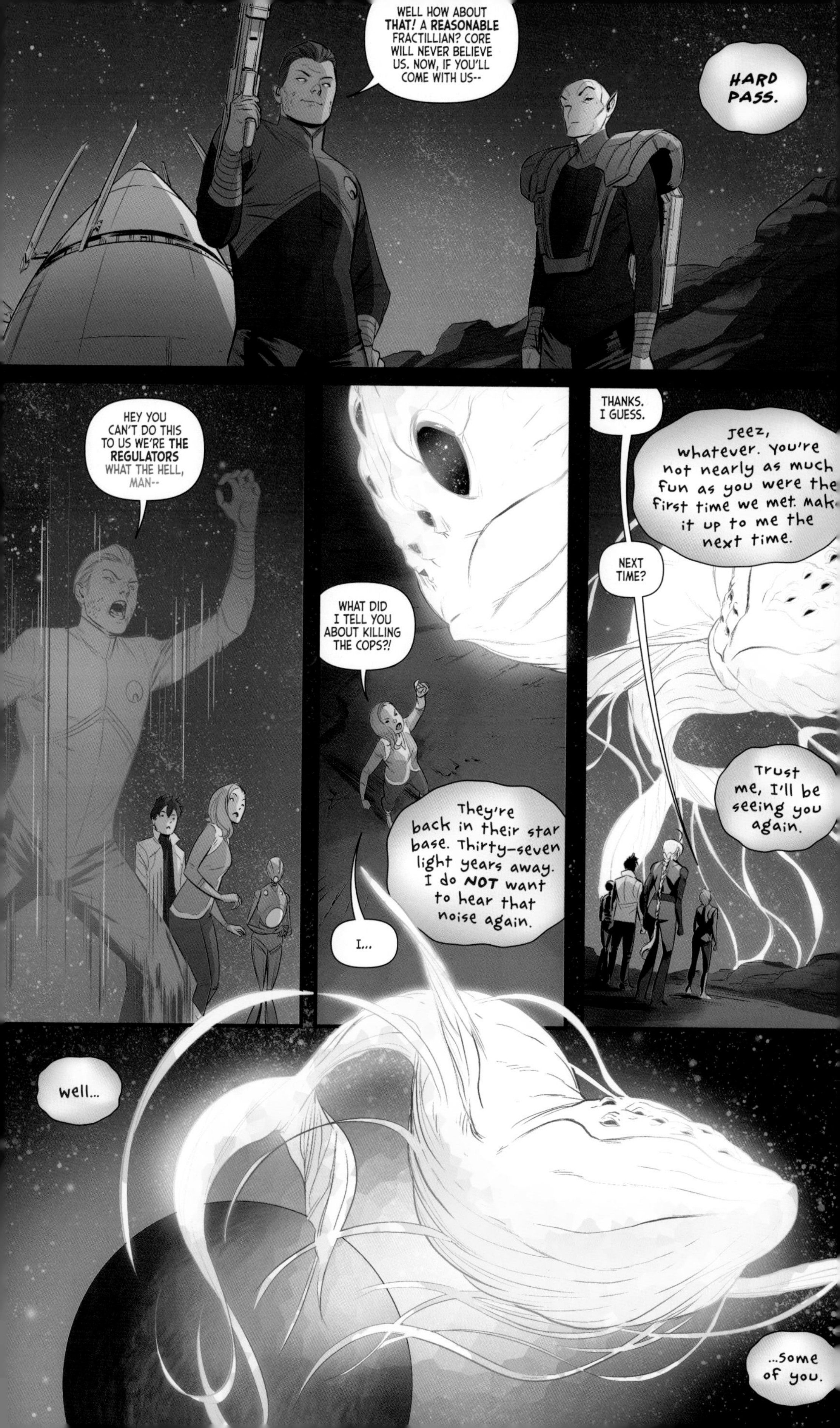
WELL HOW ABOUT THAT! A REASONABLE FRACTILLIAN? CORE WILL NEVER BELIEVE US. NOW, IF YOU'LL COME WITH US--
HARD PASS.
HEY YOU CAN'T DO THIS TO US WE'RE THE REGULATORS WHAT THE HELL, MAN--
WHAT DID I TELL YOU ABOUT KILLING THE COPS?!
They're back in their star base. Thirty-seven light years away. I do NOT want to hear that noise again.
I...
THANKS. I GUESS.
Jeez, whatever. You're not nearly as much fun as you were the first time we met. Make it up to me the next time.
NEXT TIME?
Trust me, I'll be seeing you again.
well...
...some of you.

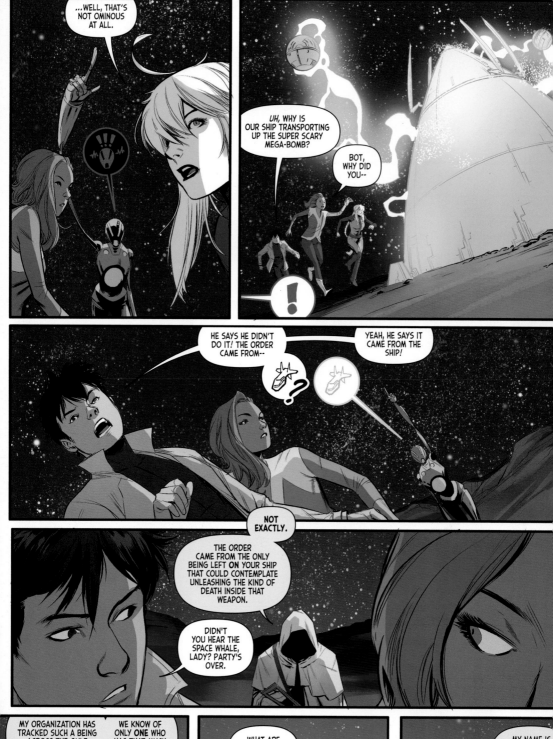

...WELL, THAT'S NOT OMINOUS AT ALL.

UH, WHY IS OUR SHIP TRANSPORTING UP THE SUPER SCARY MEGA-BOMB?

BOT, WHY DID YOU--

HE SAYS HE DIDN'T DO IT! THE ORDER CAME FROM--

YEAH, HE SAYS IT CAME FROM THE SHIP!

NOT EXACTLY.

THE ORDER CAME FROM THE ONLY BEING LEFT ON YOUR SHIP THAT COULD CONTEMPLATE UNLEASHING THE KIND OF DEATH INSIDE THAT WEAPON.

DIDN'T YOU HEAR THE SPACE WHALE, LADY? PARTY'S OVER.

MY ORGANIZATION HAS TRACKED SUCH A BEING ACROSS THE GULF OF STARS FOR MILLENNIA.

WE KNOW OF ONLY ONE WHO HAS THAT MUCH HATE IN HIS HEART.

WHAT ARE YOU TALKING ABOUT? WHO ARE YOU?

MY NAME IS MAERIE K'THO VAL'HULLIOK. BUT YOU MAY CALL ME--

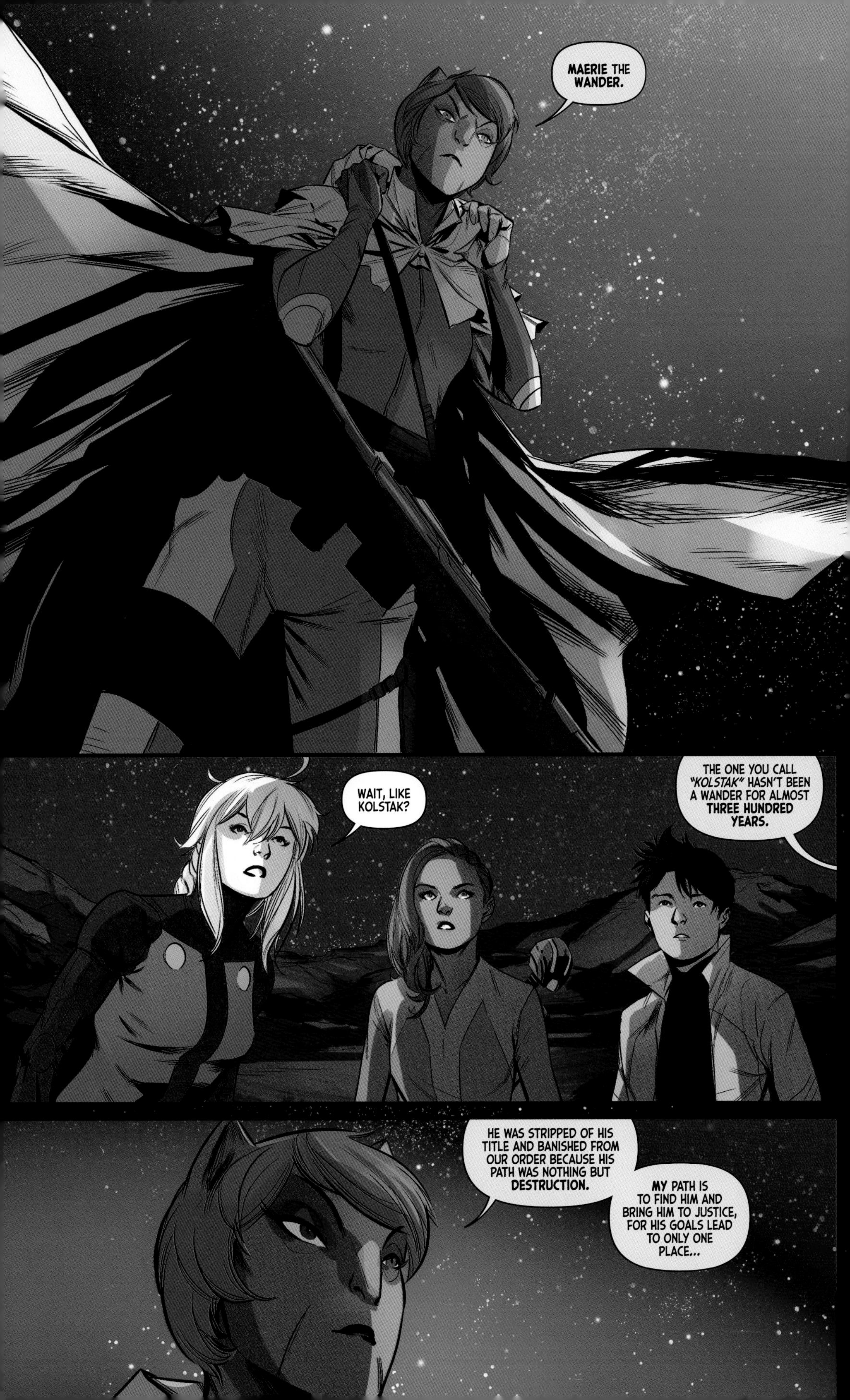
MAERIE THE WANDER.
WAIT, LIKE KOLSTAK?
THE ONE YOU CALL "KOLSTAK" HASN'T BEEN A WANDER FOR ALMOST THREE HUNDRED YEARS.
HE WAS STRIPPED OF HIS TITLE AND BANISHED FROM OUR ORDER BECAUSE HIS PATH WAS NOTHING BUT DESTRUCTION.
MY PATH IS TO FIND HIM AND BRING HIM TO JUSTICE, FOR HIS GOALS LEAD TO ONLY ONE PLACE...

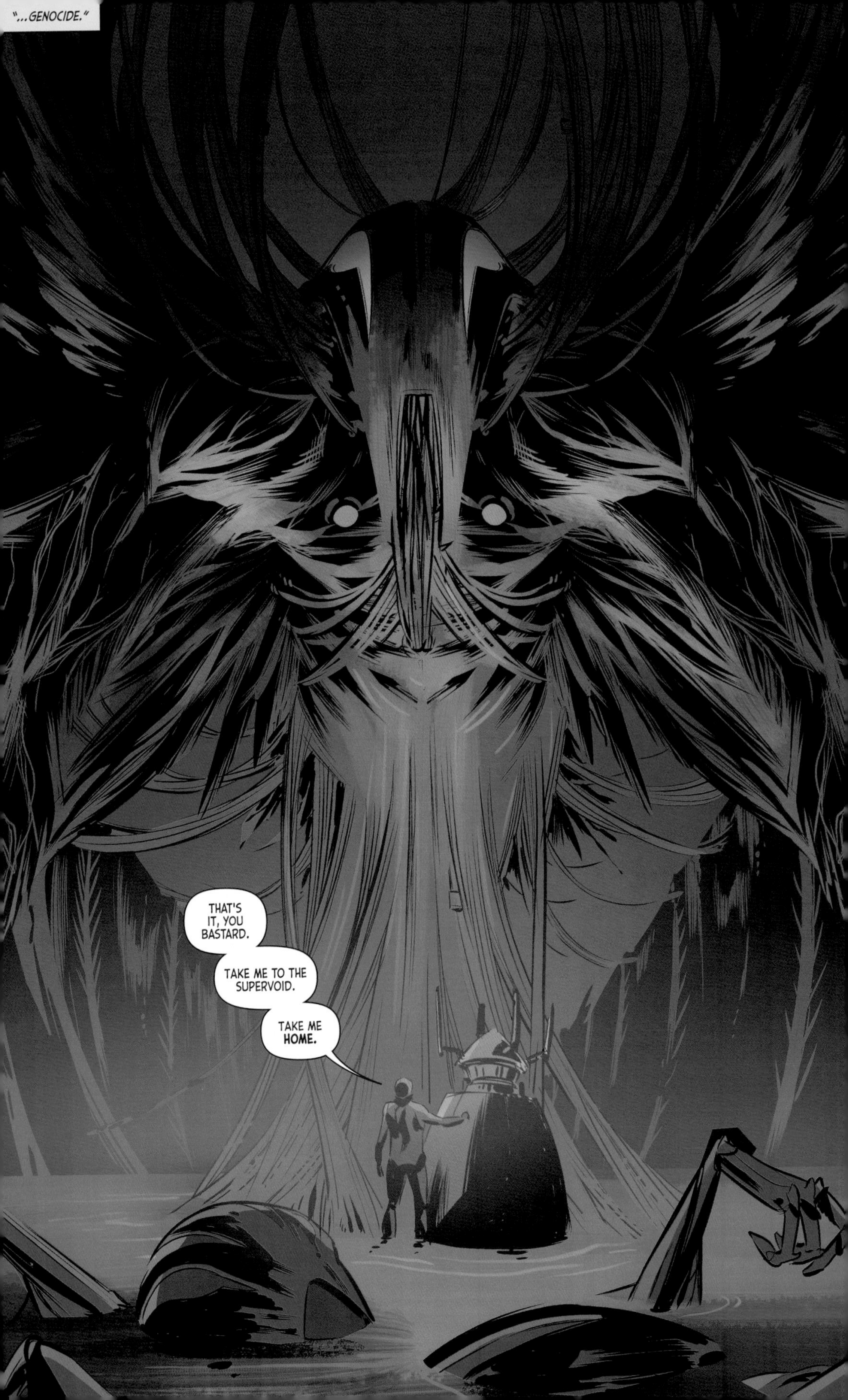
"...GENOCIDE."
THAT'S IT, YOU BASTARD.
TAKE ME TO THE SUPERVOID.
TAKE ME **HOME.**

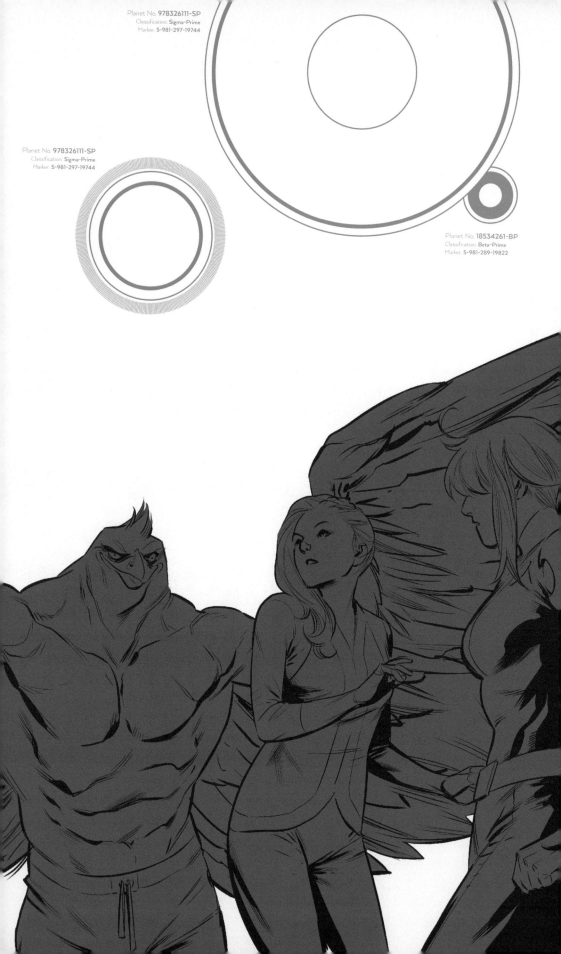

Planet No. 978326111-SP
Classification: Sigma-Prime
Marker: 5-981-297-19744

Planet No. 978326111-SP
Classification: Sigma-Prime
Marker: 5-981-297-19744

Planet No. 18534261-BP
Classification: Beta-Prime
Marker: 5-981-289-19822

CHAPTER **EIGHT**

AND THE VOID STARES BACK

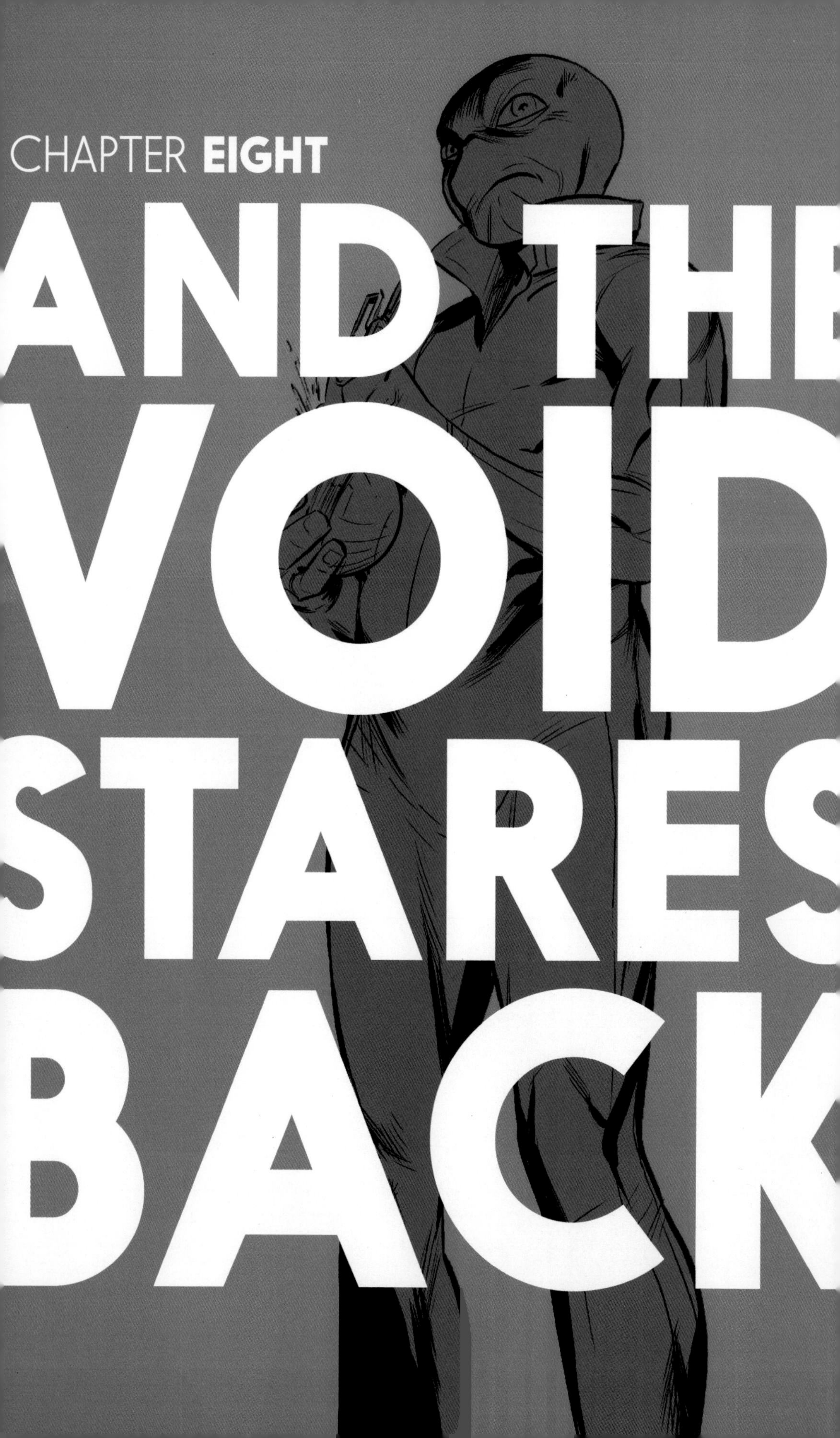

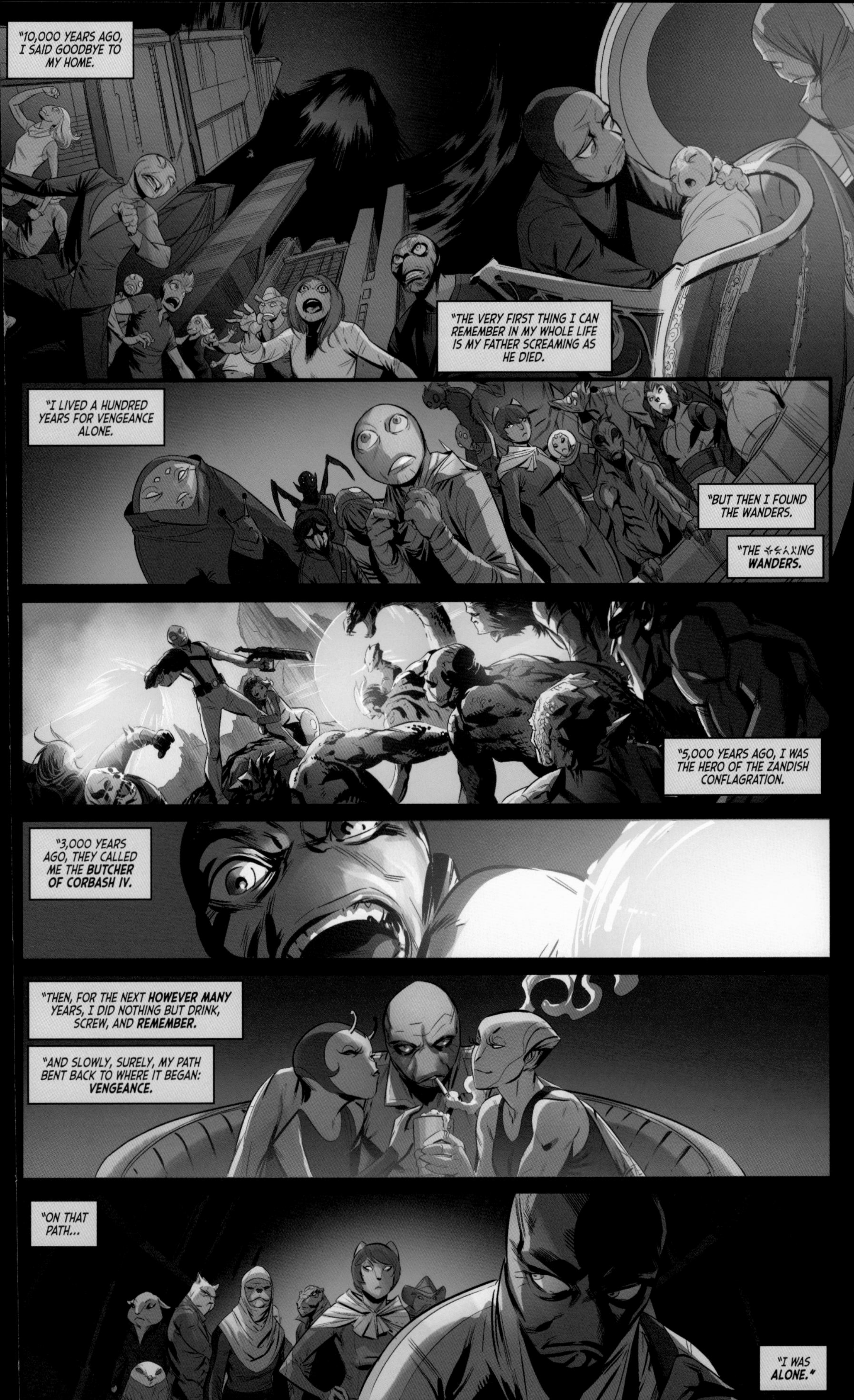
"10,000 YEARS AGO, I SAID GOODBYE TO MY HOME.
"THE VERY FIRST THING I CAN REMEMBER IN MY WHOLE LIFE IS MY FATHER SCREAMING AS HE DIED.
"I LIVED A HUNDRED YEARS FOR VENGEANCE ALONE.
"BUT THEN I FOUND THE WANDERS.
"THE ING WANDERS.
"5,000 YEARS AGO, I WAS THE HERO OF THE ZANDISH CONFLAGRATION.
"3,000 YEARS AGO, THEY CALLED ME THE BUTCHER OF CORBASH IV.
"THEN, FOR THE NEXT HOWEVER MANY YEARS, I DID NOTHING BUT DRINK, SCREW, AND REMEMBER.
"AND SLOWLY, SURELY, MY PATH BENT BACK TO WHERE IT BEGAN: VENGEANCE.
"ON THAT PATH...
"I WAS ALONE."

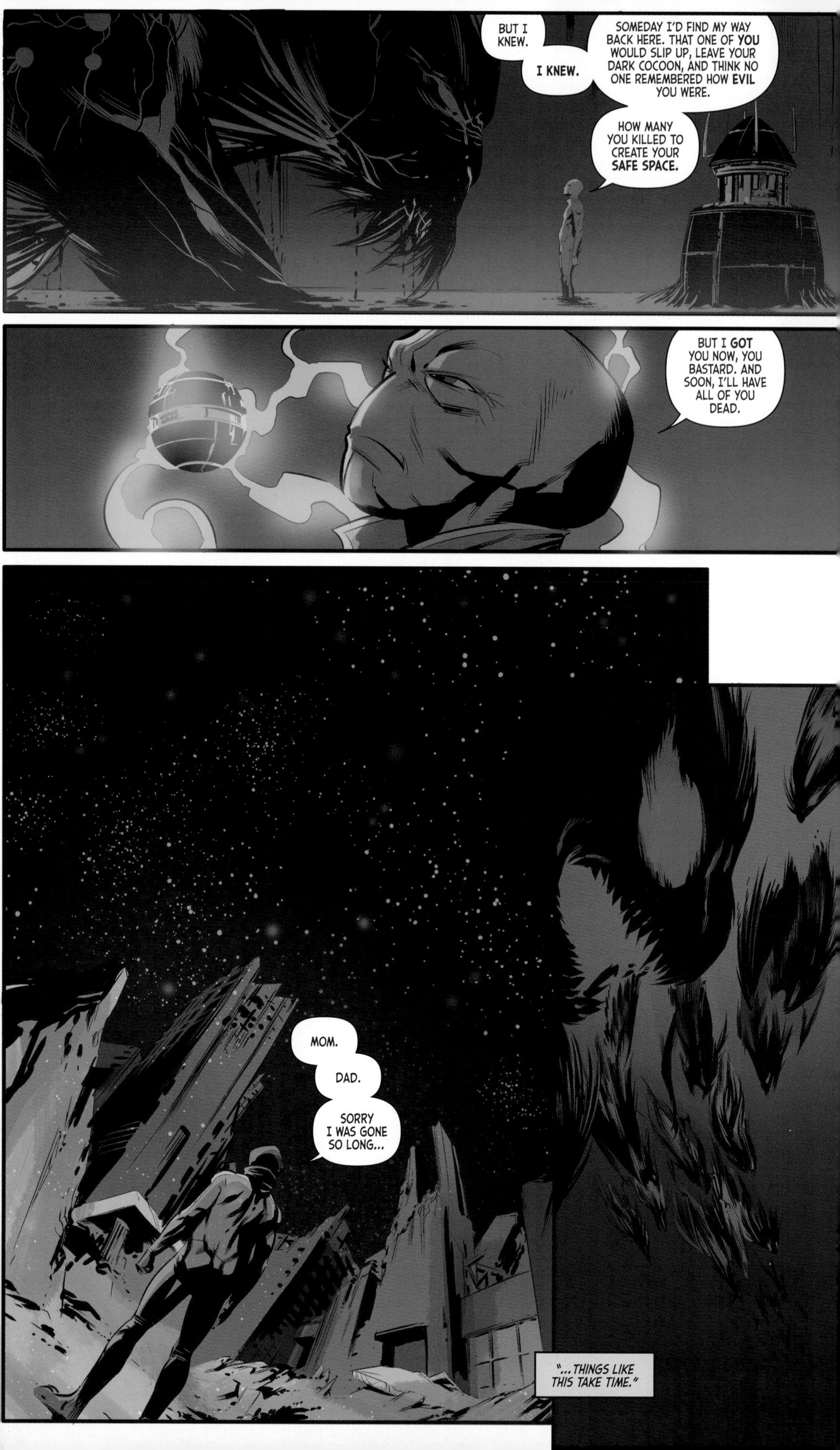
BUT I KNEW.
I KNEW.
SOMEDAY I'D FIND MY WAY BACK HERE. THAT ONE OF YOU WOULD SLIP UP, LEAVE YOUR DARK COCOON, AND THINK NO ONE REMEMBERED HOW EVIL YOU WERE.
HOW MANY YOU KILLED TO CREATE YOUR SAFE SPACE.
BUT I GOT YOU NOW, YOU BASTARD. AND SOON, I'LL HAVE ALL OF YOU DEAD.
MOM.
DAD.
SORRY I WAS GONE SO LONG...
"...THINGS LIKE THIS TAKE TIME."

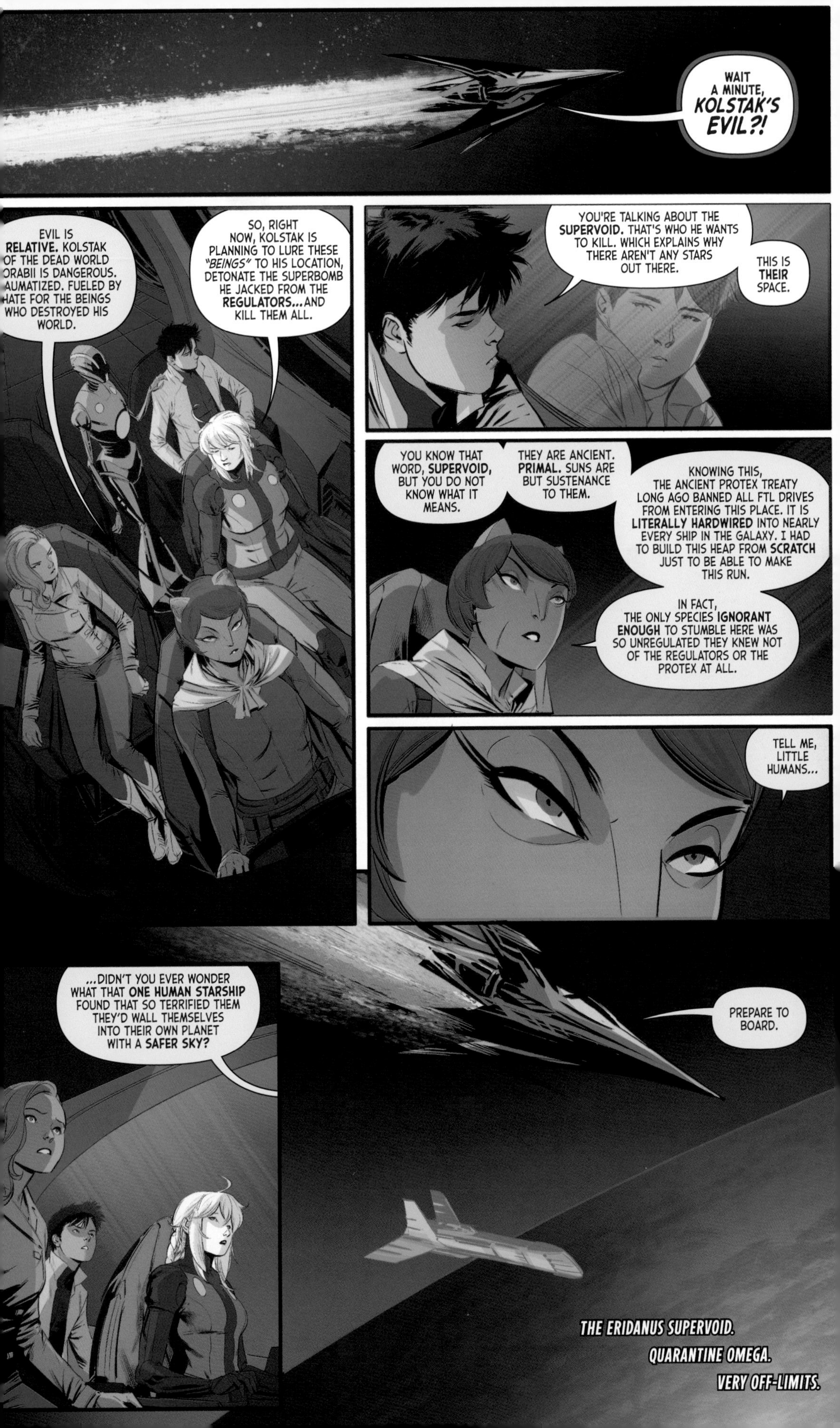
WAIT A MINUTE, KOLSTAK'S EVIL?!
EVIL IS RELATIVE. KOLSTAK OF THE DEAD WORLD ORABII IS DANGEROUS. AUMATIZED. FUELED BY HATE FOR THE BEINGS WHO DESTROYED HIS WORLD.
SO, RIGHT NOW, KOLSTAK IS PLANNING TO LURE THESE "BEINGS" TO HIS LOCATION, DETONATE THE SUPERBOMB HE JACKED FROM THE REGULATORS...AND KILL THEM ALL.
YOU'RE TALKING ABOUT THE SUPERVOID. THAT'S WHO HE WANTS TO KILL. WHICH EXPLAINS WHY THERE AREN'T ANY STARS OUT THERE.
THIS IS THEIR SPACE.
YOU KNOW THAT WORD, SUPERVOID, BUT YOU DO NOT KNOW WHAT IT MEANS.
THEY ARE ANCIENT. PRIMAL. SUNS ARE BUT SUSTENANCE TO THEM.
KNOWING THIS, THE ANCIENT PROTEX TREATY LONG AGO BANNED ALL FTL DRIVES FROM ENTERING THIS PLACE. IT IS LITERALLY HARDWIRED INTO NEARLY EVERY SHIP IN THE GALAXY. I HAD TO BUILD THIS HEAP FROM SCRATCH JUST TO BE ABLE TO MAKE THIS RUN.
IN FACT, THE ONLY SPECIES IGNORANT ENOUGH TO STUMBLE HERE WAS SO UNREGULATED THEY KNEW NOT OF THE REGULATORS OR THE PROTEX AT ALL.
TELL ME, LITTLE HUMANS...
...DIDN'T YOU EVER WONDER WHAT THAT ONE HUMAN STARSHIP FOUND THAT SO TERRIFIED THEM THEY'D WALL THEMSELVES INTO THEIR OWN PLANET WITH A SAFER SKY?
PREPARE TO BOARD.
THE ERIDANUS SUPERVOID.
QUARANTINE OMEGA.
VERY OFF-LIMITS.

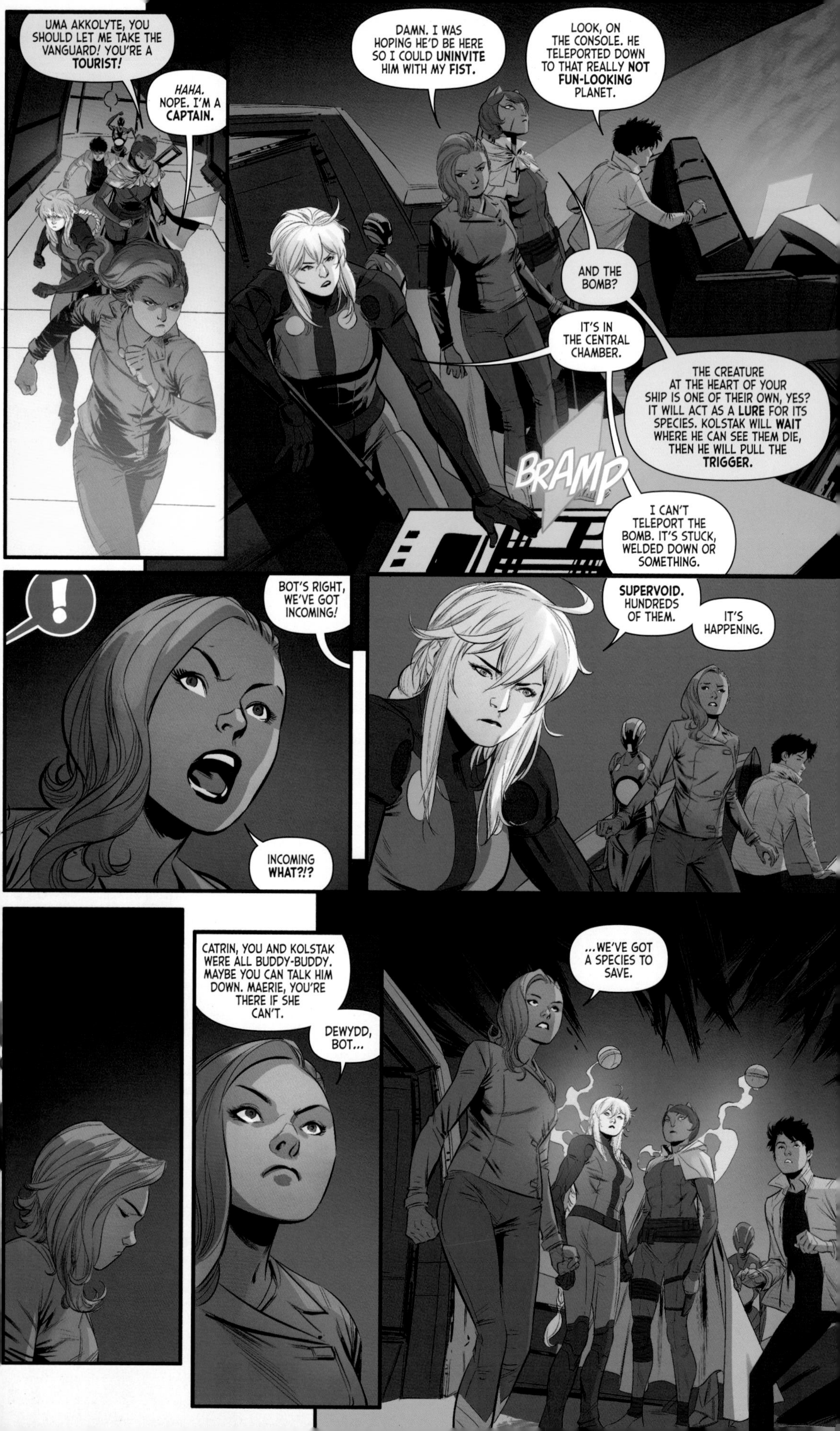
UMA AKKOLYTE, YOU SHOULD LET ME TAKE THE VANGUARD! YOU'RE A TOURIST!
HAHA. NOPE. I'M A CAPTAIN.
DAMN. I WAS HOPING HE'D BE HERE SO I COULD UNINVITE HIM WITH MY FIST.
LOOK, ON THE CONSOLE. HE TELEPORTED DOWN TO THAT REALLY NOT FUN-LOOKING PLANET.
AND THE BOMB?
IT'S IN THE CENTRAL CHAMBER.
THE CREATURE AT THE HEART OF YOUR SHIP IS ONE OF THEIR OWN, YES? IT WILL ACT AS A LURE FOR ITS SPECIES. KOLSTAK WILL WAIT WHERE HE CAN SEE THEM DIE, THEN HE WILL PULL THE TRIGGER.
BRAMP
I CAN'T TELEPORT THE BOMB. IT'S STUCK, WELDED DOWN OR SOMETHING.
!
BOT'S RIGHT, WE'VE GOT INCOMING!
INCOMING WHAT?!?
SUPERVOID. HUNDREDS OF THEM.
IT'S HAPPENING.
CATRIN, YOU AND KOLSTAK WERE ALL BUDDY-BUDDY. MAYBE YOU CAN TALK HIM DOWN. MAERIE, YOU'RE THERE IF SHE CAN'T.
DEWYDD, BOT...
...WE'VE GOT A SPECIES TO SAVE.

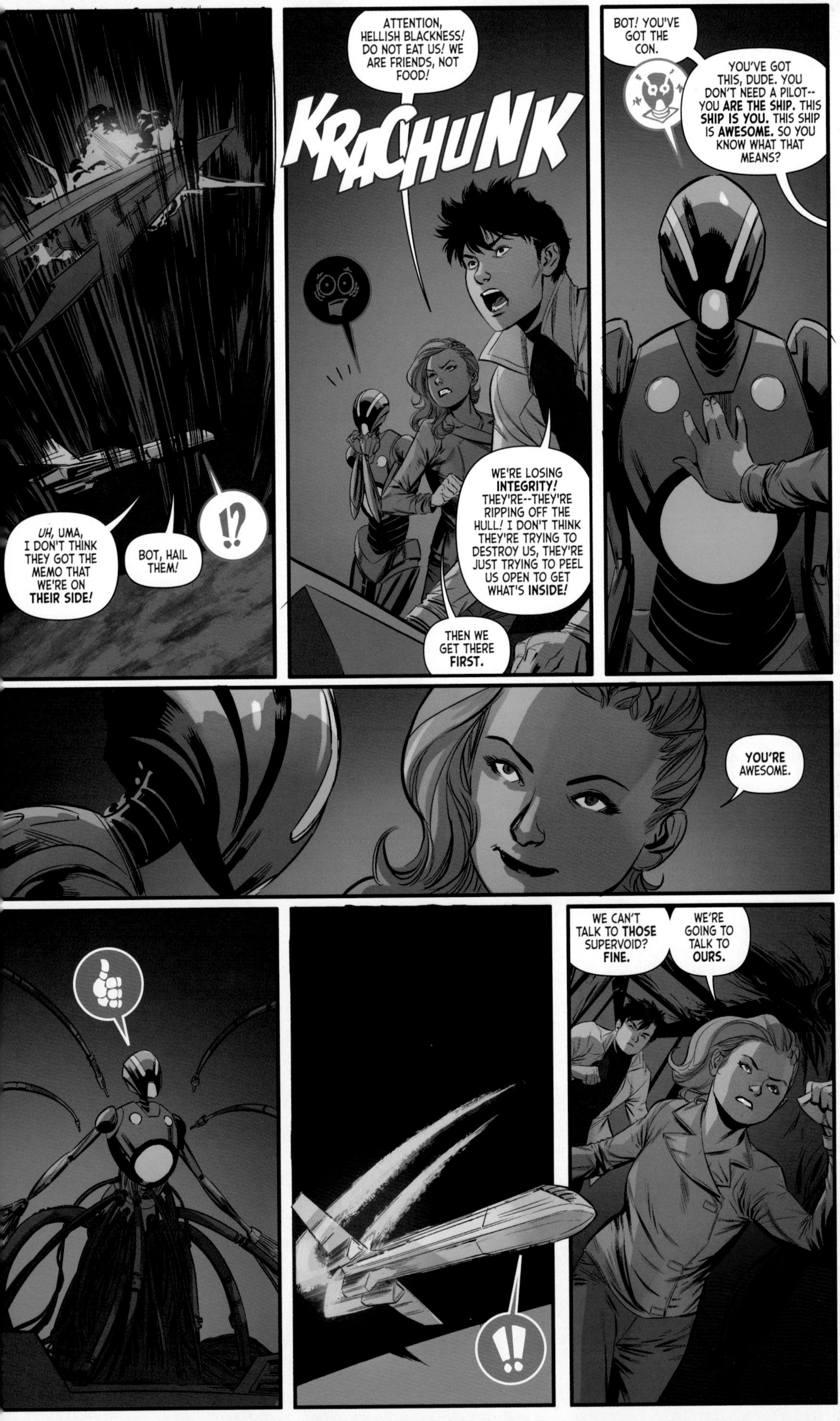
UH, UMA, I DON'T THINK THEY GOT THE MEMO THAT WE'RE ON THEIR SIDE!
BOT, HAIL THEM!
!?
ATTENTION, HELLISH BLACKNESS! DO NOT EAT US! WE ARE FRIENDS, NOT FOOD!
KRACHUNK
WE'RE LOSING INTEGRITY! THEY'RE--THEY'RE RIPPING OFF THE HULL! I DON'T THINK THEY'RE TRYING TO DESTROY US, THEY'RE JUST TRYING TO PEEL US OPEN TO GET WHAT'S INSIDE!
THEN WE GET THERE FIRST.
BOT! YOU'VE GOT THE CON.
YOU'VE GOT THIS, DUDE. YOU DON'T NEED A PILOT--YOU ARE THE SHIP. THIS SHIP IS YOU. THIS SHIP IS AWESOME. SO YOU KNOW WHAT THAT MEANS?
YOU'RE AWESOME.
!!
WE CAN'T TALK TO THOSE SUPERVOID? FINE.
WE'RE GOING TO TALK TO OURS.

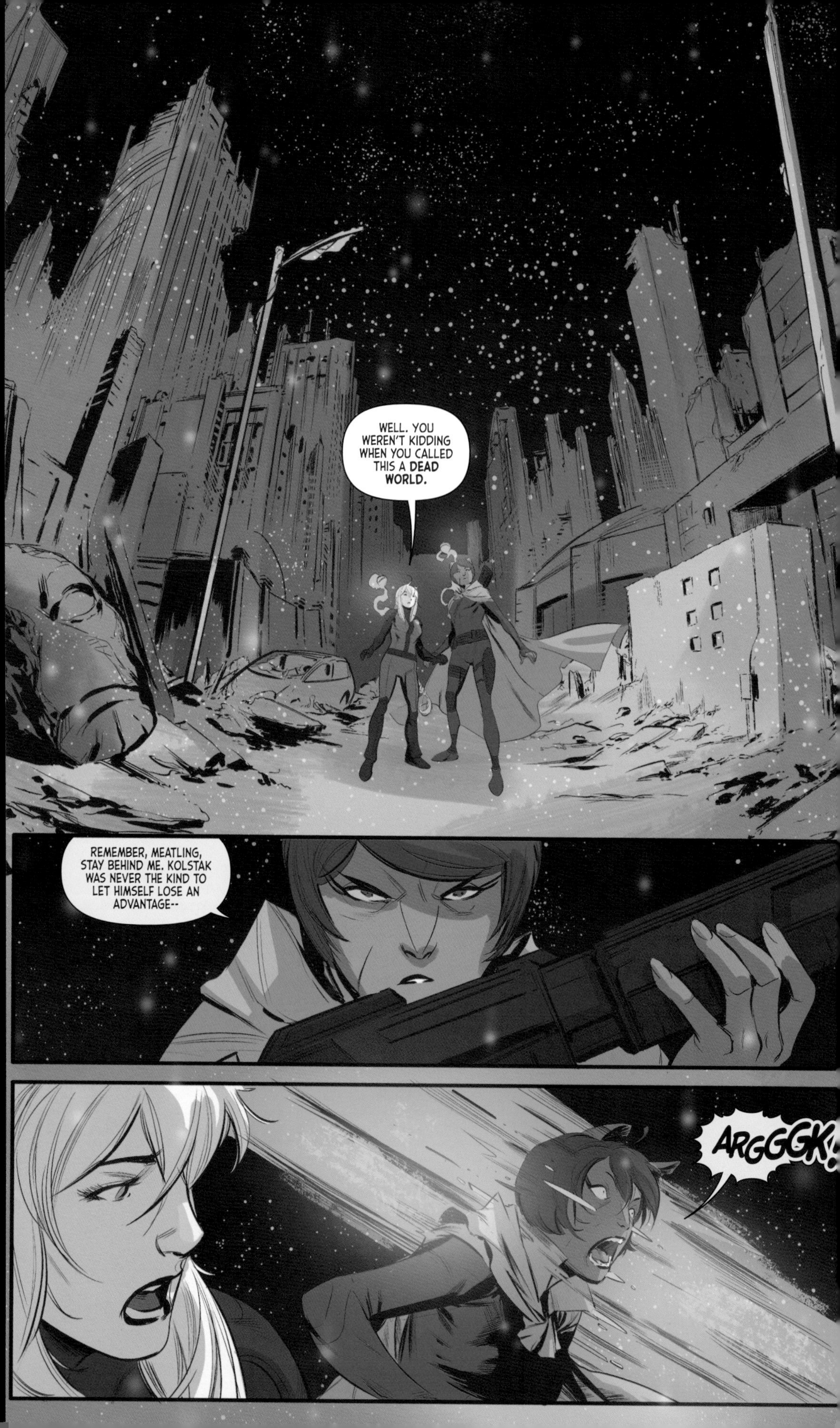
WELL. YOU WEREN'T KIDDING WHEN YOU CALLED THIS A **DEAD WORLD.**
REMEMBER, MEATLING, STAY BEHIND ME. KOLSTAK WAS NEVER THE KIND TO LET HIMSELF LOSE AN ADVANTAGE--
ARGGGK!

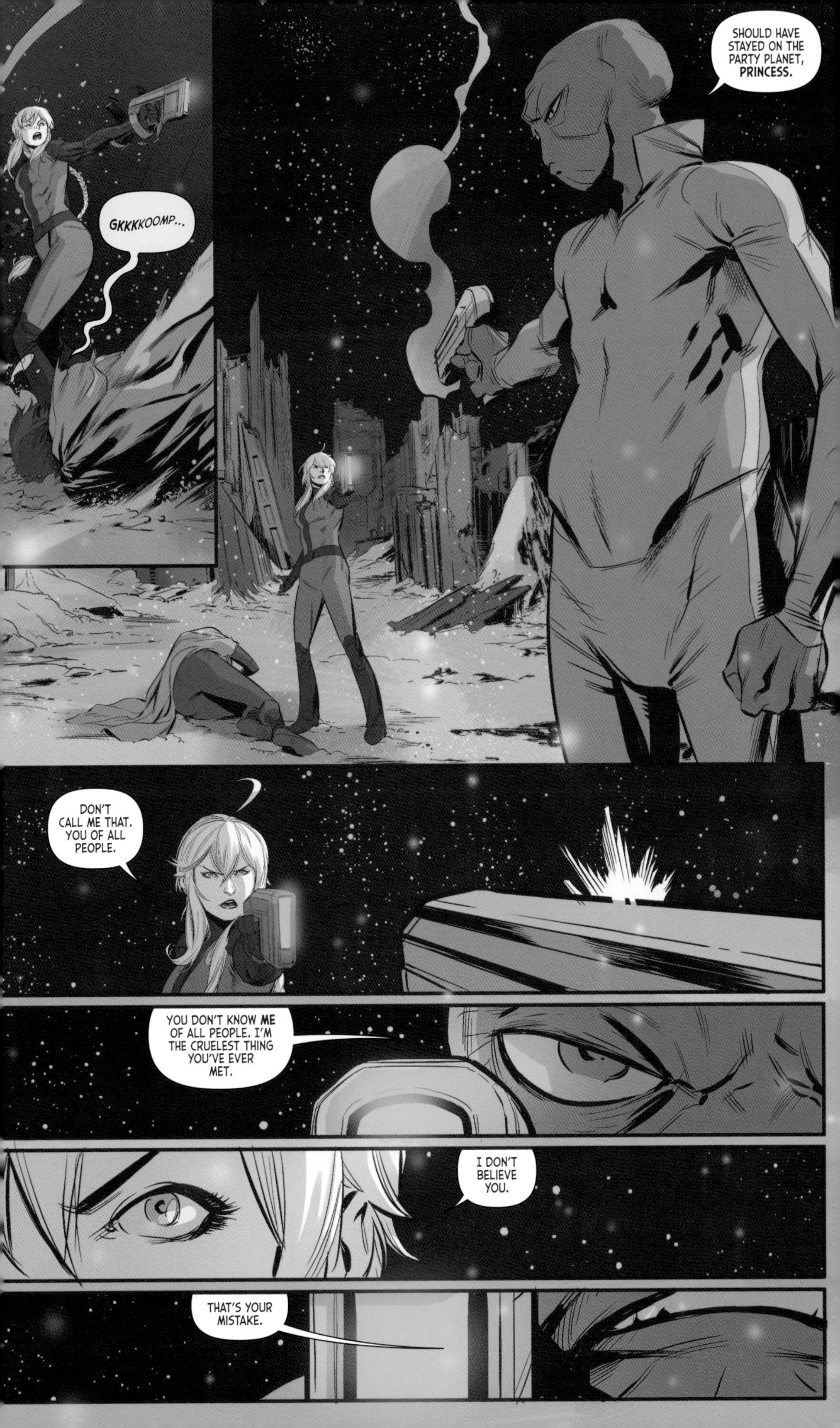
GKKKKOOMP...
SHOULD HAVE STAYED ON THE PARTY PLANET, PRINCESS.
DON'T CALL ME THAT. YOU OF ALL PEOPLE.
YOU DON'T KNOW ME OF ALL PEOPLE. I'M THE CRUELEST THING YOU'VE EVER MET.
I DON'T BELIEVE YOU.
THAT'S YOUR MISTAKE.

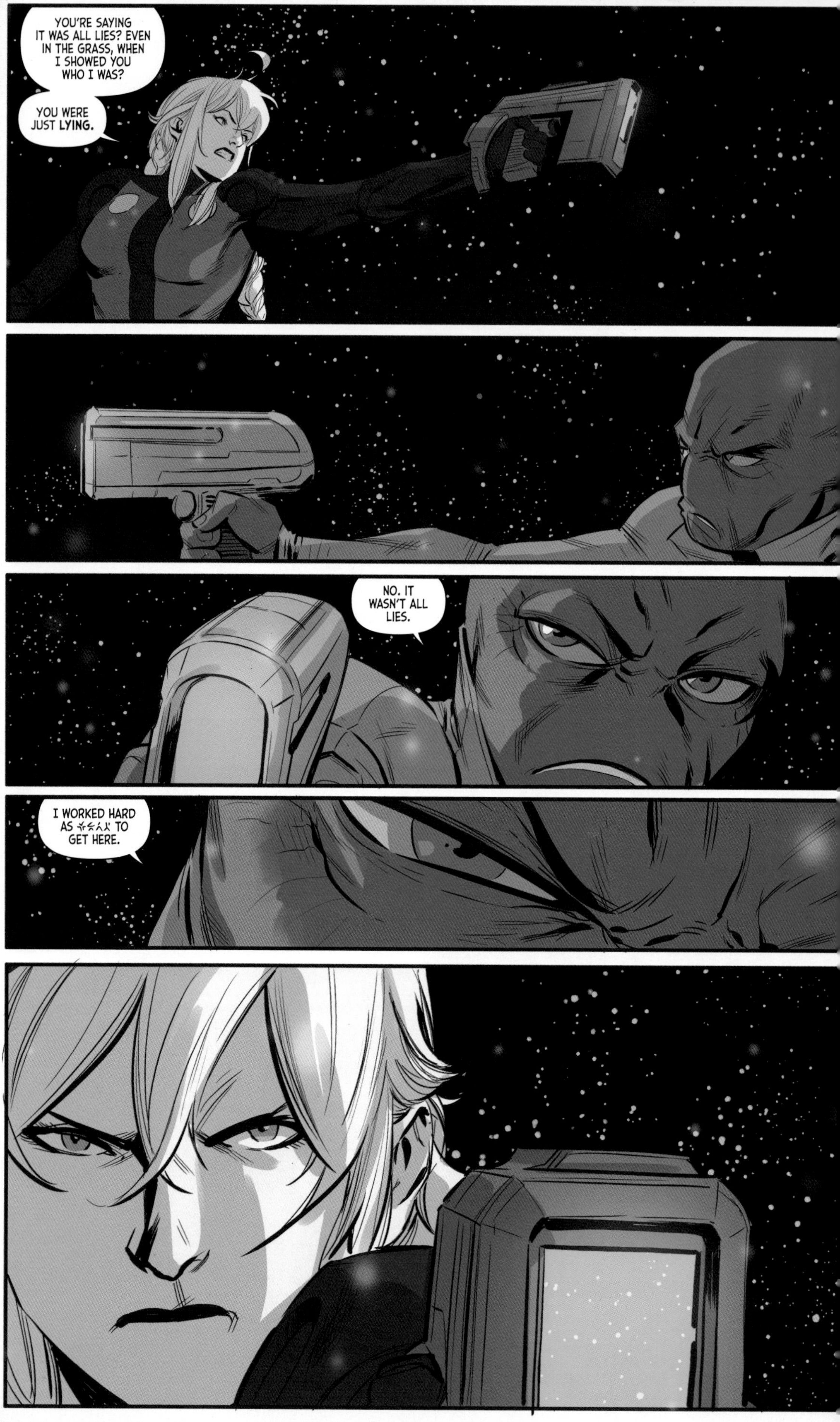
YOU'RE SAYING IT WAS ALL LIES? EVEN IN THE GRASS, WHEN I SHOWED YOU WHO I WAS?
YOU WERE JUST **LYING.**
NO. IT WASN'T ALL LIES.
I WORKED HARD AS TO GET HERE.

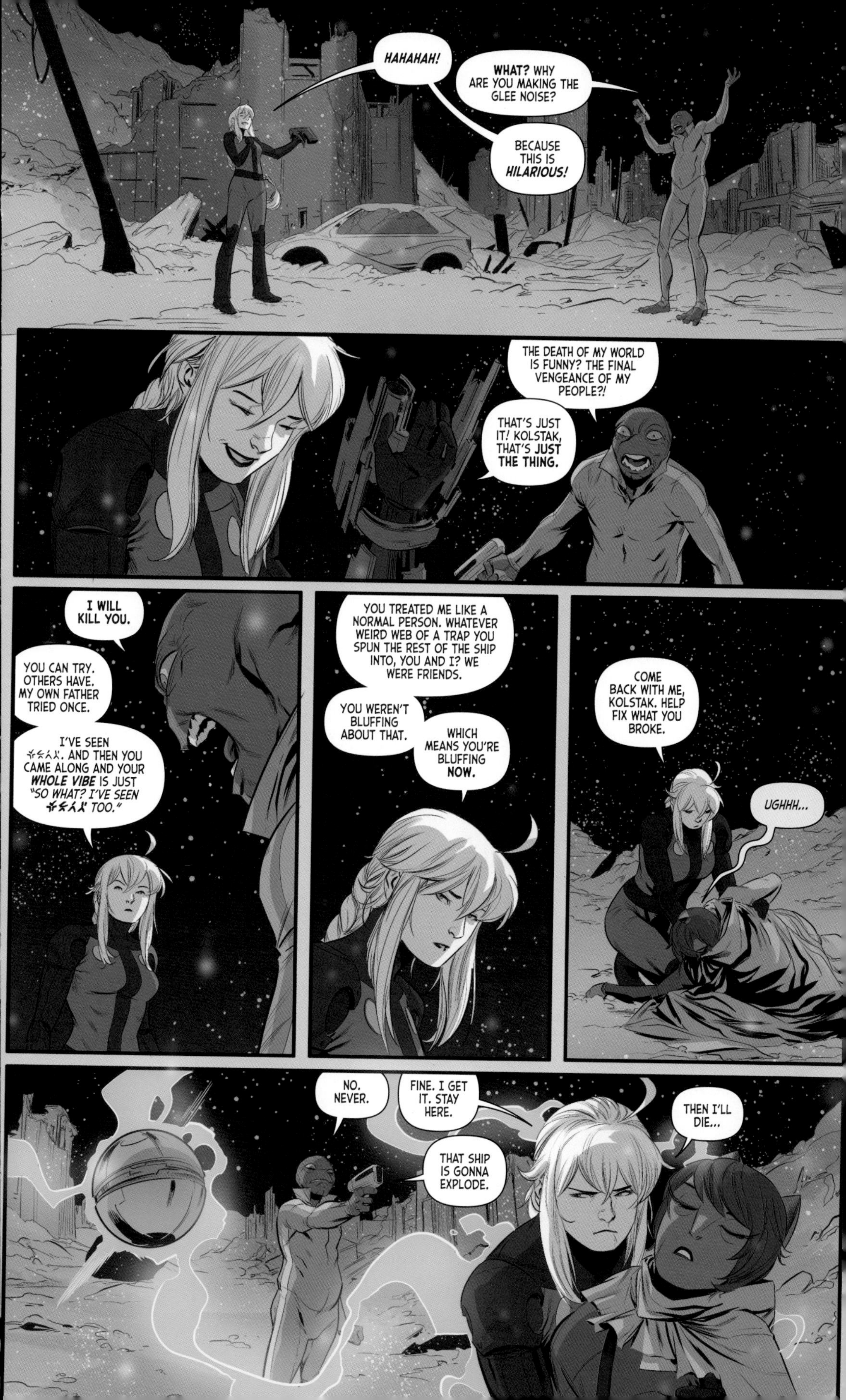

HAHAHAH!
WHAT? WHY ARE YOU MAKING THE GLEE NOISE?
BECAUSE THIS IS HILARIOUS!
THE DEATH OF MY WORLD IS FUNNY? THE FINAL VENGEANCE OF MY PEOPLE?!
THAT'S JUST IT! KOLSTAK, THAT'S JUST THE THING.
I WILL KILL YOU.
YOU CAN TRY. OTHERS HAVE. MY OWN FATHER TRIED ONCE.
I'VE SEEN . AND THEN YOU CAME ALONG AND YOUR WHOLE VIBE IS JUST "SO WHAT? I'VE SEEN TOO."
YOU TREATED ME LIKE A NORMAL PERSON. WHATEVER WEIRD WEB OF A TRAP YOU SPUN THE REST OF THE SHIP INTO, YOU AND I? WE WERE FRIENDS.
YOU WEREN'T BLUFFING ABOUT THAT.
WHICH MEANS YOU'RE BLUFFING NOW.
COME BACK WITH ME, KOLSTAK. HELP FIX WHAT YOU BROKE.
UGHHH...
NO. NEVER.
FINE. I GET IT. STAY HERE.
THAT SHIP IS GONNA EXPLODE.
THEN I'LL DIE...

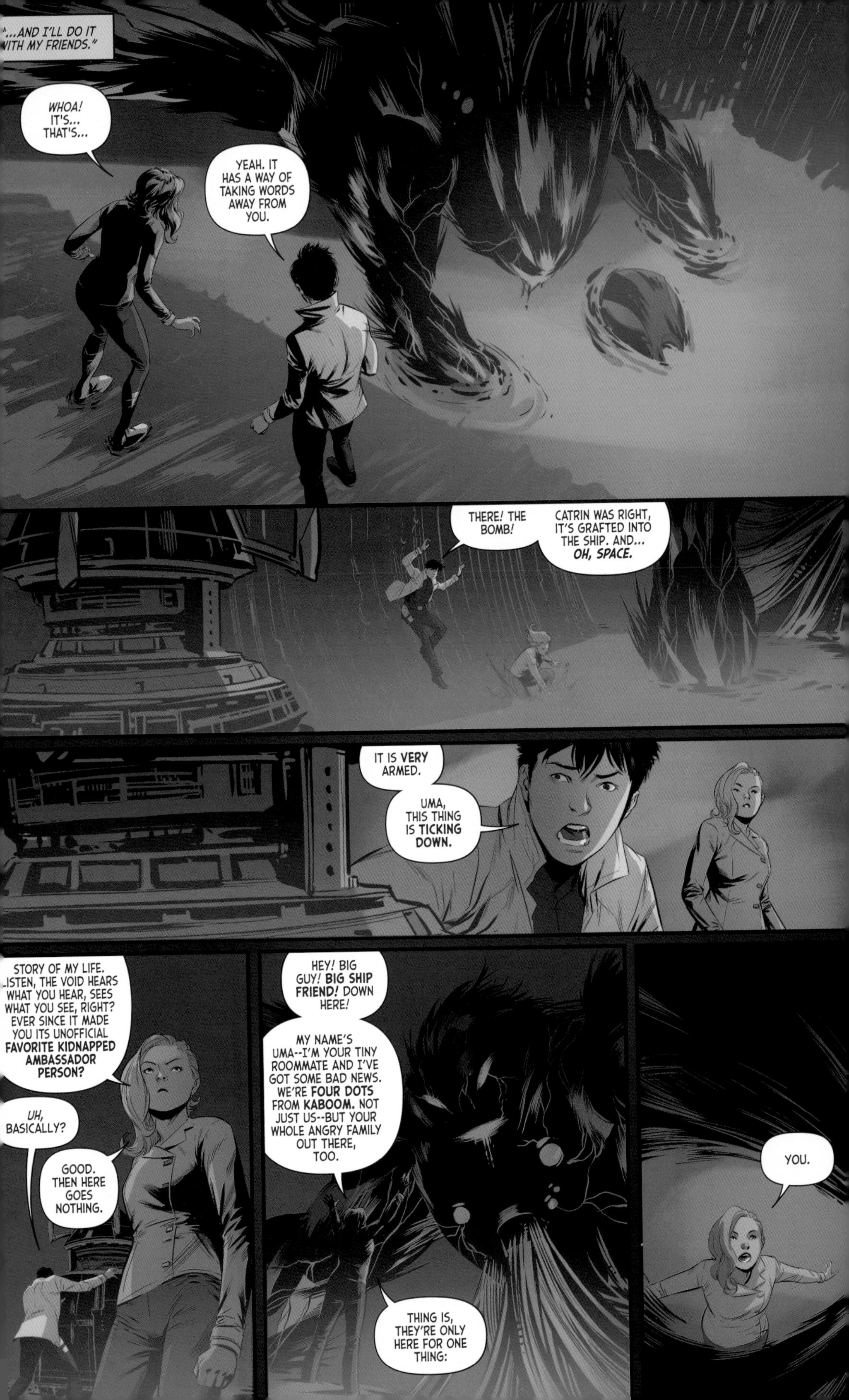
"...AND I'LL DO IT WITH MY FRIENDS."
WHOA! IT'S... THAT'S...
YEAH. IT HAS A WAY OF TAKING WORDS AWAY FROM YOU.
THERE! THE BOMB!
CATRIN WAS RIGHT, IT'S GRAFTED INTO THE SHIP. AND... OH, SPACE.
IT IS VERY ARMED.
UMA, THIS THING IS TICKING DOWN.
STORY OF MY LIFE. LISTEN, THE VOID HEARS WHAT YOU HEAR, SEES WHAT YOU SEE, RIGHT? EVER SINCE IT MADE YOU ITS UNOFFICIAL FAVORITE KIDNAPPED AMBASSADOR PERSON?
UH, BASICALLY?
GOOD. THEN HERE GOES NOTHING.
HEY! BIG GUY! BIG SHIP FRIEND! DOWN HERE!
MY NAME'S UMA--I'M YOUR TINY ROOMMATE AND I'VE GOT SOME BAD NEWS. WE'RE FOUR DOTS FROM KABOOM. NOT JUST US--BUT YOUR WHOLE ANGRY FAMILY OUT THERE, TOO.
THING IS, THEY'RE ONLY HERE FOR ONE THING:
YOU.

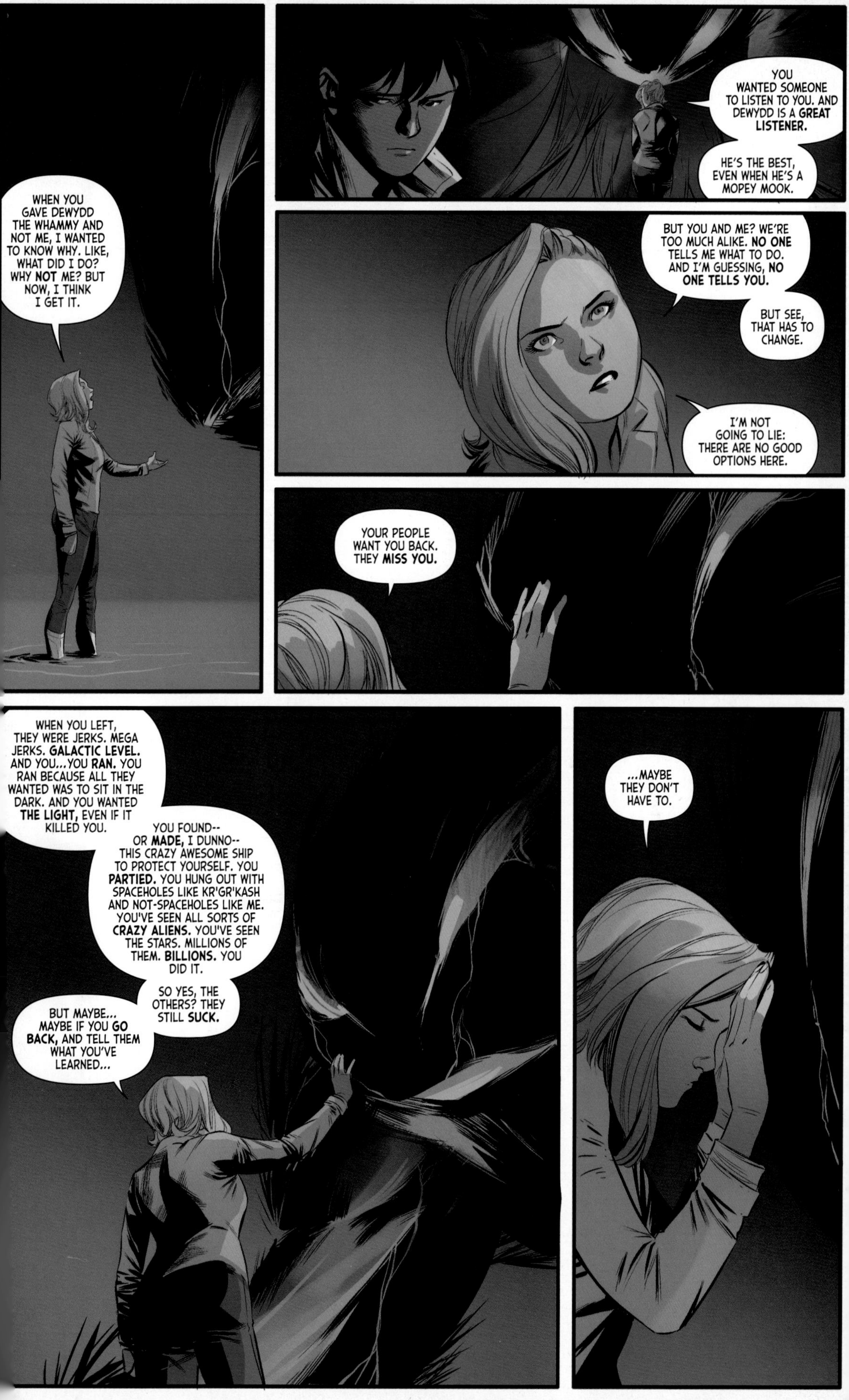
WHEN YOU GAVE DEWYDD THE WHAMMY AND NOT ME, I WANTED TO KNOW WHY. LIKE, WHAT DID I DO? WHY NOT ME? BUT NOW, I THINK I GET IT.
YOU WANTED SOMEONE TO LISTEN TO YOU. AND DEWYDD IS A GREAT LISTENER.
HE'S THE BEST, EVEN WHEN HE'S A MOPEY MOOK.
BUT YOU AND ME? WE'RE TOO MUCH ALIKE. NO ONE TELLS ME WHAT TO DO. AND I'M GUESSING, NO ONE TELLS YOU.
BUT SEE, THAT HAS TO CHANGE.
I'M NOT GOING TO LIE: THERE ARE NO GOOD OPTIONS HERE.
YOUR PEOPLE WANT YOU BACK. THEY MISS YOU.
WHEN YOU LEFT, THEY WERE JERKS. MEGA JERKS. GALACTIC LEVEL. AND YOU...YOU RAN. YOU RAN BECAUSE ALL THEY WANTED WAS TO SIT IN THE DARK. AND YOU WANTED THE LIGHT, EVEN IF IT KILLED YOU.
YOU FOUND-- OR MADE, I DUNNO-- THIS CRAZY AWESOME SHIP TO PROTECT YOURSELF. YOU PARTIED. YOU HUNG OUT WITH SPACEHOLES LIKE KR'GR'KASH AND NOT-SPACEHOLES LIKE ME. YOU'VE SEEN ALL SORTS OF CRAZY ALIENS. YOU'VE SEEN THE STARS. MILLIONS OF THEM. BILLIONS. YOU DID IT.
SO YES, THE OTHERS? THEY STILL SUCK.
BUT MAYBE... MAYBE IF YOU GO BACK, AND TELL THEM WHAT YOU'VE LEARNED...
...MAYBE THEY DON'T HAVE TO.

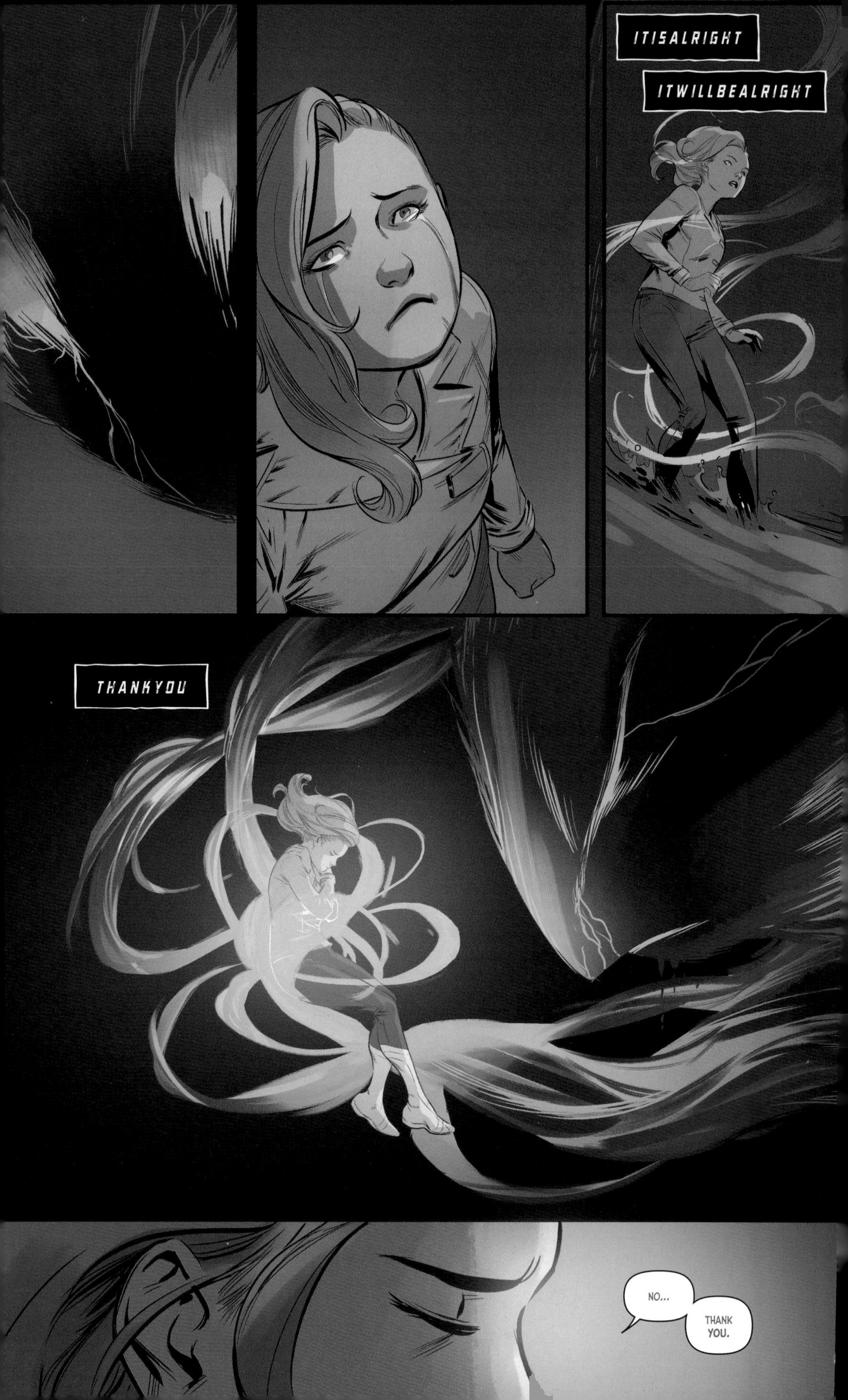
ITISALRIGHT
ITWILLBEALRIGHT
THANKYOU
NO...
THANK YOU.

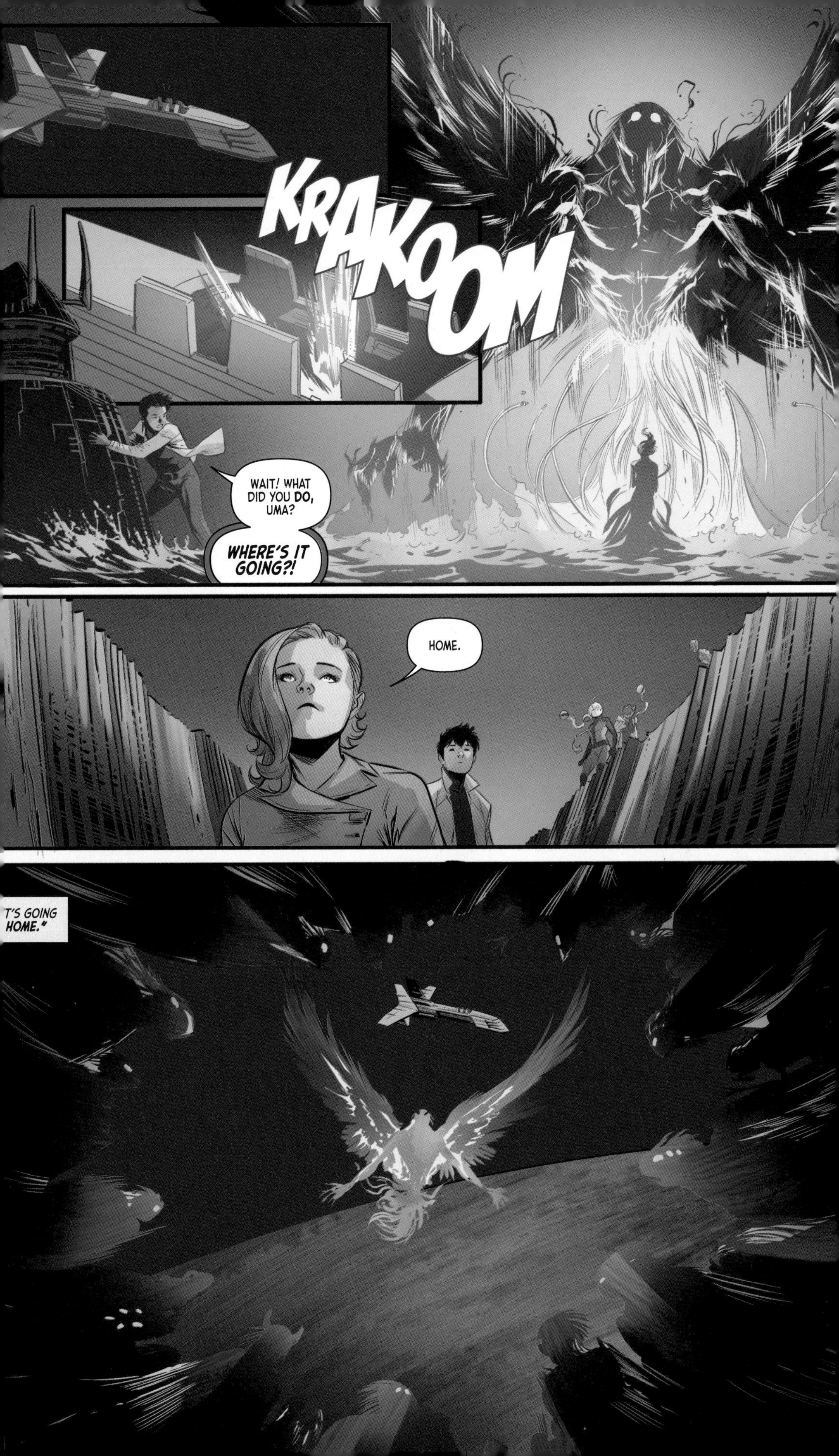
KRAKOOM
WAIT! WHAT DID YOU DO, UMA?
WHERE'S IT GOING?!
HOME.
T'S GOING HOME."

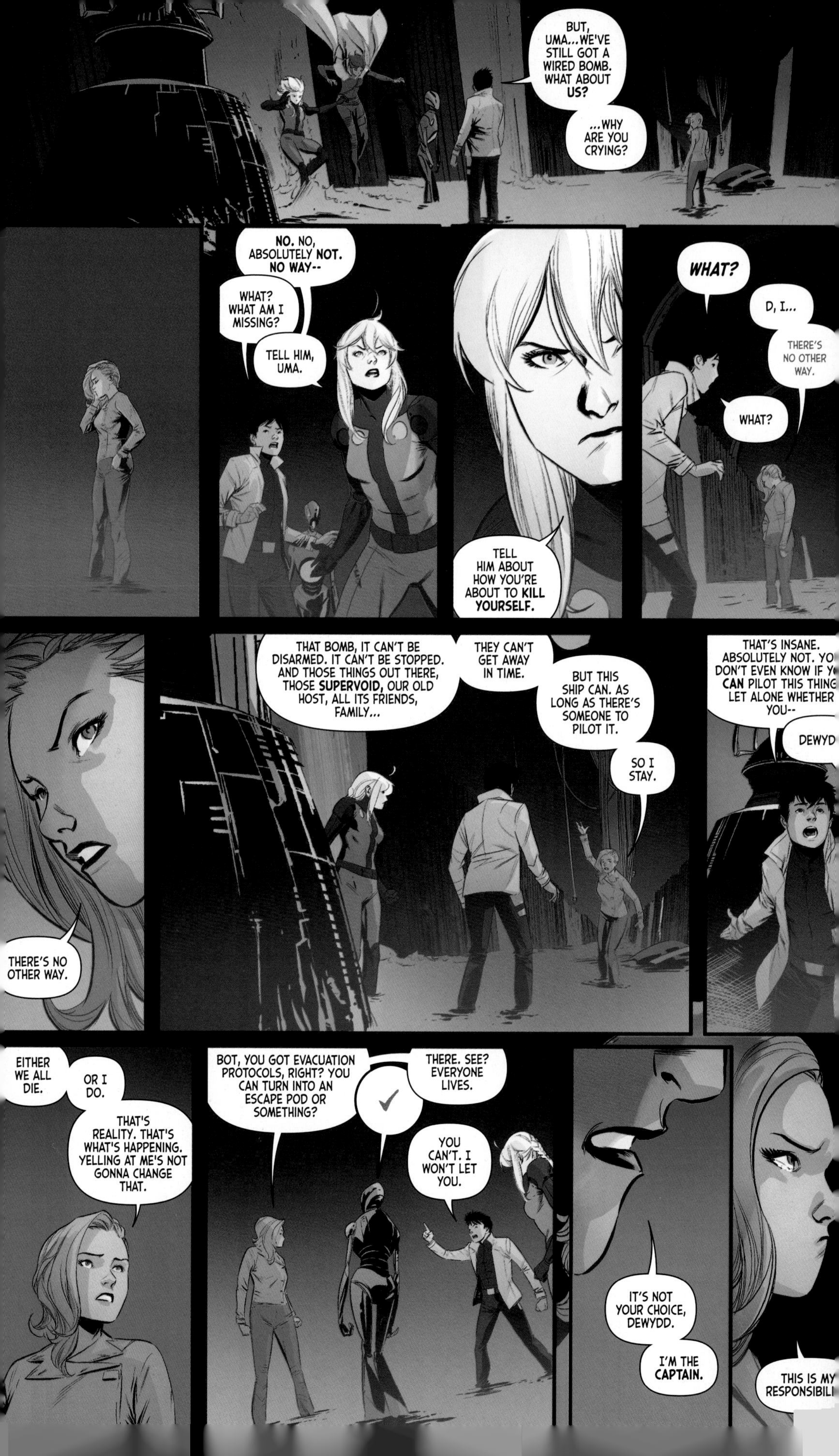

BUT, UMA...WE'VE STILL GOT A WIRED BOMB. WHAT ABOUT US?
...WHY ARE YOU CRYING?
NO. NO, ABSOLUTELY NOT. NO WAY--
WHAT? WHAT AM I MISSING?
TELL HIM, UMA.
TELL HIM ABOUT HOW YOU'RE ABOUT TO KILL YOURSELF.
WHAT?
D, I...
THERE'S NO OTHER WAY.
WHAT?
THERE'S NO OTHER WAY.
THAT BOMB, IT CAN'T BE DISARMED. IT CAN'T BE STOPPED. AND THOSE THINGS OUT THERE, THOSE SUPERVOID, OUR OLD HOST, ALL ITS FRIENDS, FAMILY...
THEY CAN'T GET AWAY IN TIME.
BUT THIS SHIP CAN. AS LONG AS THERE'S SOMEONE TO PILOT IT.
SO I STAY.
THAT'S INSANE. ABSOLUTELY NOT. YO DON'T EVEN KNOW IF Y CAN PILOT THIS THING LET ALONE WHETHER YOU--
DEWYD
EITHER WE ALL DIE.
OR I DO.
THAT'S REALITY. THAT'S WHAT'S HAPPENING. YELLING AT ME'S NOT GONNA CHANGE THAT.
BOT, YOU GOT EVACUATION PROTOCOLS, RIGHT? YOU CAN TURN INTO AN ESCAPE POD OR SOMETHING?
✓
THERE. SEE? EVERYONE LIVES.
YOU CAN'T. I WON'T LET YOU.
IT'S NOT YOUR CHOICE, DEWYDD.
I'M THE CAPTAIN.
THIS IS MY RESPONSIBILI

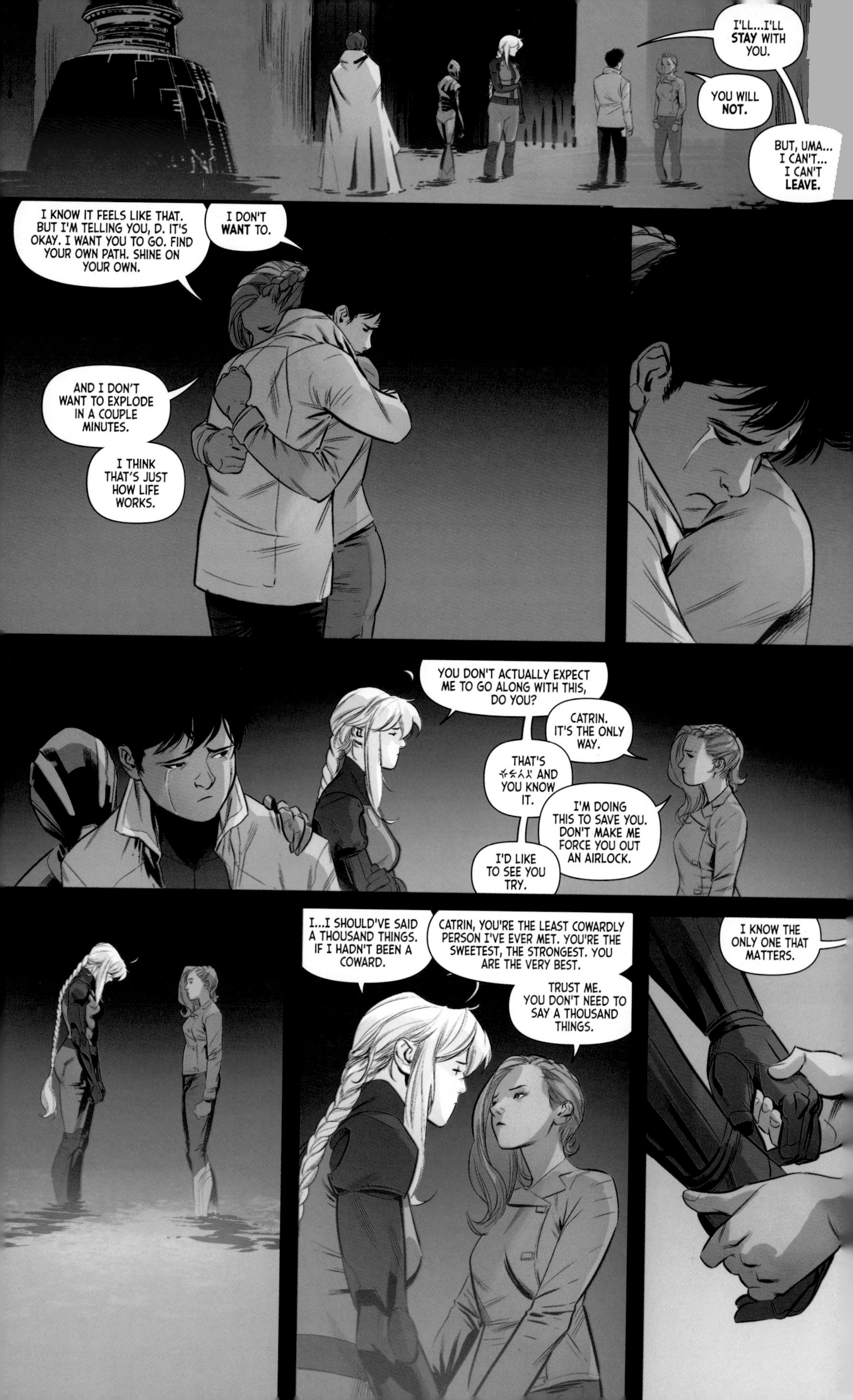
I'LL...I'LL STAY WITH YOU.
YOU WILL NOT.
BUT, UMA... I CAN'T... I CAN'T LEAVE.
I KNOW IT FEELS LIKE THAT. BUT I'M TELLING YOU, D. IT'S OKAY. I WANT YOU TO GO. FIND YOUR OWN PATH. SHINE ON YOUR OWN.
I DON'T WANT TO.
AND I DON'T WANT TO EXPLODE IN A COUPLE MINUTES.
I THINK THAT'S JUST HOW LIFE WORKS.
YOU DON'T ACTUALLY EXPECT ME TO GO ALONG WITH THIS, DO YOU?
CATRIN. IT'S THE ONLY WAY.
THAT'S
AND YOU KNOW IT.
I'M DOING THIS TO SAVE YOU. DON'T MAKE ME FORCE YOU OUT AN AIRLOCK.
I'D LIKE TO SEE YOU TRY.
I...I SHOULD'VE SAID A THOUSAND THINGS. IF I HADN'T BEEN A COWARD.
CATRIN, YOU'RE THE LEAST COWARDLY PERSON I'VE EVER MET. YOU'RE THE SWEETEST, THE STRONGEST. YOU ARE THE VERY BEST.
TRUST ME. YOU DON'T NEED TO SAY A THOUSAND THINGS.
I KNOW THE ONLY ONE THAT MATTERS.

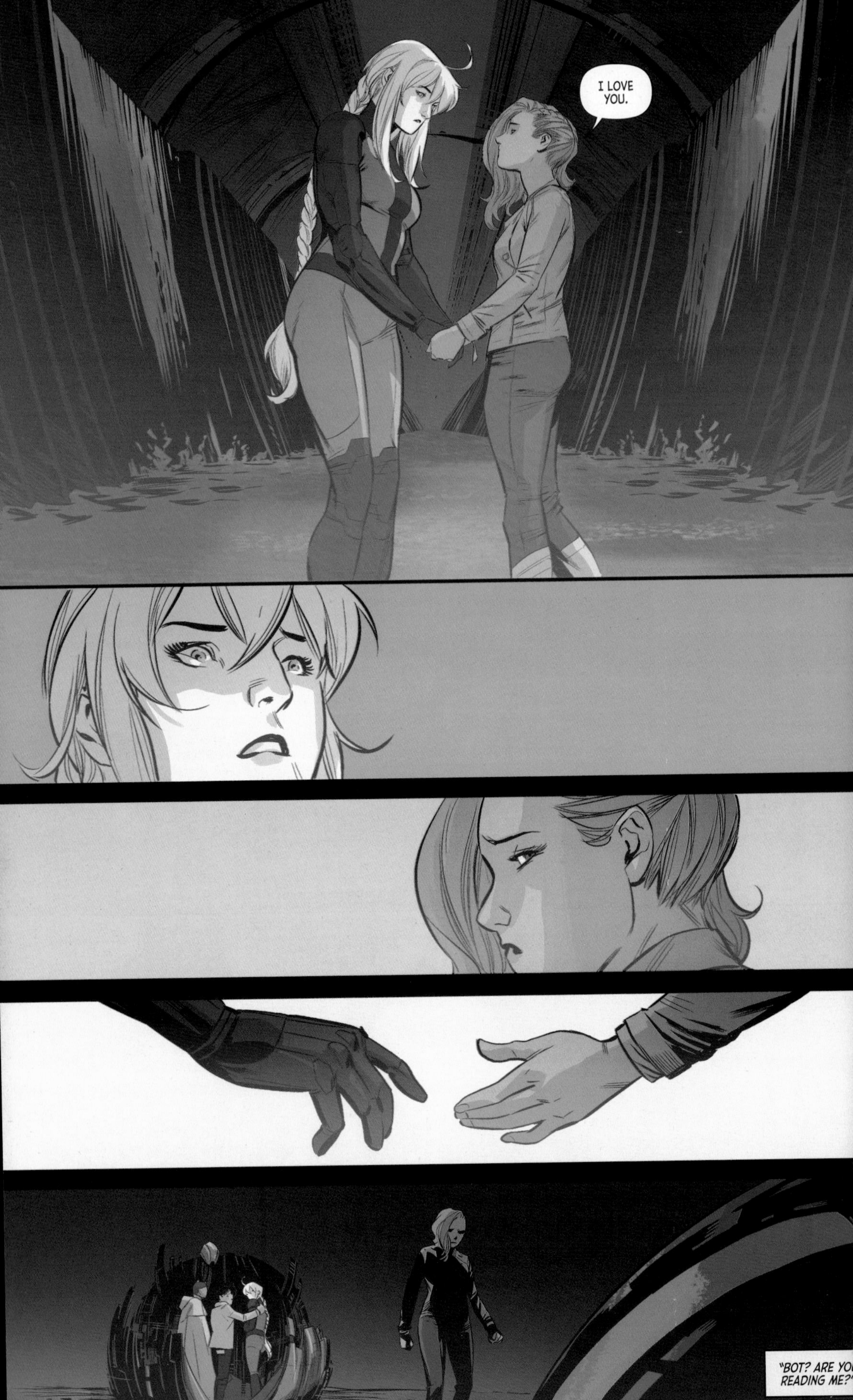
I LOVE YOU.
"BOT? ARE YO
READING ME?

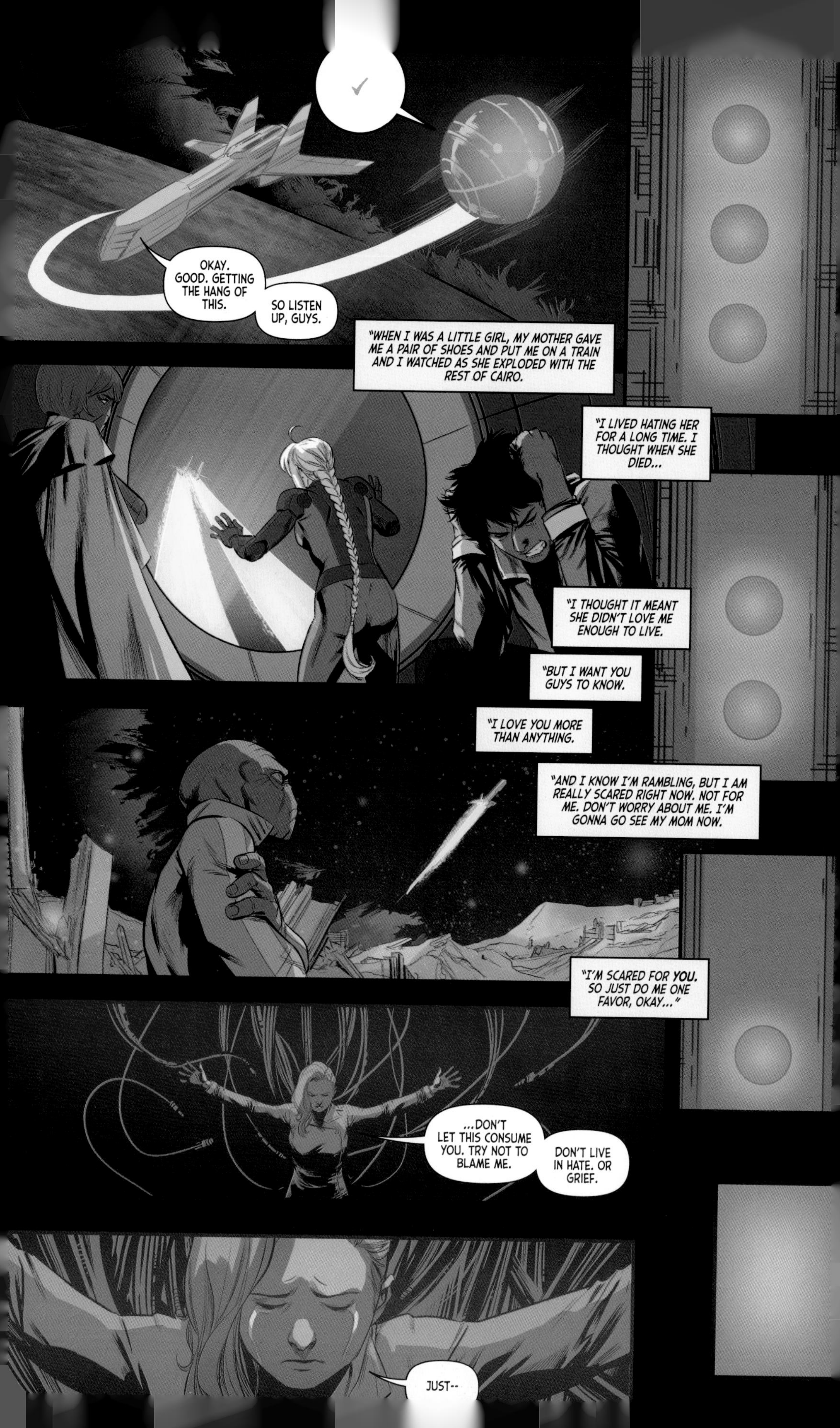
✓
OKAY. GOOD. GETTING THE HANG OF THIS.
SO LISTEN UP, GUYS.
"WHEN I WAS A LITTLE GIRL, MY MOTHER GAVE ME A PAIR OF SHOES AND PUT ME ON A TRAIN AND I WATCHED AS SHE EXPLODED WITH THE REST OF CAIRO.
"I LIVED HATING HER FOR A LONG TIME. I THOUGHT WHEN SHE DIED...
"I THOUGHT IT MEANT SHE DIDN'T LOVE ME ENOUGH TO LIVE.
"BUT I WANT YOU GUYS TO KNOW.
"I LOVE YOU MORE THAN ANYTHING.
"AND I KNOW I'M RAMBLING, BUT I AM REALLY SCARED RIGHT NOW. NOT FOR ME. DON'T WORRY ABOUT ME. I'M GONNA GO SEE MY MOM NOW.
"I'M SCARED FOR YOU. SO JUST DO ME ONE FAVOR, OKAY..."
...DON'T LET THIS CONSUME YOU. TRY NOT TO BLAME ME.
DON'T LIVE IN HATE. OR GRIEF.
JUST--

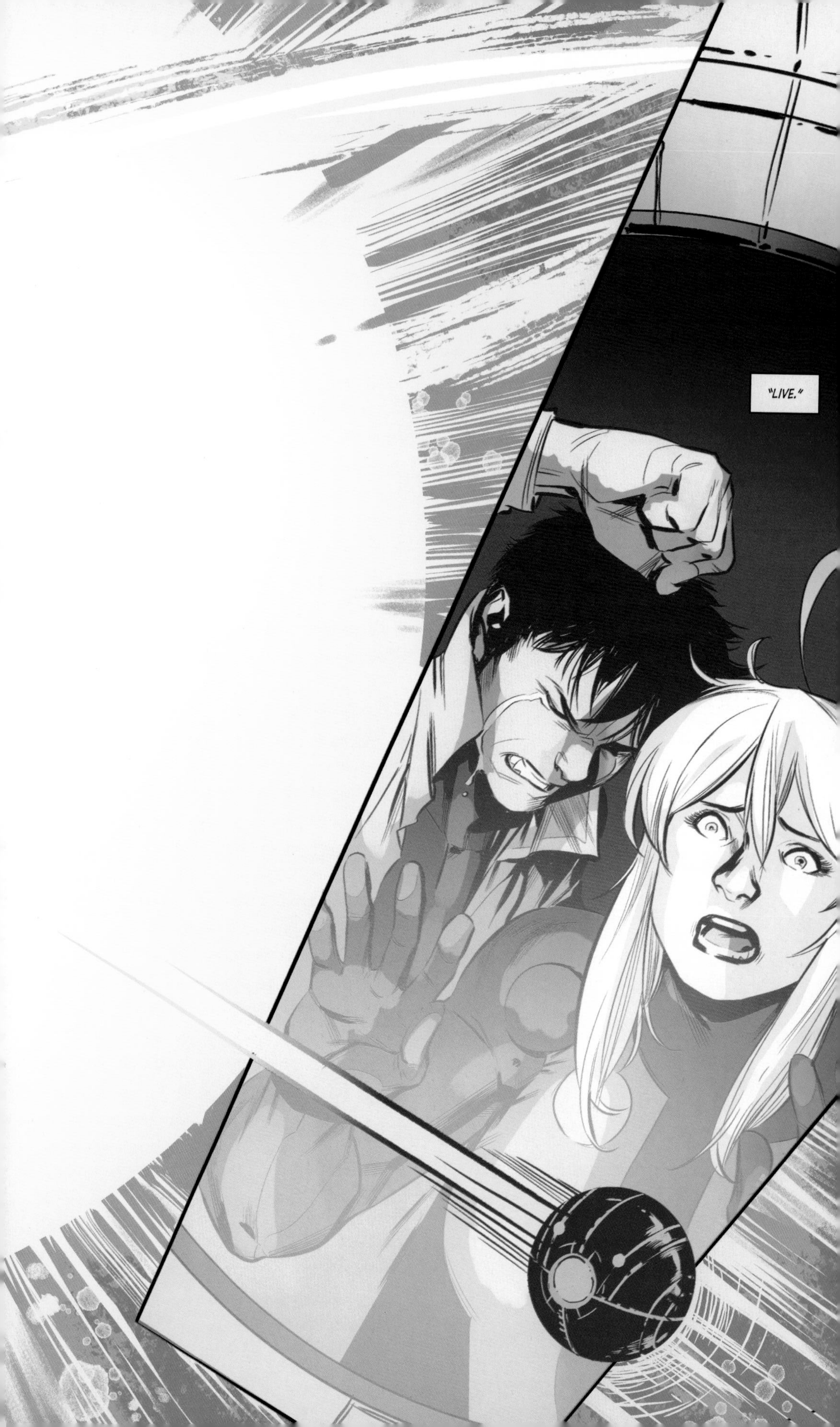
"LIVE."

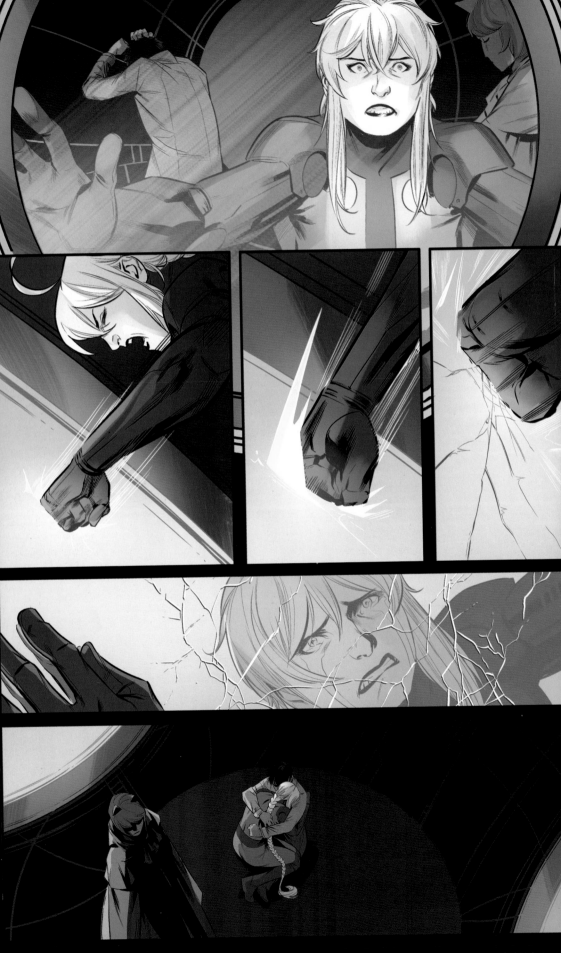

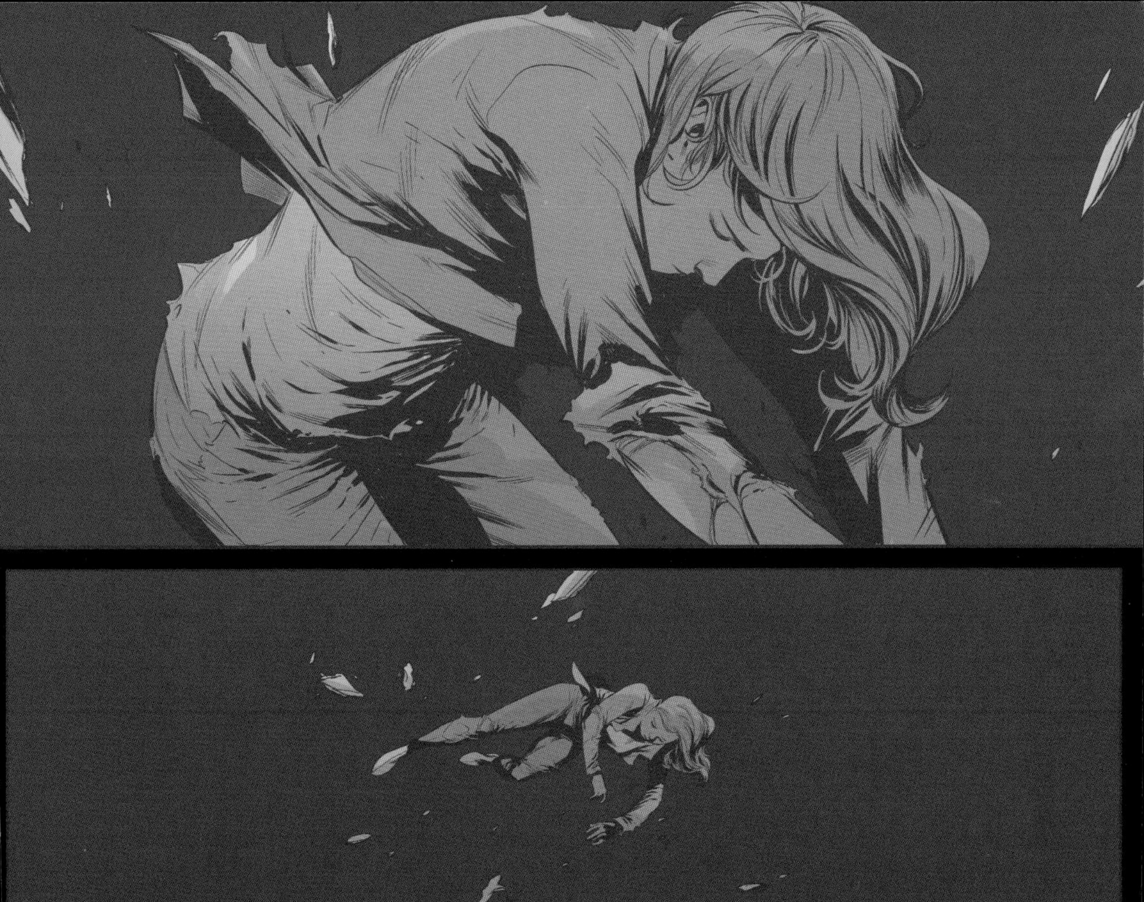

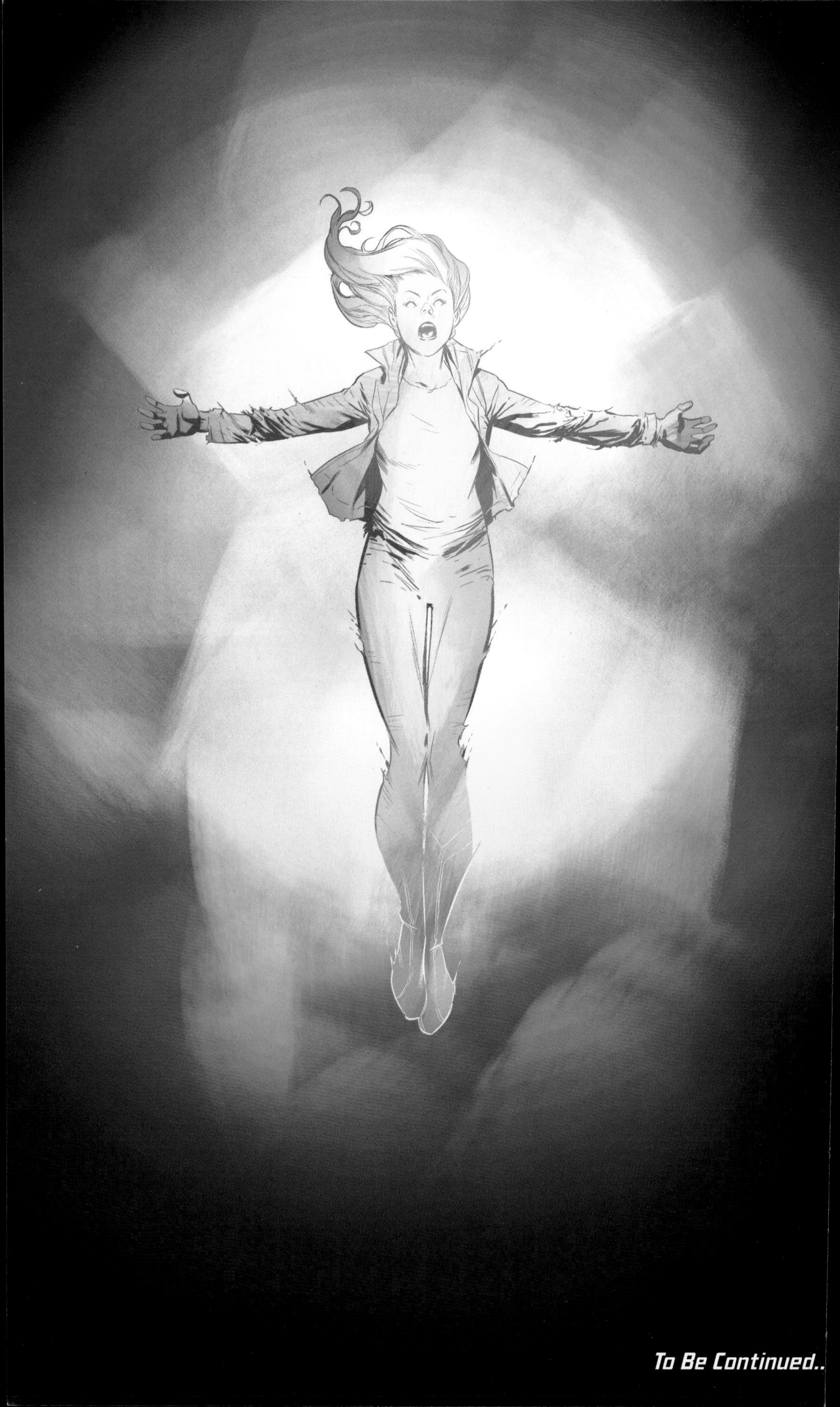
To Be Continued..

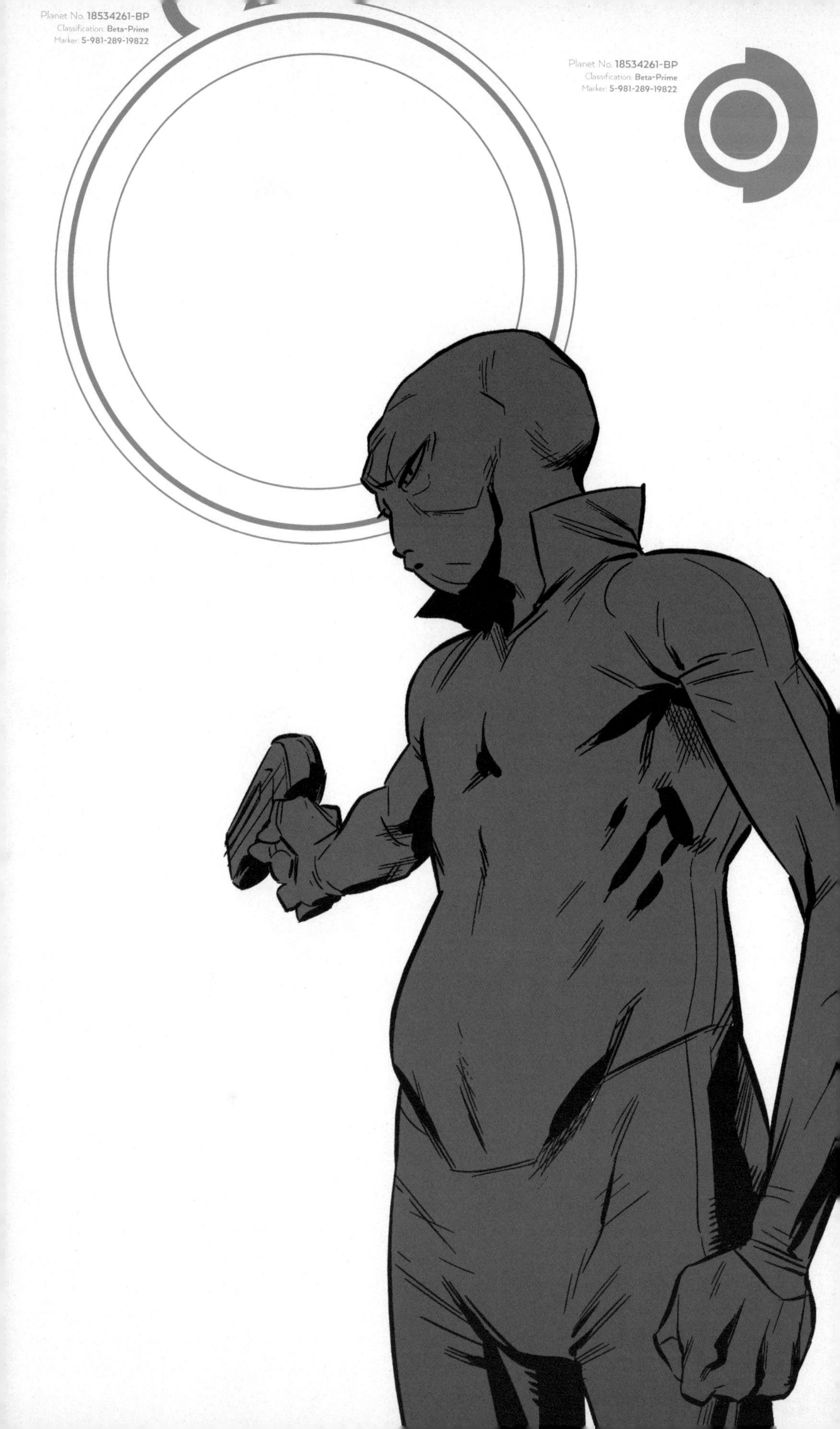
Planet No. 18534261-BP
Classification: Beta-Prime
Marker: 5-981-289-19822
Planet No. 18534261-BP
Classification: Beta-Prime
Marker: 5-981-289-19822

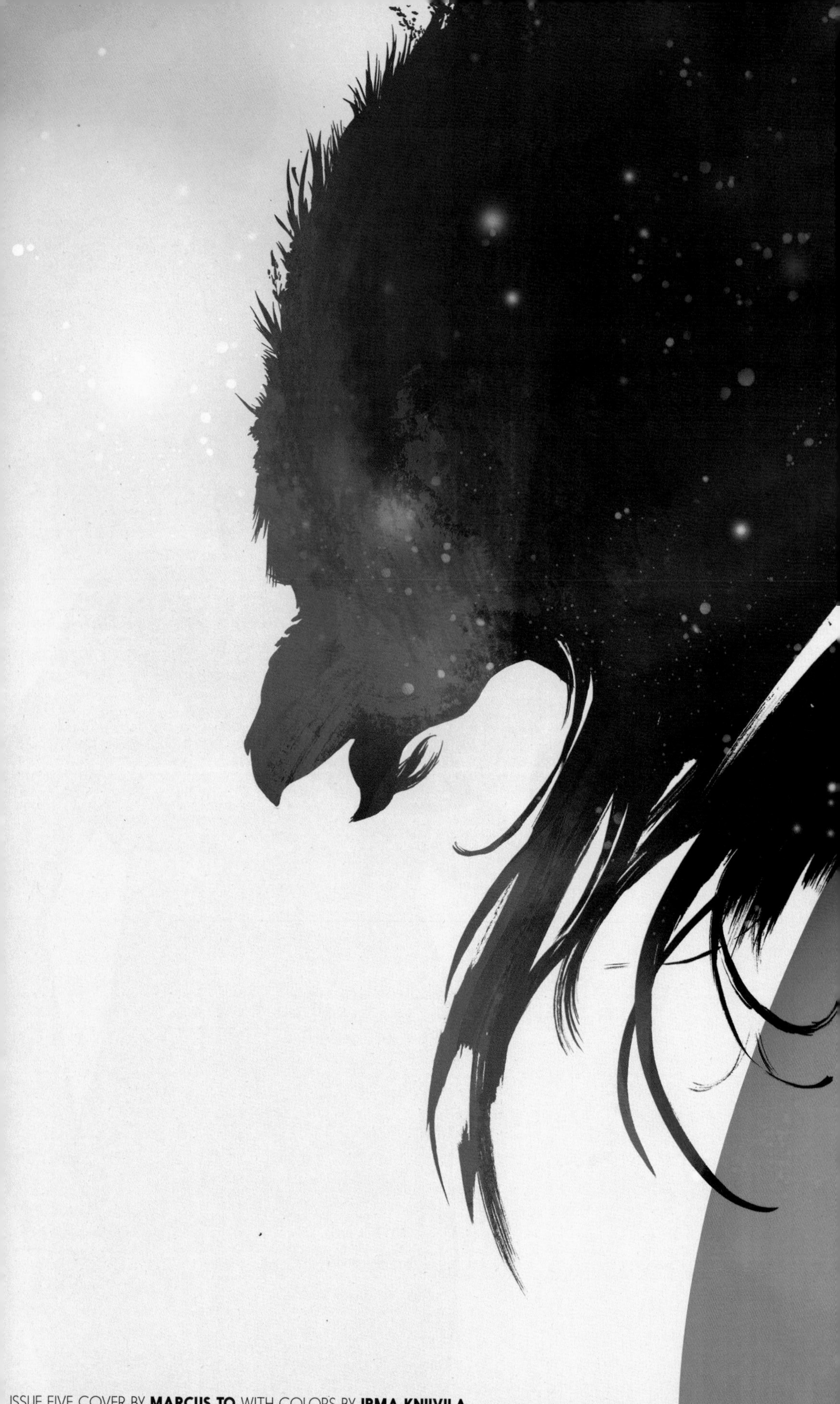

ISSUE FIVE COVER BY **MARCUS TO** WITH COLORS BY **IRMA KNIIVILA**

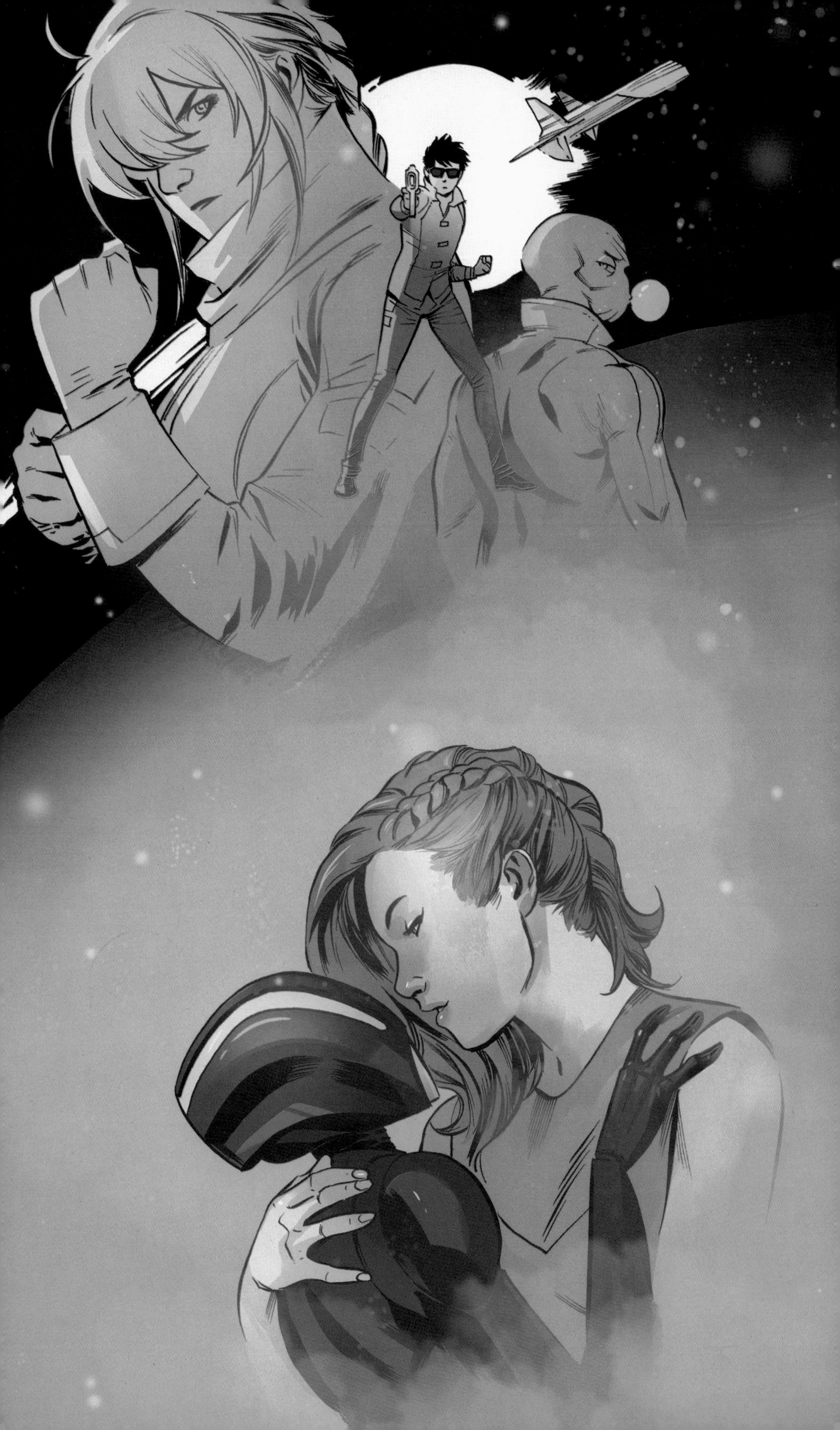

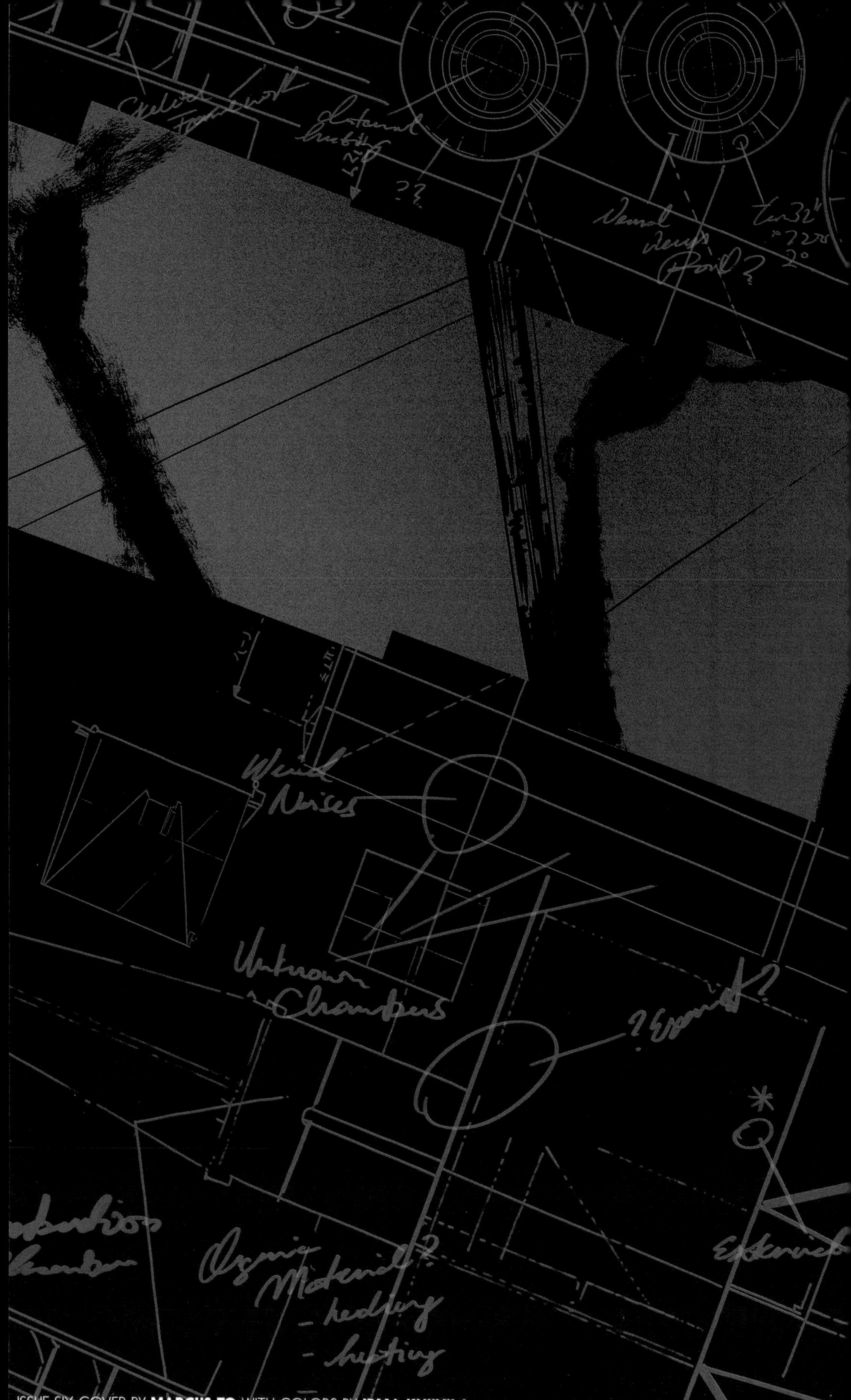
Weird Noises
Unknown Chambers
Organic Material?
- healing
- hunting

ISSUE SIX COVER BY **MARCUS TO** WITH COLORS BY **IRMA KNIIVILA**

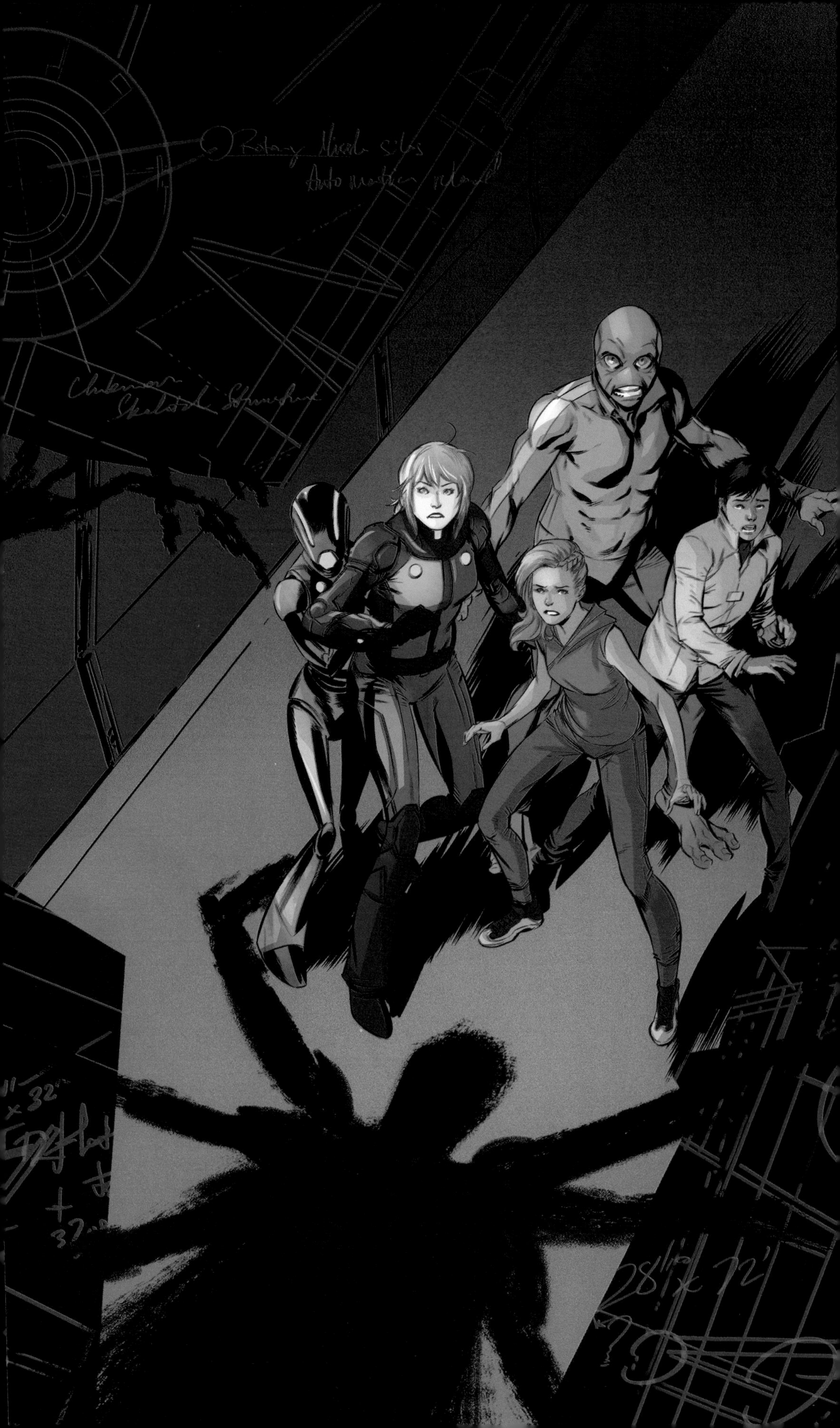

ISSUE SEVEN COVER BY **MARCUS TO** WITH COLORS BY **IRMA KNIIVILA**

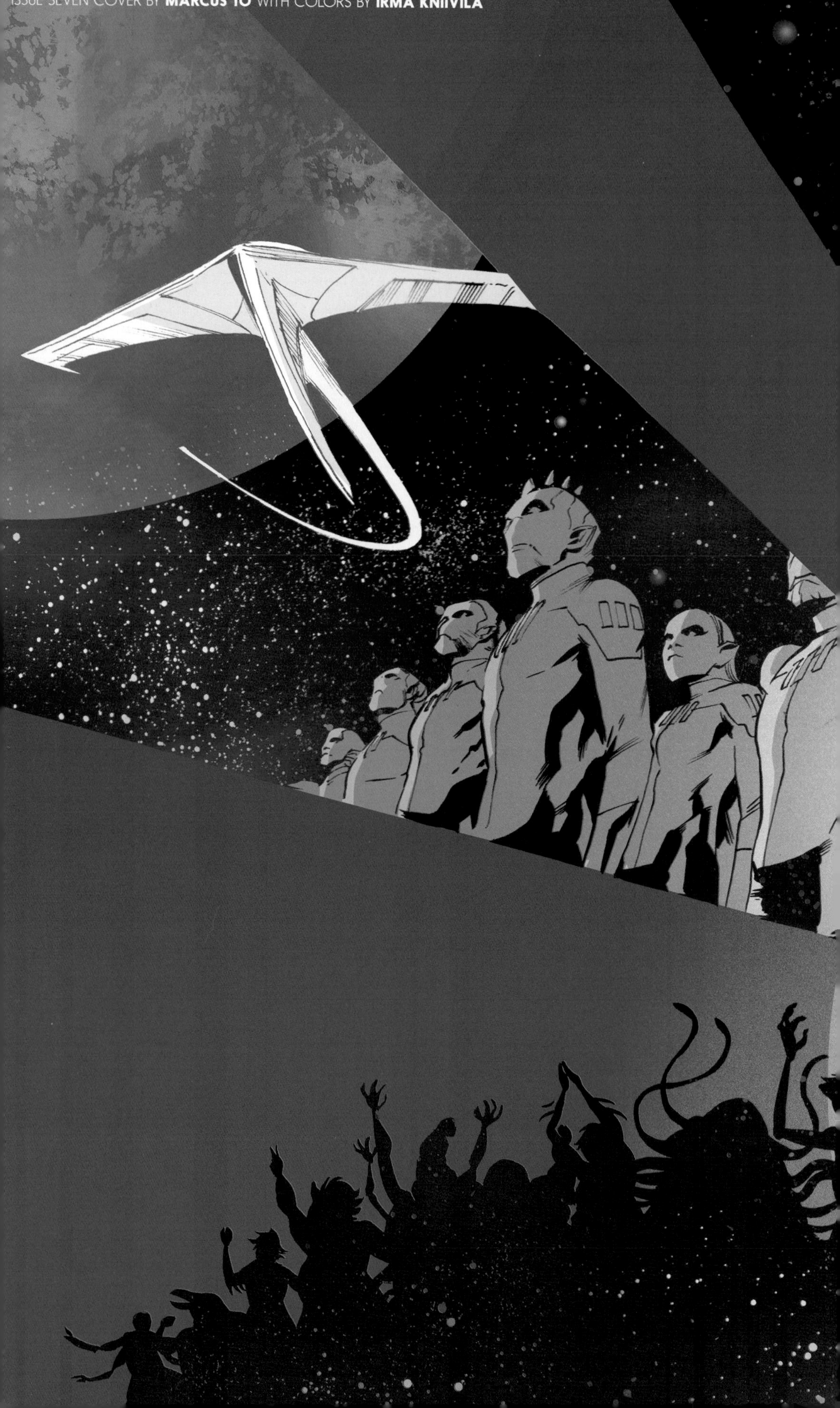

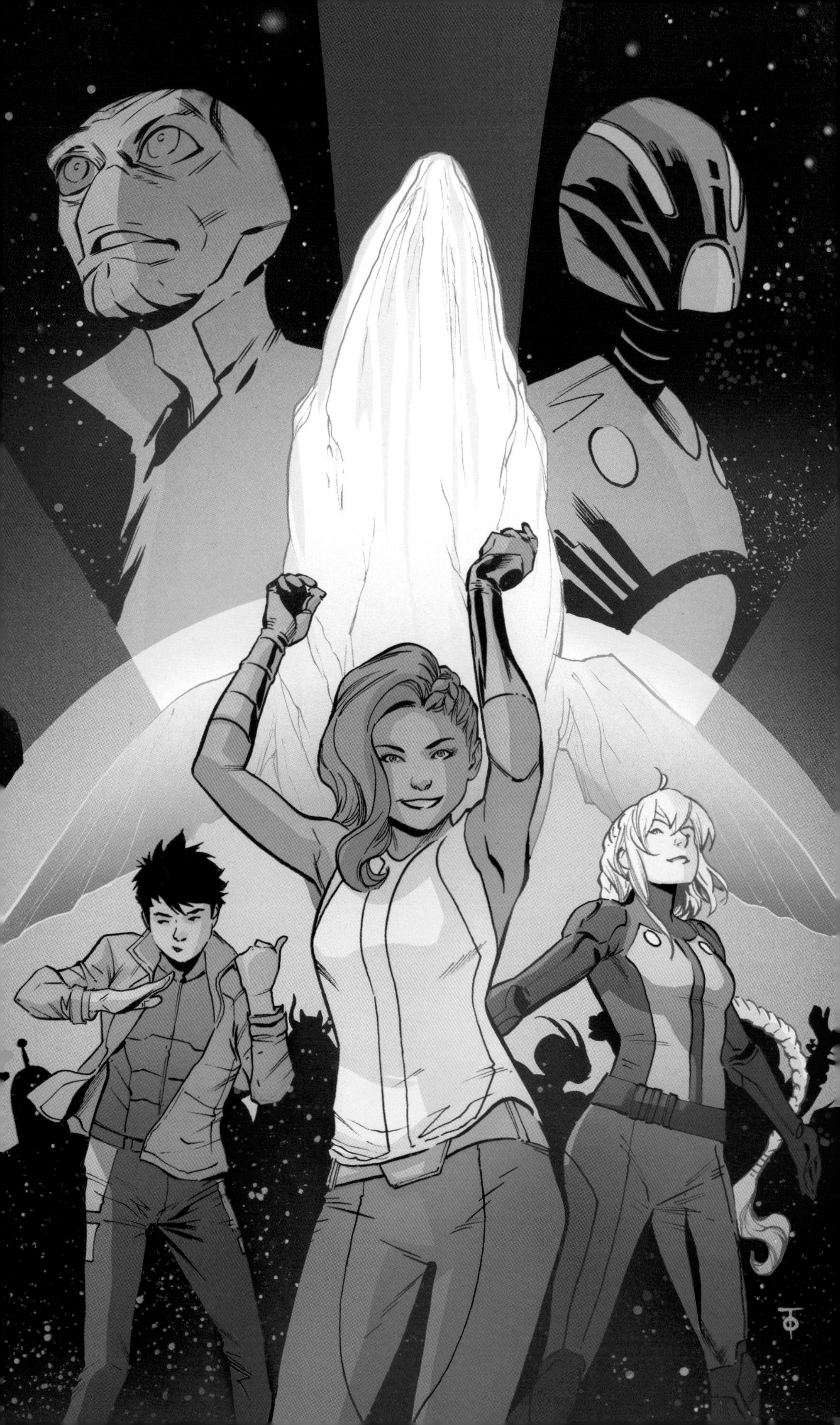

ISSUE EIGHT COVER BY **MARCUS TO** WITH COLORS BY **IRMA KNIIVILA**

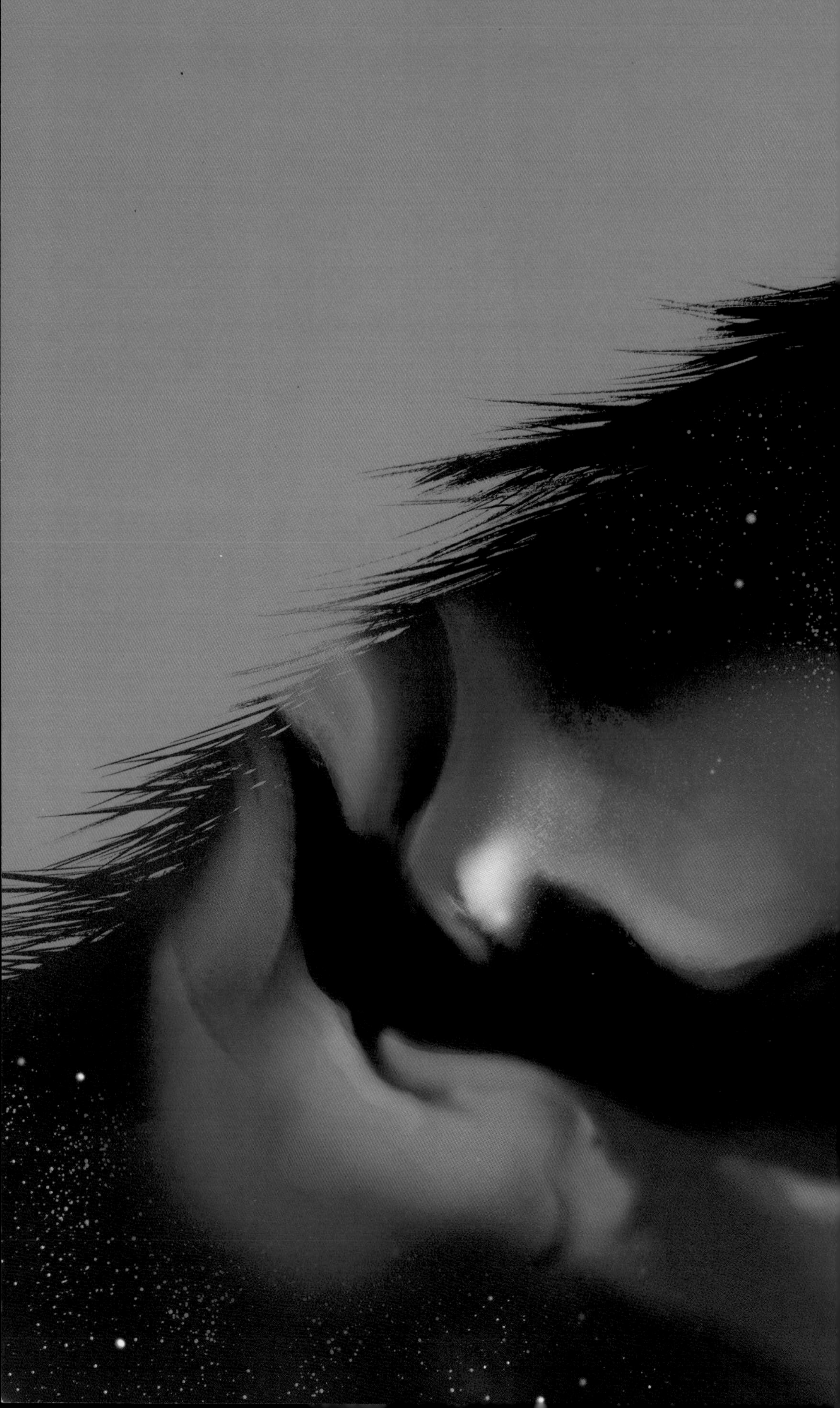

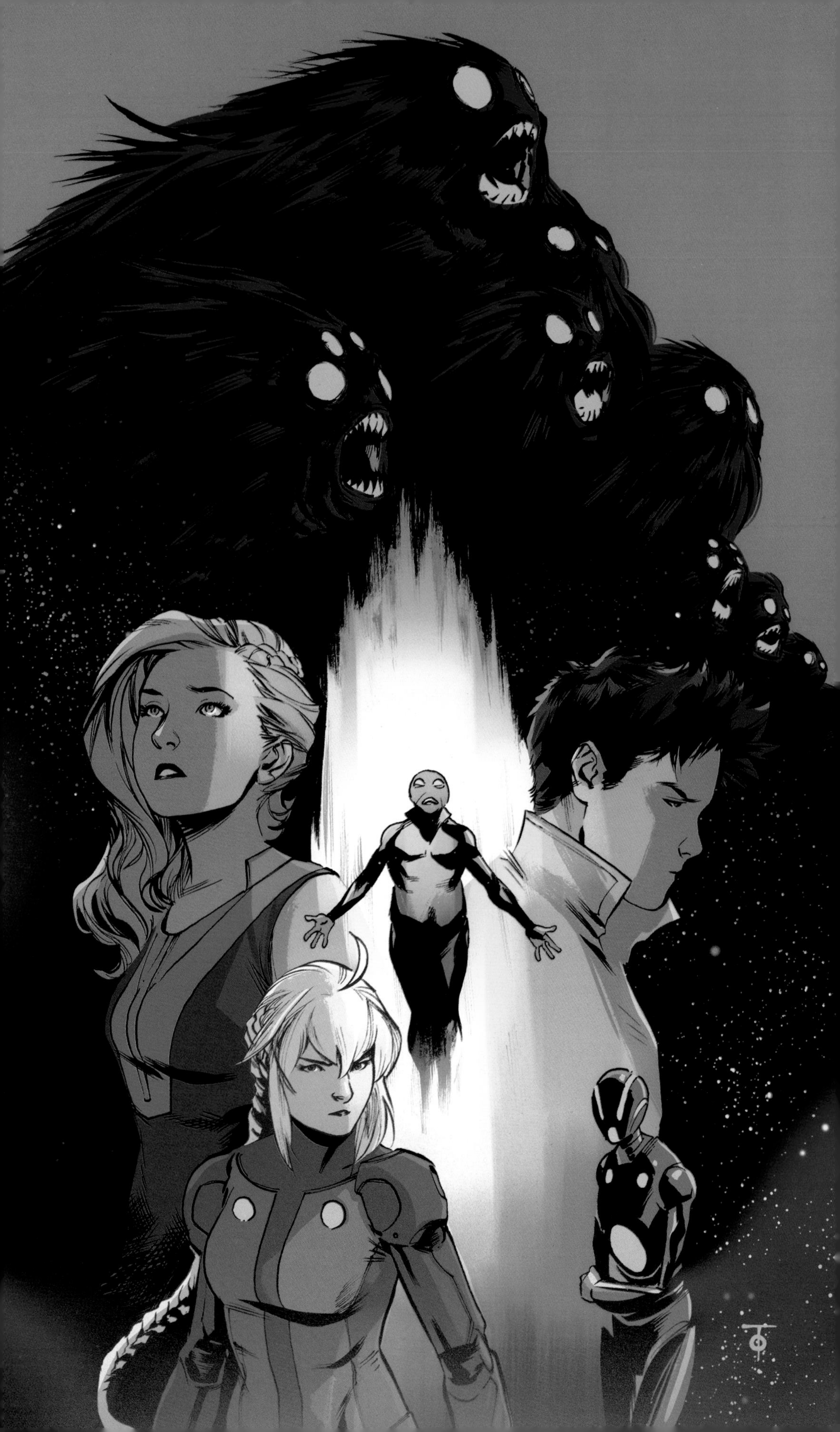

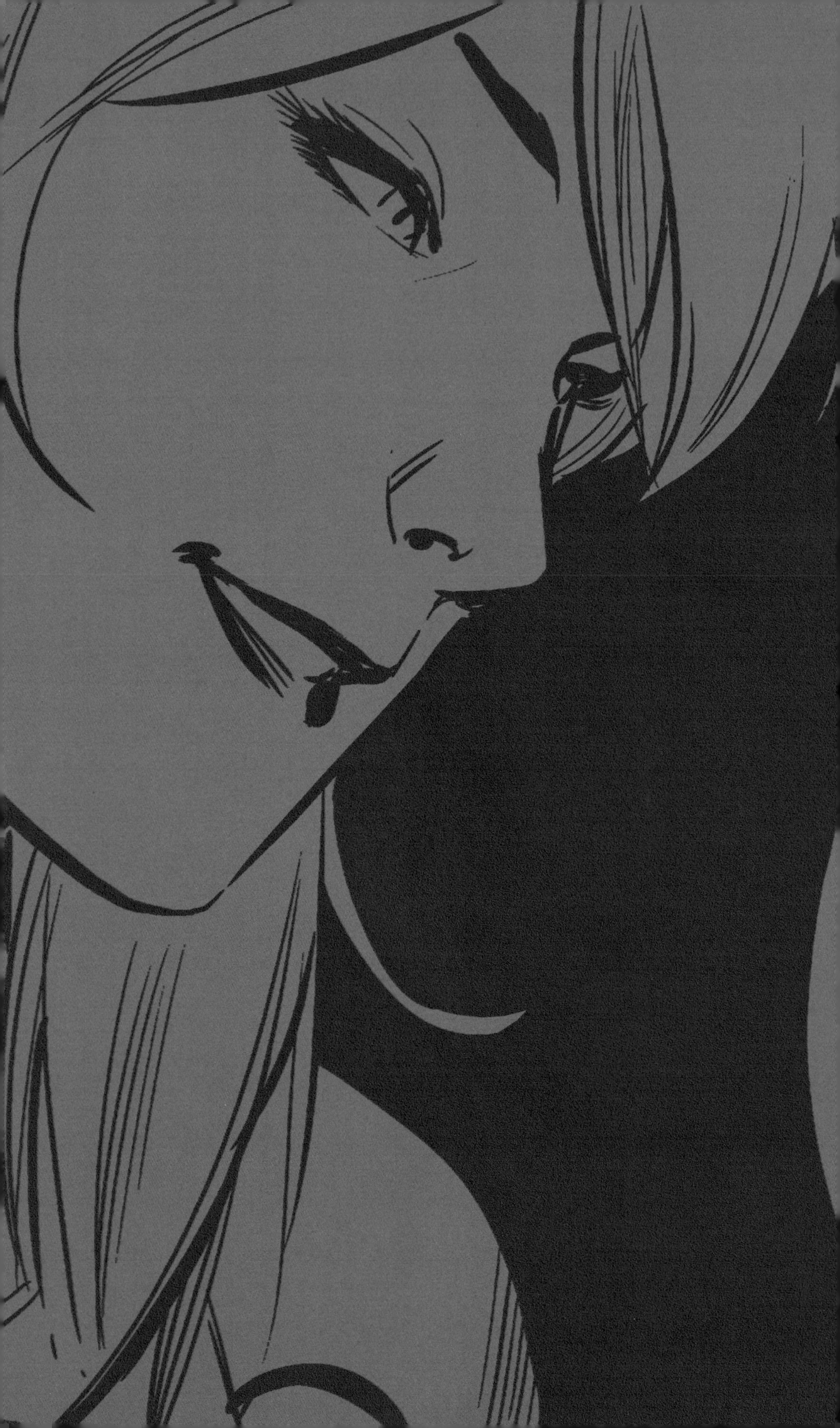

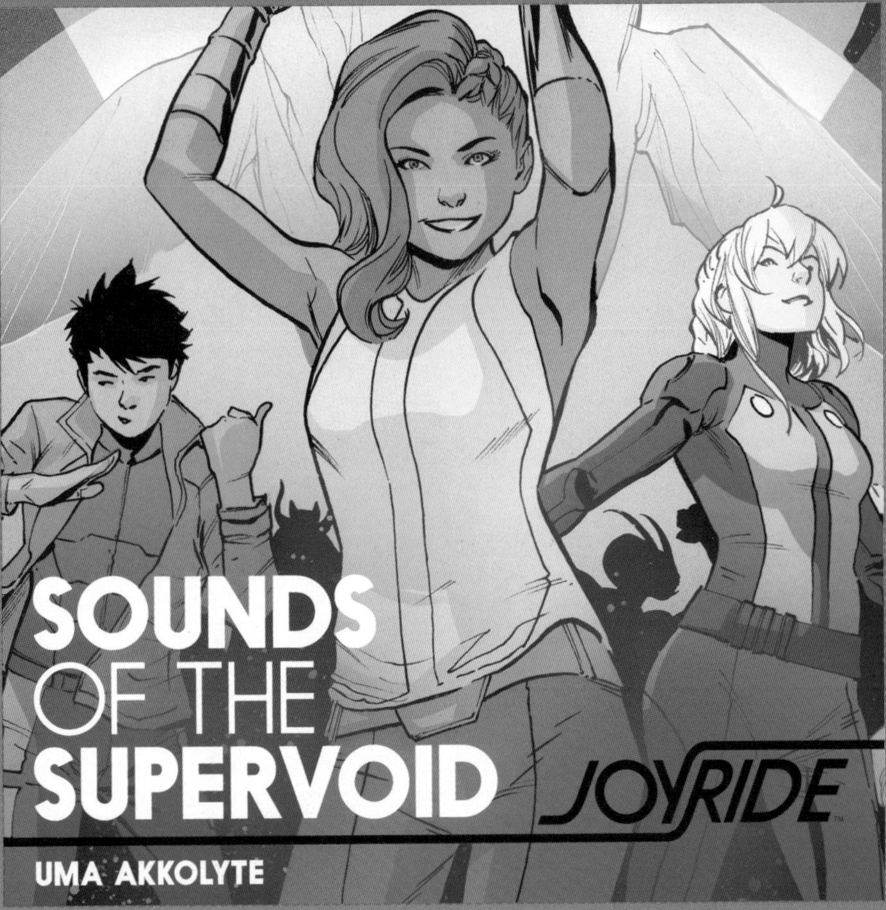
SOUNDS
OF THE
SUPERVOID
JOYRIDE
UMA AKKOLYTE

JOYRIDE SOUNDS OF THE SUPERVOID **UMA AKKOLYTE**

The Woods San Fermin
Contact High Architecture In Helsinki
Blacktop Julien Baker
Here Alessia Cara
Don't Let Me Be Misunderstood Lana Del Rey
Heavy Metal Detox Wavves
Cool Girl Tove Lo
Try to Be Helpful The Spook School
Control Majical Cloudz
Lady La De Da Jessie Jones
Bury It CHVRCHES
Human Engine Kate Boy
Break The Rules Charli XCX
Regulate Warren G, Nate Dogg
On The Regular Shamir
Departure Stage Roly Porter
I Will Follow You Into The Dark Death Cab for Cutie
Gravity Rides Everything Modest Mouse
In the Aeroplane Over the Sea Neutral Milk Hotel
All My Friends LCD Soundsytem

LISTEN TO PLAYLIST **HERE**

WHAT I AM IS **FREE**

BOOM! STUDIOS
WWW.**BOOM-STUDIOS**.COM

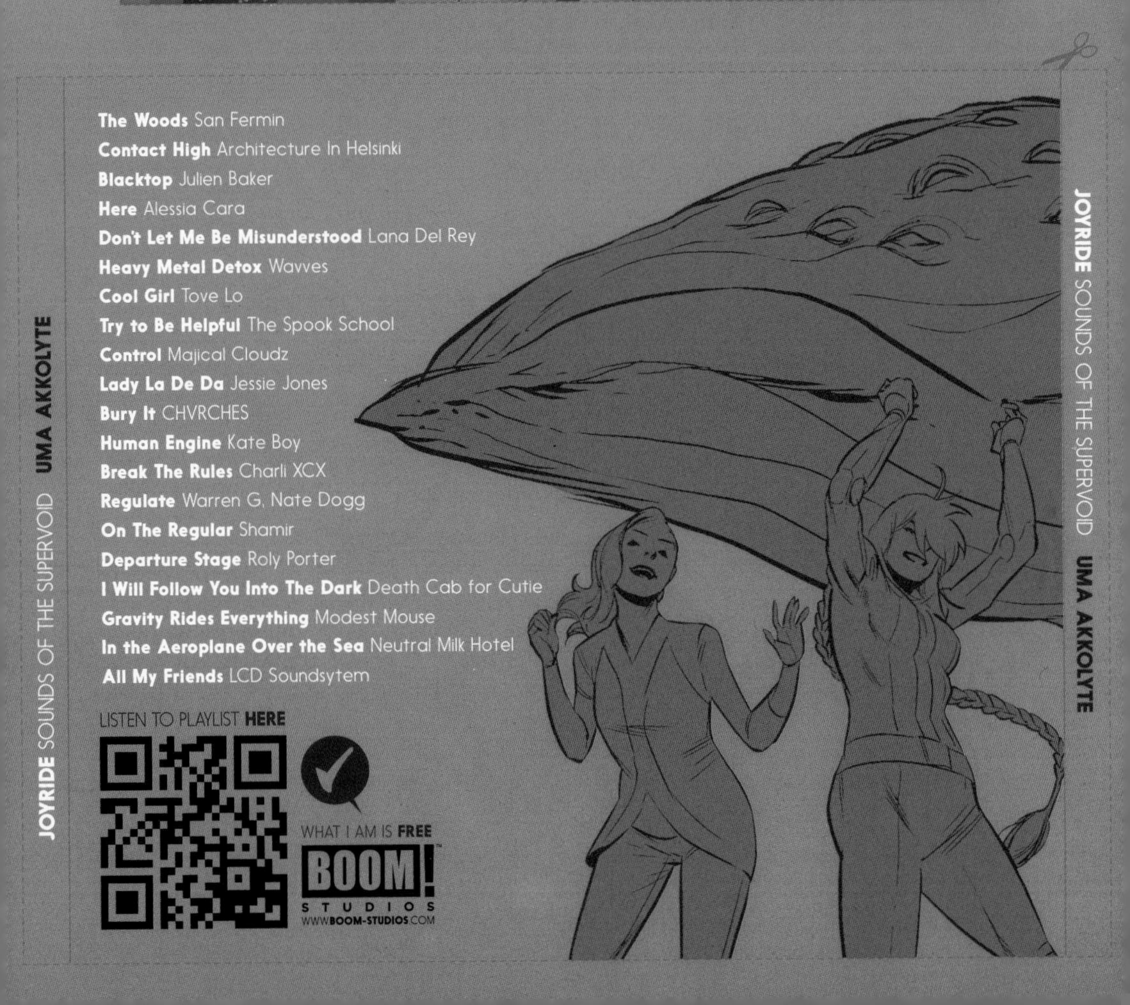

JOYRIDE SOUNDS OF THE SUPERVOID **UMA AKKOLYTE**

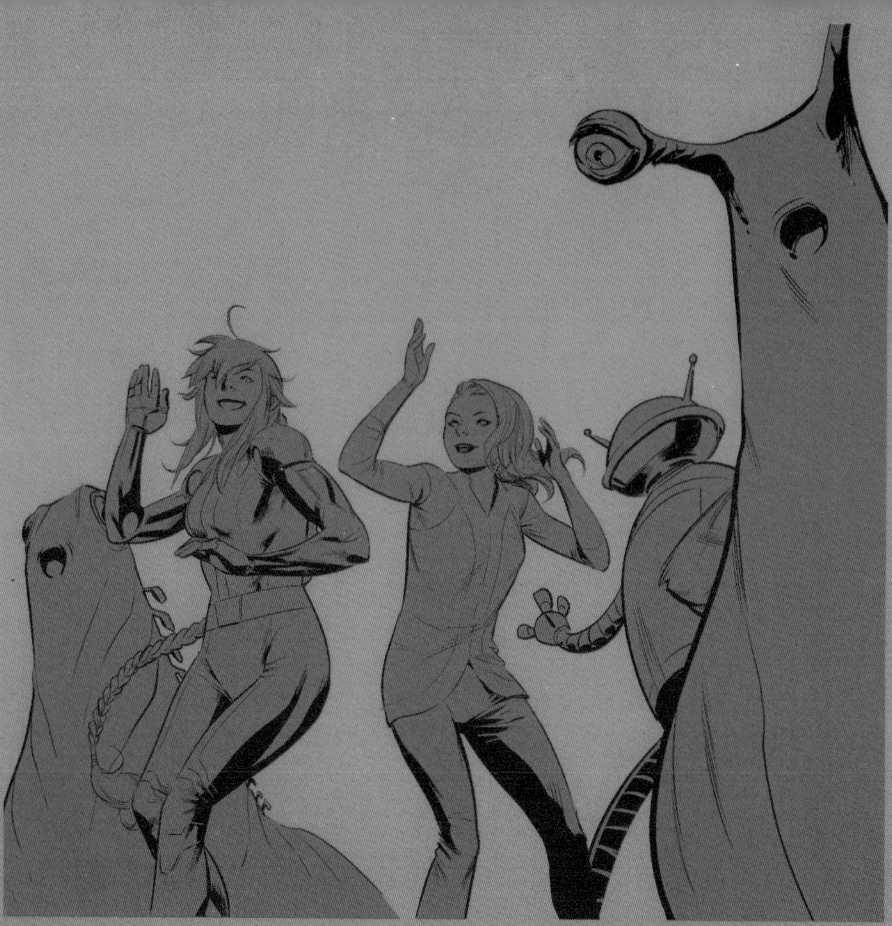

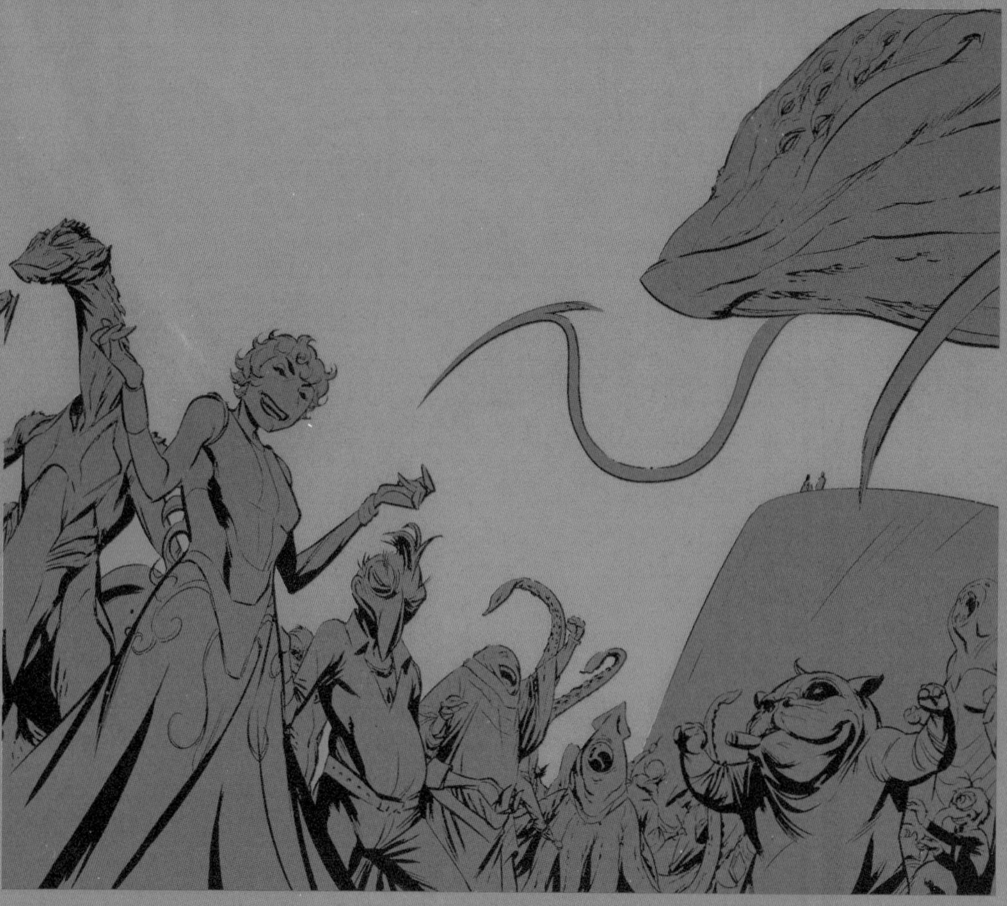

JOYRIDE SOUNDS OF THE SUPERVOID **UMA AKKOLYTE**